GONZO MARKETING

WITHDRAWN

9/06

GONZO MARKETING

Winning through Worst Practices

CHRISTOPHER LOCKE

PERSEUS
PUBLISHING

A Member of the Perseus Books Group

Copyright © 2001 by Christopher Locke

www.gonzomarkets.com

Cataloging-in-Publication Data is available from the Library of Congress
ISBN 0-7382-0769-1

Perseus Publishing is a member of the Perseus Books Group.
Find us on the World Wide Web at http://www.perseuspublishing.com
Perseus Publishing books are available at special discounts for bulk purchases in the U.S. by corporations, institutions, and other organizations. For more information, please contact the Special Markets Department at the Perseus Books Group, 11 Cambridge Center, Cambridge, MA 02142, or call (617) 252-5298.

Text design by Jeffrey P. Williams
Set in 11-point ITC Garamond by the Perseus Books Group

First paperback printing, October 2002

1 2 3 4 5 6 7 8 9 10—04 03 02

contents

for

LAURIE DOCTOR

your mind my sky
your eyes my fire

www.lauriedoctor.com

ACKNOWLEDGEMENTS

BITS AND PIECES OF THIS BOOK FIRST APPEARED IN DIFFERENT FORM— they've since been sliced and diced through my gonzo Vegematic— in various hardcopy and online publications: *Agency* (the journal of the American Association of Advertising Agencies), *byte.com* (thanks to Daniel Dern), *Digitrends, Harvard Business Review* (thanks to John Landry), *Publish, sweetfancymoses.com* (thanks to Matt Herlihy), *Feed* (thanks to Steven Johnson), and *Release 1.0* (thanks to Kevin Werbach). I'd like to especially thank Esther Dyson for her support and inspiration over the past 15 years, even when she wasn't aware she was providing it. Esther, you're a brick.

Chris Anderson, formerly with *The Economist* and now at *Wired*, jousted with me over sundry issues surrounding e-commerce. His good natured yet insistent prodding led to the beginnings of *The Cluetrain Manifesto*, in which book I neglected to thank him. As those ideas are still operative in the present work, it's not too late to say thanks. So thanks.

I'd also like to thank my *Cluetrain* co-authors David Weinberger, Doc Searls, and Rick Levine for keeping the flame(s) alive, David at *JOHO* (hyperorg.com), Doc through his excellent blogging (doc.weblogs.com), and Rick at Word of Mouth (www.wom.com).

To my agent David Miller, I owe a great deal. And not just for the great deal he cut on this book. The outfit he cut it with, Perseus Publishing, is the best company I've ever worked with. David Goehring, Elizabeth Carduff, Lissa Warren, and my new editor Nick Philipson have all been wonderful: smart, understanding, and loads of fun. Jacqueline Murphy, who was my editor through the main construction phase, has since moved on. But in ways too numerous to catalog, this is her book.

Many thanks to Eric Norlin of The Titanic Deck Chair Rearrangement Corporation (tdcrc.com) for his thoughtful feedback on early drafts, and for sending the Everclear and Eminem CDs. Eric is beyond a doubt the world's most capable CEO.

J.P. Rangaswami (of Dresdner Kleinwort Wasserstein) and Fritz Gutbrodt (of Swiss Re) both make brief appearances here. Too brief. They were fabulous hosts in London and Zurich, respectively, and I learned much from our conversations.

My sister, Elizabeth Locke, gave me more suggestions than I knew what to do with; for instance, about arcane matters like reciprocal ethnography. Liz, you're a trip, but you already knew that. Selene, my 11 year old daughter, also provided innumerable cool ideas. I believe her insight into the current state of marketing practice remains unparalleled.

Though Laurie Doctor appears on the dedication page, what is not apparent to anyone but myself is *her* dedication, for which no amount of gratitude will ever be sufficient.

Finally, I'd like to thank the thousands of (valued) *EGR* readers, who have not only endured my abstruse prolixity and unwarranted abuse, but who continue to grant me the invaluable permission to publicly discover what I mean to say.

Participating in the Scene

Only the insane take themselves quite seriously.

—SIR MAX BEERBOHM[1]

THIS IS A SERIOUS BOOK. NO FOOLING.

Now right off the bat that has to make you wonder, right? Because most books, especially business books, pretty much take it for granted that you believe that going in. Of course the book is serious. That's why you bought it. Either that, or you needed an over-the-counter alternative to your regular insomnia medication. Don't laugh. Recent studies show that seven out of ten business book buyers are really looking for semantic Sominex. And, as Harley Manning of Forrester Research points out in his insightful report—"The Snooze Factor: Sleepy Time in the Management Aisle"—these consumers find what they're looking for in 82% of all online book transactions.[2]

But seriously. In his seminal work, *Homo Ludens: A Study of the Play Element in Culture,* the Dutch cultural historian Johan Huizinga riffs on the perennial theme of wisdom, from the Latin *sapientia.* "A happier age than ours," he wrote, "once made bold to call our species by the name of Homo Sapiens." However, he wonders how appropriate this label remains today. "In the course of time we have come to realize that we are not so reasonable after all as the Eighteenth Century, with its worship of reason and its naive optimism, thought us." So someone came up with Homo Faber: Man the Maker. Better, Huizinga says, but still no cigar. Homo Ludens, he then proposes: Man the Player.[3]

While some will find the notion ludicrous, play is no less an important aspect of business than it is of life. This is probably because, contrary to widespread popular belief, commerce is a subset of life and not the other way around. Therefore, as Huizinga goes to great lengths to point out, play is serious business. Or something like that. I only read the foreword.

In 1962, the French anthropologist Claude Levi-Strauss wrote a book called *The Savage Mind*, in which he says "Language is a form of human reason and has its reasons which are unknown to man." Man, I don't even know why I quoted that, except that it sounds pretty cool.[4] More to the point, he talks about a concept for which English has no equivalent: *bricolage*.[5] In essence, bricolage is what tinkers do—collecting odd bits of stuff they think may be potentially useful, then using whatever bits seem to work in the context of some later repair job. Simple. And yet profound. Because the bits the bricoleur ends up using were not designed for the use they end up being put to. Figuring out which bits to collect and how to apply them to some task at hand requires a completely different kind of thinking than the procedural algorithmic thought processes business has become so dependent upon. While the Internet may have convinced some businesses to think "out of the box," most are still not even sure what box they're in, much less which way to turn for emergency egress. If some unprincipled individual were to yell "fire!" right about now, the entire edifice of global commerce might suddenly collapse.

Fire! Fire!

What the hell. Because, while few corporations seem to realize it, the entire edifice of global commerce is collapsing already—under its own top-heavy weight. And this is happening at the very moment business is crowing loudest about its own gross tonnage: the biggest media mergers, biggest advertising budgets, biggest aggregation of eyeballs. Yuck, what an image. In short, the messiest, massiest mass-marketing morass the world has ever seen. It's ironic.

In a wonderful *Newsweek* article titled "Will We Ever Get Over Irony?" David Gates writes about the postmodern inclination to rip (off) ideas from a broad range of historical contexts and recombine them in odd and often glaring ways. "Such juxtapositional ironies flourish in the 20th century's most characteristic artistic mode: call it collage, assemblage, bricolage, pastiche or (to be less Frenchified and more *au courant*) sampling."[6] Aha! Now we're getting somewhere—though these equivalents make the overall effect no less odd. The glare produced is still a kind of cognitive dissonance. Things that don't fit together in expected ways can make your head hurt. However, under the right conditions, this pain can also produce insight. It can illuminate not only the box, but the EXIT sign as well.

I can see already that you're skeptical, gentle reader. This isn't sounding entirely level-headed, is it? Doesn't quite have that grim-visaged wrinkle-browed aura of unassailable fact. Hmmm, must be time for a quote from *Harvard Business Review*. "Pragmatic managers. . . know what resources are available and how to round up more on short notice," write a couple of bona fide Ph.D.s, doubtless recalling how they managed to scrape by on assistant professor salaries. "We call this aspect of pragmatism bricolage . . . Effective managers are bricoleurs . . . They play with possibilities. . . They tinker. . . ."[7]

Now you believe me? Well, good. Oh yeah and by the way, Levi-Strauss says bricolage is analogous to the mythical thinking typical of primitive peoples. Savages. You know, the kind of uncivilized barbarians you get in places like Harvard, Borneo, New Guinea and the World Wide Web.[8] So, taking all the above into account (along with a grain of salt and two aspirins), think of this book as playful bricolage involving serious matters. As sampling. As a hip-hop cover of boring old best practices played backwards and burned into a bad-ass MP3 dance remix download. At times, the recombinant results may strike you as freakish, as frivolous. Feel free to sue me. However, you'll get far more satisfaction by thinking of yourself as I do: as a Raider of the Lost Arc. To sample once again the comedy stylings of Johan Huizinga. . .

The reader of these pages should not look for detailed documentation of every word. In treating of the general problems of culture one is constantly obliged to undertake predatory incursions into provinces not sufficiently explored by the raider himself. To fill in all the gaps in my knowledge beforehand was out of the question for me. I had to write now, or not at all. And I wanted to write.[9]

As Lou Gerstner, chairman and CEO of IBM once said, "Hey, I can dig it."[10] The concept of gonzo marketing would never have come together at all if I'd had to rigorously research every damn thread we're about to touch on. Will some of these lead us into curious intellectual culs-de-sac? Yeah, probably. Are you likely to encounter grievous gaffes and disquieting half truths? Sure, but what else is new? By screwing up royally here, I hope to provide a new kind of model demonstrating to business that it not only can, but *must* move beyond its unhealthy fear of error and imprecision. Today, it is certainty that is not an option. Failure is almost guaranteed.

In addition to being a sort of indie-Indy, I also think of myself as An Amateur and a Dilettante. The caps are there to echo the title of the movie, *An Officer and a Gentleman*—though as you're already finding out, I'm neither. At its heart, gonzo is animated by an attitude of deeply principled anti-professionalism in the best sense. And there is a best sense. Historian and former Librarian of Congress Daniel J. Boorstin once wrote: "Democracy is government by amateurs. . . . The survival of our society depends on the vitality of the amateur spirit. . . . The representative of the people . . . must be wary of becoming a professional politician."[11]

Here, amateur clearly doesn't mean incompetent or unskilled. It doesn't mean unprofessional. But professional-*ism* is something altogether else. Over time, any functional specialization tends to forget its relationship to the larger social context it was created to work within and serve. Instead, it concentrates on developing an inner sanctum of specialists who talk among themselves in a private language inaccessible to outsiders. Almost without exception, such professionals despise amateurs. Or worse, accord them a patronizing form of faux eye-rolling patience.

Related to "amateur" is the even more pejorative term *"dilettante"*—someone who practices a craft or studies a field of knowledge in which he or she is not a "recognized professional." But the etymological roots of these words tell a different story. Amateurs do what they do for love (from the Latin *amare*), while dilettantes are not mere casual dabblers, but instead are inspired by delight (from the Italian *dilettare* by way of the Latin *delectare*). But delight and passion for the work are precisely the qualities professionals tend to lose first. The opposite of professionalism is what Zen master Shun-ryu Suzuki called *"beginner's mind"*—an ability to look at the world with fresh eyes and an open spirit.[12]

Boorstin's observation can be equally applied to the commercial sphere. In marketing, just as in government, professionalism tends to hew unimaginatively to its own timid orthodoxy. It does not provide leadership, enthusiasm or the kind of impassioned personal engagement that has come to be called gonzo. In stark contrast, business professionalism tends to be arid and passionless, narrowly focused, self-involved. However, this doesn't mean that everyone in business fits this damning characterization. Far from it. In my own experience, there are many more lively intellects at work in the workplace than the misbegotten "corporate communications" coming out of those places would lead one to believe. There's often more going on in today's corporation than today's corporation would care to admit. New life is growing between the cracks in the corporate edifice, and it's spreading like a weed.

In the past year or so, I've had the opportunity to test many of the ideas in this book before *very* live business audiences from Maui to Bangalore. At places like Peoplesoft, Gartner Group, Sun Microsystems, SAP, First Union Bank, the Direct Marketing Association, and Andersen Consulting—now, for their sins, renamed Accenture. To be fair, my Accenture-nee-Andersen audience was great. It was clear they'd been around the block. They'd seen it all. They laughed in all the right places. On the other hand, the Direct Marketing crowd was thoroughly unamused. Understandable. The rending of garments and gnashing of teeth would have been appropriate responses.

The day before I spoke at Swiss Re (the Re is for reinsurance, a hugely lucrative niche), my hosts opened an impressive mucho-multimillion-dollar conference facility called Rüschlikon. The festivities included a Chinese dancer performing on a rooftop in the snow to piano music piped to her wireless headset and further accompanied by nocturnal animal cries taped in some Southeast Asian jungle. In addition, there was an extremely Zen-looking Japanese guy playing a 2000-year-old stone flute that appeared to be nearly as ancient as himself, and a terrorist-looking dude with his face weirdly painted in striking primary colors, who read long strings of numbers in German, timed to a strobe light. "Acht hundert neun und zwanzig, sieben hundert vier und dreizig. . ." Yeah, just another day of business as usual. The center's director, Fritz Gutbrodt, told me over a wonderfully animated dinner that he still teaches literature at the University of Zürich.

The investment banking firm of Dresdner, Kleinwort, Benson was a slightly different story. IT director J. P. Rangaswami runs offsite swat teams that take a real problem, break it down, come up with a solution, code it, and integrate the results into the corporate computing infrastructure—all within a week. In an industry where this sort of thing is usually measured in months, quarters or years, such results are astounding. Everyone on the team is expected to drink copious amounts of beer, liberally provided, between the impossibly long, often round-the-clock, hacking sessions. J. P. is working on a book about certain structural and management challenges facing large corporations. Working title: *Fossil Fools.* We had many deep exchanges about what's truly important in this industry at the moment. He turned me on to a Dire Straits bootleg. I convinced him to buy a pricey but totally kickass Roland guitar synth. "Damn you," he wrote later in email, "you are starting to cost me real money!"

The Dresdner gang isn't cheap, though. They gleefully fete me with sumptuous dinners in Mayfair, theater tickets, limousines. Would I care to take in The Tate? They put me up in the Docklands, an outrageous suite overlooking the Thames. I drop some laundry off with the valet and it comes back wrapped in rich brocade, my socks and underwear not only *ironed*—what were they thinking?— but also tied into little bundles with red ribbons that say "Four Seasons Hotel—Canary Wharf." It's totally over the top. I love it. But finally I have to get out, get real again. I give my talk on gonzo marketing, then ditch the chauffer. I take a train, then a bus. I get lost. London is better at eye level. . .

Waiting for History

"There was a demon that lived in the air. They said whoever challenged him would die. Their controls would freeze up,

their planes would buffet wildly, and they would
disintegrate. The demon lived at Mach 1. . .
They called it the sound barrier."

—FROM THE MOVIE *THE RIGHT STUFF*

"We're never gonna survive unless we get a little crazy . . . "

—SEAL

I round the corner in Covent Garden and hear what sounds like
Coltrane wafting up the block. Bent into his horn as if in fervent
prayer, a musician is laying down fat splashy bop notes in the rain,
punctuating the oblivious crowds of pre-Christmas shoppers. His
saxophone case is open for donations and I drop in a ten pound
note. He's surprisingly good to be playing in the street. Seeing the
denomination, he jumps up and presses a compact disc into my
hand. I turn it over. Karlsax Online it says.

The rain forests of the world constitute a cauldron of biological
ferment and co-evolutionary experimentation, a living ecosystem
where few parts exist independent of the whole. Lianas and ma-
hoganies, primates and insect colonies, jaguars and bromeliads,
slow-moving sloths and dazzling butterflies, intermittent light and
impenetrable darkness, the endless cycle of rain and evaporation,
transpiration and erosion, all weave together to produce a tapestry
of nearly unimaginable color and complexity. The human world is
no less complex, and the Internet reflects a similarly rich inter-
weaving, the customs and experience of myriad diverse societies
and cultures. The net is a planet-spanning virtual ecosystem, a cognitive rain forest teeming with new concepts and connections, issues and inquiries, studies and speculations, proposals, predictions
and unlimited potential.

Something's shaking, something's up. But we're none of us quite
sure what it is, what it all adds up to. How long will we have to
wait for the history books that explain this amazing period we're
living through? Fifty years? A hundred? I don't know about you, but
I don't have that long. As you may recall, we die. My dates are the
same as Jackson Browne's. "In '65 I was 17," he sang in "Running
on Empty." Plus: "gotta do what you can just to keep your love

alive"—immediately thereafter warning of the dangers of confusing that with whatever you need to do to survive, to "make a living" as we say. And now you're wondering again: *Jackson Browne?* Hey, when you write these sorts of penetrating and insightful business books for busy executive types, you take your inspiration wherever you find it.

In the meantime, the time of our lives, all we have is intuition and stories to try to make sense of the world, to provide some sort of vision of where we're at and where we may be headed. But that's not so bad. As a species, it's all we've ever had.

Gonzo marketing is the shorthand I use for the work I do—work I fell into almost accidentally, rather than as a path I set out on knowing in advance where it would lead. At first, I looked for models, guidelines, some sort of framework that would make sense of the business world I suddenly found myself inhabiting. But what I found seemed oddly broken, or ill-conceived from the outset. Perhaps because I came to the computer industry from such a contrasting set of experiences—brain surgery (yes, really), railroad braking, goat husbandry, boat carpentry, pharmaceutical, uh. . . mergers and acquisitions—most of what I saw passing for best practice seemed naïve to the point of being ridiculous. Even from the inside, it felt demeaning.

At first I thought I'd get the hang of it with time. But I never did. Along the way, I've become less and less professional. To make a living, I had to find something I could do that actually worked. And to work for my company or client, first it had to work for me. Call it a character defect, but I'm no good at anything I can't put my heart into. So I explored. I followed my heart. And I began to discover that many of the things that worked were the diametric opposite of what was normal and expected in business. In fact, the more diametrically opposed, the more contrarian the approach, the more effective it tended to be. I began calling these directions, attitudes and informal rules-of-thumb "worst practices."

They aren't algorithms or recipes. They're not procedures. They're inclinations and actions that flow from a particular state of mind. And states of mind don't lend themselves very well to bullet points. However, they can sometimes be transmitted through stories. Stories don't deal in definitions and formulas. Instead, they convey impressions, colors, connotations. Their effect is cumulative. The whole encompasses more than the sum of the parts, suggesting new ways to look at problems. And sometimes, imaginative new approaches to solving them.

I once heard a talk on aircraft design in which the speaker explained the aerodynamic basis for a scene in a movie I saw as a kid. I can't recall the name of the film, but I've often used this scenario as an analogy for solving critical problems by going against "the rules" dictated by the sort of sanity and logic that would apply under normal conditions. In the movie, various test pilots attempt to fly an experimental plane capable of supersonic speed. As the plane approaches Mach 1, something strange happens to the controls. Instead of causing the plane to climb, pulling back on the stick puts it into a dive, with terminal consequences for both plane and pilot. Finally, our hero, Chuck Yeager, breaks the sound barrier and lives to tell about it by reversing the normal procedure. As the plane begins to bore in, he pushes forward on the stick instead of pulling it back. The story may be apocryphal, but the point is that the pilot never would have survived unless he did something that was—according to all available evidence up until that time—a little crazy.

This story was retold by Tom Wolfe in *The Right Stuff*, the 1979 book from which the movie was made four years later. Wolfe was fascinated by people who did the wrong thing at the right time—like Ken Kesey and the Merry Pranksters dropping way too much LSD in *The Electric Kool-Aid Acid Test*. But that was later. In 1973, six years before *The Right Stuff*, Wolfe wrote another book called *The New Journalism*, in which he included Hunter S. Thompson's story "The Kentucky Derby is Decadent and Depraved." Here Thompson answers a worried question from his illustrator, Ralph Steadman:

"Is it safe out there? Will we *ever* come back?"

"Sure," I said. "We'll just have to be careful not to step on anybody's stomach and start a fight." I shrugged. "Hell, this clubhouse scene right below us will be almost as bad as the infield. Thousands of raving, stumbling drunks, getting angrier and angrier as they lose more and more money. By midafternoon they'll be guzzling mint juleps with both hands and vomiting on each other between races.

The whole place will be jammed with bodies, shoulder to shoulder. It's hard to move around. The aisles will be slick with vomit; people falling down and grabbing at your legs to keep from being stomped. Drunks pissing on themselves in the betting lines. Dropping handfuls of money and fighting to stoop over and pick it up."

He looked so nervous that I laughed. "I'm just kidding," I said. "Don't worry. At the first hint of trouble I'll start Macing everybody I can reach."[13]

And Dr. Thompson has been Macing everybody he could reach ever since. He's reached quite a few. Merriam-Webster defines *gonzo* as "idiosyncratically subjective but engagé." As dictionary definitions go, this one's delicious. A bit fruity perhaps, but a great nose and a nice finish. It also means "bizarre" the lexicographers add rather woodenly, ruining the whole effect.

Thompson created gonzo journalism, a genre in which high humor meets bad taste. *Fear and Loathing in Las Vegas* burst onto the literary scene with tsunami force in 1971. It was shocking, electrifying. He was simultaneously writing for *Rolling Stone* magazine, and the rock-and-roll connection was no accident. There's a clue here the size of Everest that, to this day, remains invisible in plain sight. Around the same time, the Temptations were singing "Papa Was a Rolling Stone," the Rolling Stones were singing "I bet your mama was a tent show queen," and Thompson was writing: "Moments after we picked up the car, my attorney went into a drug coma and ran a red light on Main Street. . . "[14] It makes the historian's task a real bitch when everything is connected and nothing is what is seems.

But gonzo is far more than the shock tactics it employs. "*The writer must be a participant in the scene while he's writing it,*" Thompson said. Being a full participant in events, having a point of view, a deeply personal perspective: gonzo is about being *engaged*. It's not distanced, impartial or "objective"—it cares about outcomes. When Hunter Thompson wrote about Nixon, he wasn't just writing about one of two presidential candidates. He was writing about someone he hated—hated to the point of intimacy, so much that he almost loved the man. When Thompson got done with Nixon, Nixon wasn't an abstraction. He was as real as a hurricane hitting into the Keys. As concrete as a head-on train wreck.

Gonzo journalism represented a significant shift in news reporting, or at least the option of a new direction. It granted other writers the permission to be human, to stop pretending they were automatic cameras recording events about which they had no opinion, in which they had no personal stake. And it granted this permission even to writers who *didn't* sprinkle acid on their morning cornflakes.

While the so-called legitimate press (where does *that* come from?) has not exactly risen to the occasion in overwhelming numbers, plenty of net-heads have. In the next X years, billions of dollars worth of news, information, entertainment and what I like to call "The Artist Formerly Known As Advertising" are going to do a full 180. That is, a very large proportion of these media functions will no longer be delivered top-down, as in the broadcast model, but will be coming bottom-up from creative individuals on the Internet. X may be two years or five years or ten—the question is not if but when. These changes are inevitable for reasons the balance of this book will explore more deeply.

Business created mass markets through broadcast advertising, the same stentorian voice of command-and-control it used on workers, but in this case applied to the marketplace. "Shut up and do what you're told" is not that much different a proposition from "shut up and buy our product." The "shut up" part was built in to broadcast, as there was never any back-channel—never a way to ask questions. The 30-second jive-and-jingle TV spot was never an invitation to converse.

The Internet brings something different into the world. It has connected people person-to-person, and the people so connected are today talking among each other about things they truly value. People are telling stories. From the dawn of human society, people have been drawn together by storytellers who not only shared their interests but also had a special quality of speech—let's call it *voice*. True voice is not just the ability to speak, but the ability to speak effectively. The best measure of this effectiveness is whether a particular voice can attract and hold an audience. This is as true today as it was in Neolithic times.

Tom and Ray Magliozzi are Click and Clack, the self-styled Tappet Brothers of National Public Radio's "Car Talk" show. They're funny, engaging, and they know their stuff cold. I don't know what a carburetor even looks like, but I could listen to these guys for hours.

While "Car Talk" is an offline phenomenon—and as NPR's largest non-news program it is a phenomenon—another critical factor comes into play when the Internet is involved. Because the barriers to entry are so low, storytelling and voice do not necessarily have much to do with what business usually cares most about: the size of the audience. An online audience can be microscopic by mass-media standards. Nonetheless, the micro audiences just now taking shape on the net are also potential micro *markets*. web-based micromarkets are currently coalescing in real-time around articulate, entertaining, knowledgeable voices.

Take Motley Fool, which began as a minuscule dot in the petri dish of AOL's greenhouse incubator.[15] Today, these "fools" touch millions of personal investors. Micromarkets needn't remain micro. Internet communities have always been self-selecting—audiences gather around content of high personal interest. In this natural aggregation, online is far more efficient than conventional media. People find what they want not as much through advertising as through far more credible word-of-mouth from friends and colleagues.

The mass markets traditionally served by broadcast media have been steadily fragmenting for decades as a result of global competition. Evidence of this erosion are market segmentation and targeting techniques, which attempt to track the detritus of once-mass markets the way an astronomer tracks the remnants of a burnt-out supernova. As competition for even tiny niches has intensified, market segments have become smaller and more refined, to the point that business is currently in hot pursuit of concepts like personalization and one-to-one marketing. However, many of these "mass customization" approaches still rely on analytic tools developed for conventional market segmentation, which in turn require some sort of historical market data—e.g., left-handed red-headed 18–25 year old males tend to buy more Snickers bars than right-handed blond 25–32 year old females.

But what happens when such historical data does not exist? Entirely new micromarkets are emerging on the web today. The real challenge lies not in predicting the behavior of markets this small, but in determining their existence. Because they are currently much smaller than existing market segments, they don't show up on conventional market radar screens. Because they have no history and don't behave like the markets that grew up around broadcast media, demographic segmentation is of little use in determining who constitutes these new micromarkets.

These new realities are presented above as seen from a corporate vantage point. From an Internet perspective, web micromarkets don't think of themselves as markets at all, but rather as nascent communities of interest. They tend to gravitate around articulate, knowledgeable, entertaining voices—individuals or small groups driven by a passion to communicate their views. Because entry costs require high returns on investment, broadcast media rarely offer such emergent voices a hearing. However, the Internet reverses this trend, providing many low-cost vectors for small-scale publishing—Usenet newsgroups, email lists, weblogs, web pages. Think of these as "*micromedia*" as opposed to mass media.

Such micromedia will replace a great deal of current advertising. They will quickly become the best source of user-supplied news about products and services (Amazon.com broke new ground along these lines by inviting customer reviews). Potential buyers will not have to hunt down this information, but will find it in the online venues to which they naturally gravitate according to their interests. Companies that engage in this type of dialogue will forge powerful relationships with micromarkets that will soon—continuing a trend toward market fragmentation that's been in effect for many decades—become their major source of revenues.

The Internet constitutes a market for ideas—real ideas that interest real people, not just the feel-good fantasies of product vendors. What's missing today is an effective method of *marketing* those ideas undistorted by hype and hucksterism. Mass production, whether of goods or information, has always depended on broadcast marketing in which markets are viewed as top-down targets from the lofty vantage point of long-established power and control. The Internet has destroyed that vantage. Wave after wave of new arrivals have eroded the cliffs it's built upon and the castle is crumbling into the sea.

It's about time.

Net markets are micromarkets, reflecting not the mass of humanity, but rather the voluntary alliance of individuals around deeply shared interests. Because such communities are still growing bottom-up, they have don't have the sort of demographic profiles companies have always depended on to identify new business. These micromarkets are just emerging. They hardly exist yet. Invisible to the lens of traditional marketing, they are ignored.

But don't be fooled. Micromarkets aren't insignificant markets, and given the speed of propagation the net enables, their emergence will be faster than the emergence of the Internet itself. This book describes how billions of dollars of advertising, news, information and entertainment are about to shift out of corporate control forever.

The resulting landscape will not be a neat and orderly world, any more than a rain forest, or any physical ecosystem, is neat and orderly. Rather, it will be wild in many of the senses poet Gary Snyder lists in his book *The Practice of the Wild*:[16]

> free, self-propagating, self-maintaining, flourishing in accord with innate qualities, pristine, ordered from within and maintained by the force of consensus and custom rather than explicit legislation, populated with original and eternal inhabitants, resisting economic and political domination, unintimidated, self-reliant, independent, proud, far-out, outrageous, "bad," admirable, artless, spontaneous, unconditioned, expressive and ecstatic.

Of course, artlessness and ecstatic badness don't always come in such a poetic package. The quality of wildness most lacking in commerce is play. Yet play, once again, is serious business. To the rollicking delight of online audiences everywhere, corporations seem to get easily confused trying to balance their overly earnest brand personas with their All-New SuperCool E-Brand Avatars that plead, "hey look, we're just one of the gang!" The resulting display is a little like watching baboons dress up in Barbie doll outfits: amusing for a while, but ultimately unconvincing. Play is serious stuff, profound even. While it's hard to describe, we all know it when we see it, flourishing as it tends to do, in accord with innate qualities. Even when those qualities are coming at you right straight off the wall. . .

Difficulty At The Beginning[17]

". . . you can go up on a steep hill in Las Vegas and look West, and with the right kind of eyes you can almost see the high-water mark—that place where the wave finally broke and rolled back."

—HUNTER S. THOMPSON, *FEAR AND LOATHING IN LAS VEGAS*[18]

How many days have I been racked out on this couch? Three? Four? I got back from London last week and immediately came down with the flu. Influenza the ancients called it. An evil influence from the stars. Between hits of Alka Seltzer Plus and fitful bouts of restless, fevered sleep, I've been reading Elmore Leonard's novel, *The Hunted*. Maybe that's what did it.

Somebody's banging on my door and bellowing. "Locke! Come out here you bottom-feeding scum sucker! I know you're in there. Come out or I'm coming in!" Something much harder than a fist hits the door with a sickening thud. A window shatters. I'm waking up now. More like coming to. What was I just dreaming? Something about the book. Something terrible. You know those dreams that keep repeating, won't let you go? One of those. I won't be able to finish it on time. I don't know what I'm doing, what to write. What if my publisher wants the money back? But this is worse. I stumble to the door, undo the bolt.

And find myself eye-to-eye with the uncompromising orifice of a shotgun barrel. Look how round it is. Nasty. I am definitely not ready for this. "Look," I croak, my voice breaking, "I've got a mother of a cold going on here. Could you maybe come back later?"

A rough hand reaches through the door and grabs me by the shirt, yanking me out into the cold, then hurling me back against the long bank of entryway windows. It's not the Fed-Ex guy. Not UPS or the mailman. Nobody else ever comes here. "Who are you?" I manage, "and why are you doing this?" The man looks crazed. He looks as if he's been drinking. Maybe even on drugs.

Then I notice the cigarette holder. Oh dear God. My worst nightmare come true. It's Hunter S. Thompson. In that case, definitely on drugs. "I wish I had something to offer you," I say, thinking as fast as I can, which isn't very, "but I quit drinking 17 years ago." He jacks a shell into the pump. Uh-oh, wrong approach. However, he sees that I've recognized him. Sees the confusion lifting, the fear dawning in my face.

"I understand you're writing a book," he drawls. And just lets it hang there, the whole scene suddenly framed in tableaux. I should have seen this coming. I should have called it Seven something. Or something about Simplicity or Cheese. "Look," I say . . . but that's as far as I get because the shotgun is now jammed between my teeth. "Mrphh rmble xltrig forqwad!" I protest.

"A book about gonzo," he says with towering contempt. "A book about gonzo *marketing*," he says, and spits—an ugly gesture at the best of times, and I'm thinking this isn't one of them. But at least he's pulled the gun back some, so I can talk.

"Hunter, man! It's not what you think! You're gonna love it, actually. See, the reason it's gonzo is what you said about the writer needing to be engaged in what he's writing." I compulsively add ". . . well, he or she." Big mistake. He rams the barrel into my sternum, pinning me against the window. "Yeah sure, so it's a business book, OK. But not *that* kind of business book. You know?" It doesn't look like he knows. "Listen . . ." I try again.

But he says "No, you listen to this!" And suddenly there's a blinding light and a very loud noise that I'm hearing with every auditory synapse as I watch myself, fascinated, tumbling backwards in slow motion through the glass, which has shattered into a rainbow catching the morning light, fractal, delicate, heartbreakingly beautiful.

I slam into the Sony XBR TV, my head crashing through the largest tube job on today's consumer electronics market. Circuits spark and leap. The current streams into my brain. I realize as consciousness fades that the damn thing is trying to mate with me. Artificial intelligence attempting to spawn itself on the far and fading shores of broadcast. Predictably, the attempt fails.

The phone rings.

"Hello?" Tentative. Thinking maybe this is what comes after. You get some kind of call. But it's David Weinberger. You remember him from *Cluetrain*, right? "So how's the book coming?" he wants to know, all rested and cheery. At this moment I hate him. "I've decided not to write it," I hear myself saying. "I'm afraid people won't. . . you know, they just won't *get it*." Even though it's dawning on me it was all a dream. Still . . .

"What do you mean you're not writing it!" Weinberger thunders. I can tell he's secretly pleased, though. He just signed a contract for his own book and, really, the guy is more competitive than Larry Ellison. Also, he senses something deeply neurotic with strong psychoanalytic potential. But I head him off before he can get into it. "I just realized it was too complex," I say. "These business types haven't evolved enough yet. Maybe if I live another thousand years. . . "

I don't want to tell him the truth. That Woody Creek, Colorado, is only a few hundred miles into the mountains west of here and it's all too clear that that fearful loathsome Dr. Thompson is still up there somewhere. Alive and kicking.

CHAPTER 1

Eight Miles High:
The View from 40,000 Feet

> *"All your base are belong to us."*
>
> —*ZERO WING*[1]

MARKET RESEARCH IS DEAD. LET'S HOPE SO ANYWAY, BECAUSE ALL IT does is predict we'll want the same things tomorrow that we wanted yesterday. As practiced in most of the 20th century, market research works against creativity and the kind of risk taking that's crucially prerequisite to innovative products and services. Today, there's a counter-phenomenon at work, beginning in the realm of ideas. If they're any good, ideas propagate well over networks. And ideas create new markets.

The outcome hinges on that little word *if*. If they're any good. Market research takes an idea and asks what proof there is of an audience. Will the idea fly? And if so, with whom? To start a new cable channel today, it's necessary to prove an audience of 30 million viewers. That's a lot of eyeballs. And terms like *eyeballs* are what you get when you begin to think this way. How much can you know about individual tastes and interests among that many people? Not much. But all you really want to know is the chances of whether they'll tune in, because launching such a channel is going to take megabucks and whoever is putting up the cash is going to want pretty strong assurance of seeing those bucks back someday real soon, accompanied by a handsome return on the investment.

The return will come through advertising. Or so goes the formula. Aggregate enough eyeballs, show them whatever you think they want to see—which you hope market research will tell you—and slip in as much spam as you can between the "content" segments. The spam then cooks up into a tasty profit sandwich.

Traditionally, this approach has produced a lot of money. And little else. It has produced the kind of television programming where everything is nearly indistinguishable from everything else—where the women are always beautiful, the men are always tough, neither are any too bright and everybody wants to be a millionaire. Market research says that's what we want. So we get it by the bucketful, ad nauseam.

The same formula has produced "news" in which nothing is new. Watch CNN for a day and you'll hear the same stories repeated over and over in an endless loop. You think, how amazing that so little is happening in such a big world. If something really juicy is afoot— say a football advertising personality offs his wife, or some minor British royalty buys it in a car crash—you can watch the news for months at a time without hearing about much else. God help you if some cute little Cuban kid accidentally washes up in Florida.

But then, so much gets washed up in Florida. Two hundred years of American democracy, for instance. And again, it's the same market research formula at work behind the scenes. A presidential race run like a focus group, with a couple hundred million people expressing their poll-driven proclivities for the product features of Brand X or Brand Y. The U.S. election of 2000 reflected an almost beautiful, if totally twisted symmetry. Offered no real choice, the electorate returned no real decision. The only surprise is that anyone was surprised.

So what choice have we got? If everything we see and hear is beamed at us on the theory that what we want to see and hear is what we've *always* seen and heard, it seems we're inexorably condemned to some maddening media hell where it's always Groundhog Day. No wonder Eli Lilly sells so much Prozac. Who wouldn't go batshit under such conditions? Lab rats wouldn't just display neurotic behavior. They'd explode.

But we do have a choice: the Internet. Rather than explode with anger and frustration, a flood tide of humanity has immigrated to this temporary autonomous zone. The net is like a vast global city packed with displaced persons, refugees fleeing the insanity of mass media. "The sky above the port was the color of television tuned to a dead channel," wrote William Gibson in the opening salvo of *Neuromancer*,[2] the book that coined the word *"cyberspace"* in 1984 before anyone had ever been there. Artists are outsiders. But artists are also outriders. A dense and crowded matrix of rainy street corners, the net offers little shelter from the elements. But you can pick up your guitar and play. Just like yesterday. Or your sax or your word processor or your graphics or film editing software. Like tens of millions of disaffected kids with more time than money and more brains than most record company executives, you can crank up your MP3 encoder and your CD burner. As the music industry learned from Napster—just a few days late and a couple billion dollars short—you can change the rules.

Mass media works top-down. Like Aztec temples, they concentrate power and ownership atop steep pyramids based on command and control, using broadcast as a form of human sacrifice. To the teeming millions massing from the bottom up on the net today, this is not just an overburdened metaphor. Having been treated their entire lives only as eyeballs, as fodder for this impersonal, inhuman media mill, they have no allegiance to the gods of broadcast and their unholy rituals of content licensing and windfall profit. If you change the rules, you can change the world. And the only real question has become: why not?

But as predicted, this revolution is not being televised. Business depends for its intelligence on broadcast news and market research, both of which tell it what it wants to hear. Business has its ear to the wrong ground. Happily touting the wonders of e-commerce, it is tuned to a dead channel, deaf to the voices of the dispossessed.

At first, the world at large ignored the net, missed its significance, scoffed, then jumped in with both feet, thinking it was a bandwagon, asked the wrong questions about how to make money with it, got too excited when it seemed to be something it wasn't, too depressed when it turned out to be what it is: mirrored fractal nets within nets, the collective intelligence of the human race unfolding in real time—and for the first time, on its own terms. The Internet routes around obstacles; the bigger the obstacle, the more joyous the detour. The humorless power of the state, the iron-fisted control demanded by the corporation, the sexless desire insinuated by broadcast advertising—all are falling to networked imagination.[3]

And so far, we've just been playing. The flap over Napster is merely the toy of public opinion wound up and released—a plastic duck quacking its way through the mainstream media. It's right! It's wrong! The millennium has come! The end is nigh! But who cares? Most of this "debate" is looking backward, trying to salvage constructs that no longer matter. Whose property is intellect? Whose right the right to copy what has gone before? Human culture has always been the work of thieves, beginning with Prometheus. Kill Napster today, get the fire next time.

While the music industry wrings its hands over profits lost from catchy tunes it ensnared in the twentieth-century equivalent of bad-faith treaties with native tribes, the net is already dreaming about arts and music and literatures not yet composed. About how they will travel, whose eyes and ears, whose hearts they will arrive at. Business made an unholy pact with technology, and thought it had found the keys to the kingdom. But unlocking the gates, it imported a Trojan horse into the city of commerce. Within the code is a deeper code that business does not understand.

"Today I want to talk about piracy and music," said Courtney Love to the Digital Hollywood online entertainment conference in May 2000. "What is piracy?" she asked, then answered her own question. "Piracy is the act of stealing an artist's work without any intention of paying for it. I'm not talking about Napster-type software. I'm talking about major label recording contracts."[4]

Business goes into heat at the smell of teen spirit. It dreams of new and untapped Internet markets, actionable tips on viral marketing to the stupid-turned-contagious? Yeah well, here we are now. Entertain us.

Missing the darkly nuanced reference, business does indeed seek to entertain us. What it fails to realize is that, like Whitman, we are multiple. There is no "us" that can be entertained the way America was once entertained en masse by Norman Rockwell magazine covers. Nevertheless and notwithstanding that, nearly all business approaches to the Internet shoot for a mass market. "Let's see, it'll cost us a million-five for the site and another mil for the ad campaign, but think of all the ways we can monetize a billion clicks! We'll hit break-even inside 90 days. Cool! How soon can we IPO?"

Uh-huh. But it ends up costing three times as much—and no one shows. Meanwhile, some teenager puts up a page of dancing hamsters that pulls eighty-three bajillion hits in two weeks—so many that her ISP's server melts down. Total cost: twenty nine dollars.

But does business make the correct inference from this? Does anyone in the boardroom say "Jeepers! They'd rather be looking at singing rodents than our zillion-dollar e-commerce site!" Generally speaking, this realization is strenuously deprecated. And though everyone in the organization knows it's true, giving voice to such a sentiment at any level *below* the boardroom constitutes seriously career-inhibiting behavior.

So, very few in the business scene seem to have learned much from the hamster gambit. Most companies kept on shooting for those imaginary mass markets on the web. Kept on, that is, until the dot.com bandwagon threw a wheel early in the year 2000. Too bad too, as it was during this period of Internet tulip mania that I was able to sell brooklynbridge.com. Seventeen times. And I don't even own it. But then the bottom fell out and, predictably, all these negative stories started appearing in the mainstream press. Is the Internet a Flop? Is There Any Money to be Made Online? Net Entrepreneurs Share Dumpster-Dining Tips. Etc. But the headline I kept looking for never appeared: E-commerce Exposed As Pathological Corporate Hallucination. The financial markets were worried, yes. There was deep concern on The Street. But what everyone seemed to take away from all this was what I like to call the e-berserker model. That online business plans needed to be even *more* Byzantine and grandiose. That only the super-huge and hyper-capitalized could possibly survive "the shakeout." Faster, faster, more hysteria, more hand-waving, more investment!

Among the top 10 most-visited websites as of this writing, Media Metrix lists AOL, Yahoo, Microsoft, Lycos, Excite, Go, and AltaVista. Microsoft has hit on a unique strategy for maintaining its position on this list: millions of customers trying to figure out why their computers suddenly stopped working. The rest are portals and search engines—places people go online on their way to going *somewhere else*. If you look at the most frequent queries submitted to these sites, you find an interesting pattern. Most people are looking for dirty pictures, jokes and—you already guessed it—the latest dancing-hamster equivalent. At the moment, that would be the single-page graphic of Al Gore and George W. Bush got up to look like Beavis and Butthead.

Back in there somewhere I wondered: is it a shakeout when you flush a toilet? However, not being privy to my private ruminations, the press continued to drool over the prospect of a big media mating season just ahead.

Let me propose a wager, gentle reader. I bet when you first heard about the merger of AOL and Time Warner, your reactions were . . . well, let's say a little mixed. On the one hand, impressive sums were mentioned, mountains of virtual money no one will ever see, numbers too large to count. On the other hand, you had no idea what any of it meant.[5]

The one thing you must at all costs *not* consider—it would be rude of you at best—is that it means nothing. Nada. Zero. Zip. But of course, we would never entertain such thoughts, so the rudeness issue is entirely moot. We all know it's a big deal. We all know it will shape our fortunes and our futures as surely as God made Edsels and Atari games.

You see, we now have this ultra-cool hyper-high-tech Internet, with which we must keep up. We must. And as we all know, it's moving fast—at warp 8 light speed. Faster than sliced bread moved off the shelves the day after it was invented. We're running just to stay in place. We're checking out equipment down at DigiMart. We're taking courses. We're reading manuals thicker than *War and Peace* that don't even have a basic plot. Pant-pant!

But the real problem—as you'll appreciate when you come to fully understand these things—is that the Internet is so darn slow.

Eh? Howzat?

Well, look: Sure you got your basic e-mail and your basic 100 billion kajillion web pages, but do you have true broadband? Are you fully hardwired to a 7 x 24 x 365 multiply redundant TCP/IP-enabled cable infrastructure? Because whether you know it or not, that's what you really want. It's what you need. Let's not mince words: it's what you'll fork out for. And it's been the American Dream for many years now. So much money has been spent already. Just for you.

Back around 1993, another mega-convergence deal was announced between TCI and Bell Atlantic (*"convergence"* is a technical term for hybrid—sort of like when you mate a horse with a donkey and get a mule). True, it fell apart before it came together, but you have to admit they tried. Then, just a few years later another world-class merger of media titans was announced to great fanfare—between MCI and Rupert Murdoch's News Corporation. The fact that it lasted less than a year should not blind us to its historic import, its brave and selfless attempt to bring us more precious bandwidth.

Bandwidth is an enormously complex concept, which you are probably not congenitally predisposed to understand. Here's the watered down Cliff Notes version. A word is worth one word. A picture is worth 1,000. We have the bandwidth to exchange these sorts of things online today, but they are embarrassingly low-tech. What can you really do with them? Draw some funny pictures for your home page? Write a letter to your granddaughter in China? Meet new people? Learn new things? Maybe explore another culture, or find a cure for cancer? Oh, puh-leease!

Be honest. Look your techno-fetishism in the face for once. You don't want e-mail. You don't want friends or conversations. You certainly don't want knowledge. What you want is user-selectable full-motion video-on-demand. You want golf clubs and cubic zirconiums, strange new forms of exercise equipment, otherworldly food processors. You want nonstop astrological advice and 24-hour wall-to-wall home shopping. What you really want is Jerry Springer!

And this is what AOL and Time Warner want too. It's what they want for you. Why? Because bandwidth this fat can deliver advertising like there's no tomorrow. And that, gentle reader, is worth considerably more than 1,000 words. Imagine this: It's worth a bucketful of bucks so big, so vast, so overwhelmingly impressive, that all those numbers you've seen up till now are nothing more than petty-cash chump change.

Now does it all make sense?

The AOL/Time Warner hookup represents the ultimate shared goals of mass media and mass marketing. Simply stated, the objective is to become as big as possible as fast as possible, to reach and lock in "the mass market." This sort of strategy made perfect sense at one time—when there *was* a mass market. But mass markets were fragmenting for many decades before the Internet came on-stream, and since then, the net has enormously accelerated the frag-mentation. I often refer to the new company resulting from the AOL/Time Warner merger as The Titanic Deck Chair Rearrangement Corporation (NASDAQ:TDCRC). Huge media empires with dreams of top-down mass market control are living in a past that's no longer relevant. No more can broadcast advertising shape the tastes and desires of some undifferentiated mass of humanity. In contrast to mass media, the net has liberated audiences and markets to seek out what *they* are interested in. And thereby hangs another tale entirely.

If they're any good, ideas propagate well over networks. And ideas create new markets. (Remember that bit? Just checking. . .) Unlike market research, the net provides another, more immediate way to find out if ideas are "any good." What you do is simply take the plunge. If a website or mailing list you create attracts an audi-ence, you're off and running. If not, you crash and burn. Oh well. Of course, business never thinks "oh well." It wants to know out front and top down that success is assured. It wants risk reduction and dependable size-of-audience projections. It wants a guaranteed return on its investment. But this is usually because it invests way too much based on obsolete mass-market expectations.

Here's what's wrong with approaches based on this model: all they care about is making money for investors. And here's where many business readers will pull a full-body Keanu Reeves: "Whoa!" Because isn't that what business is all about? Yeah sure. But business is not what the Internet is all about. Never was, never will be. Mass media were created to serve the marketing requirements of corpora-tions. The net had no such provenance. Companies that assume the net is there so they can sell more tend to forget why so many *peo-ple* are there: because business is *not*—at least not in the same in-trusive and unavoidable way business is there on television. People are there because of their interest in other people and what those other people are interested in. The net never promised anyone a media empire. It never purported to be the Northwest Passage to enormous corporate profits. If it turns out not to work the same way as conventional mass media—and it doesn't—whose fault is that?

Companies have always correctly assumed that people are not naturally inclined to be interested in their products. Not sufficiently interested, at any rate. However, mass media provided a perfect cure for this inattention: advertising. Advertising was an effective way to "remind" people of how much they really wanted—how much they *needed*—that new car or insurance policy or washday miracle. Companies talk about branding products, but what mass marketing is really about is branding people—stamping product impressions onto as many forebrains as possible as many times a day as possible. The product is boring? No problem. Get a bigger hammer to drive the message home. This process is what most media mediate. Commercial sponsors are their lifeblood and reason for existing.

Not so with the net. It's possible to spend days and weeks online without ever seeing an ad—if you don't count the email spam (delete, delete). Many sites have no sponsors, yet are drawing an audience. How do they make money? They don't. They are labors of love, created on nights and weekends by people deeply, often obsessively interested in their subject matter. Think about it this way. You know those horses and bison on the cave walls in places like Lascaux and Altamira? Can you imagine this conversation with one of the Neolithic artists who created them?

"Nice execution, Gork, but who's bankrolling this site? I mean, have you lined up investors yet? Any backers? And what about sponsors? Do you have a business plan *at all?*"

"Duh. Gork not think of that. Gork guess he get busboy job down at Wooly Mammoth Burgers. . . "

Think about it this way. If the business notion of best practices had been applied from the dawn of human civilization, human beings never would have achieved civilization. Art history would focus on things like ancient Roman bas-reliefs of the current Tide and Cheer equivalents, the Sistine Chapel ceiling would say "Bank With Medici!" and instead of a torch, the Statue of Liberty would be brandishing a tube of Preparation H.

Fortunately for us, product placement is a relatively new idea. But hold the phone, some will indubitably say. Without making a profit for investors. . . why business wouldn't be. . . [sputter, choke, sputter] business! Well, one thing's for sure. It wouldn't be business as usual. Hmmm. . . interesting phrase, that. David Weinberger, Doc Searls, Rick Levine and myself used it in the name of a book we wrote together—*The Cluetrain Manifesto: The End of Business As Usual*. We were as serious about that subtitle as I am about Winning Through Worst Practices. There's even a connection.

Before *Cluetrain* was a book it was a website. But long before that, it was a set of tentative, half-formed ideas. Ideas, as it turned out, that propagated well over the Internet. Ideas that not only created a new market—for a highly unusual business book—but that also began to question the whole idea of business and to redefine the very notion of markets. Years before *Cluetrain* hit *Fast Company* and *The Industry Standard*, *The Wall Street Journal* and *The New York Times*, we had no conscious plan to make a nickel off any of the ideas we were kicking around. Perhaps I'd best speak for myself from here on out. What I thought *I* was doing was destroying my (hah!) professional career. What can I say? I was bored.

Very bored. From where I was sitting five years ago—IBM as it happens—business looked like a fetid swamp. All day I would watch as overgrown dinosaurs stumbled into the La Brea tar pits of their own bottomless ignorance. Fun for a while, to be sure. Godzilla Meets Gerstnera. Fortuna–500 vs. Earth. Et cetera. But it was all reruns after about the first 90 minutes.

Hocus Focus

So I started a market research project. An Internet focus group. Only I didn't call it that. I disguised my true intentions by calling it Entropy Gradient Reversals.[6] The name should be fair warning in itself. EGR was (and still is) a webzine and email list that, from the beginning, sought to answer one burning question: does intelligent life exist in online business?

But first, a word about shameless self-promotion. Media budget in the low three figures? Don't know how you'll ever make ends meet? As four out of five net-heads and zinesters have discovered, shameless self-promotion is just the ticket! And as your dentist will tell you, it's an important part of a regular program of bottom-up gonzo marketing. It's also an important part of our core theme, so try not to look too shocked as it dawns on you that, in this case, the bogus self-effacement so typical of business books went AWOL right from the outset in this one. We now return you to another exciting episode of *Practice What You Preach,* already in progress. . .

EGR is hard to characterize. Some would say impossible. From day one, it sought to rankle, to antagonize readers, drive them crazy. In fact, one of the site's primary objectives is to get curious viewers to go away. Needless to say, this was a major step in the evolution of gonzo marketing. However, nothing I've tried has worked. The number of hits on the site, while not exactly threatening to edge out Yahoo, has always grown, never diminished. What am I doing wrong?

Since May Day 1996, EGR has been pumping out an irreverent stream of over-the-top gonzo effluvia as insurance against my ever again accepting employment in a so-called Fortune-class company. In the agonizingly slow process of aggregating an audience bottom-up, without benefit of a mega-dollar-java-animated-web-banner-advertising budget, and depending solely on its readership's goodwill and word-of-mouth peer review to attract new subscribers, here are some of the editorial mandates to which the publication has hewed religiously:

- Assume that anyone who disagrees is a patent imbecile.
- Insult readers at every opportunity; impugn their motives; question their cognitive reach.
- Use profanity with licentious abandon.
- Use arcane vocabulary demanding recourse to out-of-print editions of unabridged dictionaries.

- Make pompous offhand allusions to literary works *no one* has ever read.
- Include interviews with fictitious media "personalities," farm animals and B-movie monsters.
- Encourage loyal subscribers to unsubscribe "to make room for others."
- Publish lurid personal confessions, often entailing wanton sex and the use of illegal pharmaceuticals.
- Drop gratuitous equal-opportunity racial, religious and gender slurs.
- Brutally mock potential sponsors.
- Threaten to hand over subscribers' personal information to spammers.
- Demand payment from readers for no apparent reason, then abruptly change tack and announce: "We wouldn't take your stinking money if you paid us!"
- Make endless lists about which no one in their right mind could reasonably be presumed to give a rat's ass.

. . . and so on; you catch the general drift. Or perhaps you don't. But either way, what did all this bombastic rant-and-raillery set out to accomplish? What could it possibly have hoped to prove?

EGR is largely written by spectral constellation of psychic flotsam who insists on calling himself RageBoy®. There are days I'd like to forget about him, believe me. He is the product of what Poe called the imp of the perverse, a certain inexplicable inclination to self-destruct just as everything is going well. You're standing at the edge of an abyss, Poe says—just taking in the scenery—and suddenly you feel this incredible urge to throw yourself off the edge. That's the imp of the perverse, the ultimate font of worst practices.

RageBoy is all my own worst qualities and character defects, somehow split out into a separate personality that, allowed free range on the web, has attained a disturbing measure of autonomy. He is my science-fiction monster run amok. My albatross. And probably my well-deserved karma for past offenses against various deities. But I can't get rid of him. He's also my cash cow. When new clients call up, do they want to talk to me? No way. "Is RB available?" they ask, as if I'm just the office boy. This is so unfair. Me,

I've worked really hard all my life to develop ideas that made some sort of logical sense. I've struggled to express them clearly and persuasively. I think I've even succeeded a few times. But nobody cared about that. It was so boring people fell asleep reading the stuff. Some even died.

RageBoy, on the other hand, is insane. I don't mean this metaphorically, you understand. The guy is certifiably nuts. When I think of all the times he's threatened to destroy my career, I cringe. When I was working at IBM, he published a lengthy interview with Mr. Ed. That's right, the talking horse. He pretended that Ed was secretly running the whole worldwide media scene—and intimated that he regularly overdosed on psychedelics. It was horrible. What if my employer had found out about this? As if that weren't bad enough, he started "interviewing" ranking individuals at IBM itself, including its chairman, Lou Gerstner. Jesus Christ!

I lived in terror of what he'd do next. I still do.

But it's weird. RageBoy also has this knack of getting it precisely right by following these whacked-out inclinations. At times, anyway. Plenty of people hate him—with just cause—but there are also plenty who love him dearly and, against all logic, go to great lengths to do his insalubrious bidding. One time he got email from this business guy in the UK. "You really don't give a shit, do you?" he wrote. "I am incredibly impressed." RB framed that one. I tell you, the guy's a total lunatic, but what can I do? He does all the writing and the interviews. He's now bringing all the income into this operation.

OK, so we're the same person in reality, or whatever passes for that around here. But you see how it is. To be generous, a bit confusing. I've learned to live with this fractured personality setup, however, because it has taught me something. Everyone needs an outlet for that part of themselves that usually isn't allowed to speak at all. Not always to be sure, but often, that part has something vital to say. It has a certain wisdom, but we repress it, thinking it's too weird, too untamed, too out of control.

This is one sense of gonzo. Whenever I've thought about *Gonzo Marketing* up till now (this book has been brewing for years), I've thought I would say that this *daemon*, this wild and somewhat dangerous element wasn't really essential. Yes, it's a dimension I've explored, I was going to say, but it isn't something you need to consider yourself. I thought I could get away with it. Hey, if I didn't have to spook anybody, bigger market for the book, right?

But I can't get away with it. As I write these paragraphs, I realize how wrong that separation sounds. While there are other, hugely important dimensions of gonzo (which we'll get to in due time), I now see that gonzo marketing can't possibly work without at least some measure of, well. . . call it fear and loathing. There has to be some sense of going over the edge, taking a leap into the unknown, going against all those internal alarms that pose as instincts but are really just paranoid defense mechanisms. There has to be some real sense that you're not only breaking the rules, but burning the bridge to boot. And that has to scare you. Otherwise, how would you become fearless?

To speak from the heart is to become who we truly are, and that's always risky, or at least surprising. If I strategize my speech, anticipate what I think you want me to say, things may go more smoothly on the surface. Certainly, there will be less confusion. Things will be simpler and more predictable. Fearful of exposure, we read from the expected social script. But we haven't really met. We haven't yet entered into that terra incognita where genuine communication becomes possible. Voice is far more than the sounds we make.

Noting that corporate notions of markets were not based on real people but on cardboard cutout models of customers so straight and so stupid it's hard to imagine anyone except maybe Ward and June Cleaver ever fit the mold, I wondered out loud (or RB wondered, I forget) what impact all this might have on current approaches to online marketing. Like maybe all the hysterical e-commerce hoopla was a crock. But no one was really listening anyway. Or so I thought.

In December 1999, under the heading "The wisdom of RageBoy," *The Economist* wrote:

> For the past four years, Mr. Locke has exorcised his demons with an irregular e-mail screed sent under the name of his one-man consultancy, Entropy Gradient Reversals. . . As often as not, he writes in the voice of his psychotic alter-ego, RageBoy, in a profanity-laced ramble that occasionally touches on the subject of Internet business strategy, ridiculing all it sees. There are plenty of nuts out there

firing off crazed e-mails, but what is extraordinary about Mr. Locke is that he has attracted some 3,500 devoted readers from some of the Internet's largest firms. After months of paging through his abuse, they eventually realise that it is all a subversive demonstration of his big idea, "gonzo marketing". . . [7]

Unfortunately, the magazine didn't quite grasp this big idea—assuming it was a way for "big companies to reach a new class of young, hip consumer with edgy, humorous and self-deprecating web content." Uh, no. . . not exactly. Though it would certainly be refreshing if companies could be less humorless and self-congratulatory—a style, you may have noted, that I've adopted as a subversive demonstration of ham-fisted irony. *The Economist* did hit the mark in one respect, however. "Being right," the article observed, "has not made Mr. Locke rich. . . "

Yes, my readers expressed sincere and deeply warped delight. They egged me on. They begged for more. But I asked myself why I was doing this. It seemed thoroughly insane. Over the past five years, I have invested an absurd amount of time in this zine. And for what? At the moment, EGR is up to about 5,000 subscribers. By online business standards, this doesn't even rank in the pathetic showing category. However, what they lack in numbers, these readers make up for in raw intelligence, boundless skepticism and massive net savvy. They're smart. They're unconvinced. They're wired to the eyes. Oddly enough, many do work in major corporations.[8]

In *The Cluetrain Manifesto* I wrote, "The word that's passing like a spark from keyboard to screen, from heart to mind, is the permission we're giving ourselves and each other: to be human and to speak as humans." And that's exactly what happened when the book hit. Before the publisher could launch its marketing campaign, *Cluetrain* was already climbing the charts. The sales rank figures on Amazon had to be a mistake. It started out way too high. But it stayed in the top 50 for months; in the top 100 for most of the year.

While much has been written about viral marketing, most of it is crap—carrot-dangling to corporate sales droids who desperately want to believe their lackluster product come-on will go platinum on the net. Not bloody likely. But *Cluetrain* did go platinum, did go viral. Why? Because it passed on that permission to be human. And it passed it on via gonzo marketing—which is *not* some slick new trick for corporations to manipulate the young, the hip, the edgy. Gonzo marketing is market advocacy, the marketplace speaking in its own behalf.

Cluetrain was hardly what you'd call a *nice* book. Not nice to business, at any rate. It railed, it ranted, it used bad words. It told corporations that everything they knew about the net was wrong. And not just wrong, but laughably deluded. Then, adding injury to insult, it refused to provide any sort of guidelines. You're on your own, it said. But suddenly, companies like BP Amoco, Citicorp, Conde Nast, Conoco, J. Walter Thompson, Nordstrom, Ogilvy & Mather, Reuters, Young & Rubicam were reading my harsh, implacable words. Buying them, in fact, in several senses. And making me rich as a result (it's always so nice to disprove the financial press). I almost began to feel guilty. *Almost.* The problem was this. Many companies seemed to agree with what I'd written in the manifesto: "Conversations among human beings *sound* human. They are conducted in a human voice. . . People recognize each other as such from the sound of this voice." And companies wanted to know, therefore, how they too could sound human. But I didn't think they could. And I still don't. I felt bad about it sure, especially with all those outfits purchasing *my* product for a change. But there it was. Bummer, dudes. Impasse. You just can't get here from there. *Cluetrain* said that a metaphorical Berlin Wall was separating the corporate conversations inside companies from the market conversations outside.

Ripping Out the Wall

". . . we don't need no thought control."

—PINK FLOYD, *THE WALL*

In February 2000 something extraordinary happened. One company—a very large one—ripped out the wall. Ford announced it was giving home PCs and Internet access to all 350,000 of its employees worldwide. The first sentence of the press release said: "Ford Motor Company is taking a step forward to reach its vision of being on the leading edge of technology and connect more closely with its customers."

This bold move was reported prominently on the front pages of *The Washington Post* and *The New York Times*. However, these articles focused on who would be supplying the computers, how much the program would cost, how the move was good for labor relations, and detailed specs of the hardware. The *Post* quoted Jac Nasser, Ford president and CEO as saying, "We're committed to serving consumers better by understanding how they think and act. Having a computer and Internet access in the home will accelerate the development of these skills, provide information across our business and offer opportunities to streamline our processes."

But other than this clip, neither paper said anything about the company connecting more closely with customers. And none of the coverage that I saw quoted Nasser's far more detailed remarks in making the actual announcement:

> . . . we want to be able to improve communications—two-way communications—and make sure that our employees—every one of us—is connected to what's going on in the marketplace, so that we know where consumers are heading, what's happening to market trends, what's happening to product trends, and make it easier for our employees to have a better understanding of the shift that's happening out there. . . .[9]

Maybe that doesn't make for a great sound bite on the six o'clock news, but it's the heart of the story—a story the mainstream press completely missed. The real deal here is that Ford has unleashed 350,000 independent—and genuinely intelligent—agents to fan out online and listen carefully.

But not just listen—"two-way communications," Nasser said. These computers and net connections will not be under corporate control. They will not be monitored in any way. Ford has unleashed 350,000 people to whom it has tacitly granted permission to speak on its behalf. Not in a legal sense, but in a much more powerful way. These are people who will tell their own stories, in their own voices, any way they see fit. Ford not only got out of their way, it provided the tools and the encouragement to use them. That's smart. Replacing paranoia and control with no-strings permission is always smart.

The next day, Delta Air Lines announced a similar offer to its 75,000 employees. American Airlines, Intel and Bertelsmann have since followed suit, and I expect we'll hear many more such announcements. This trend alone could revolutionize current notions of Internet marketing. I suspect it will pick up momentum as the attendant advantages accruing to these companies become obvious to competitors and industry analysts.

And Ford had even more strange news up its sleeve. In May, the company issued a "corporate citizenship report" in which it noted that sports utility vehicles—including its own Explorers and Expeditions—kill more people than tend to get killed in non-SUV crashes. Ford also said it wasn't too happy about the lousy gas mileage these vehicles get, as it's damaging the planet. When the media expressed surprise that the company would be so forthright on such potentially damning issues, Debbie Zemke, Ford's director of corporate governance, said "For heaven's sake, everybody else is talking about it, so why shouldn't we?"[10]

Perhaps Ford's willingness to tell the truth comes as even more of a surprise because, being digital and all, we've been conditioned by the simplistic wired/tired dichotomy of Nicholas Negroponte that bits are way cool but atoms are old hat. Ford is a very atomic company—a rustbelt NYSE discrete manufacturer, not a NASDAQ dot.com darling—so it must not "get it," right? Wrong. Companies like Ford were among the first to feel the fire of global competition, and it was no picnic. Ford was the first major U.S. company to bring in Deming and go through the Total Quality transformation. The company had to radically rethink its entire purpose. Perhaps most important, as Deming demanded, it had to drive out fear.

Fear masks arrogance, which in turn masks the kind of ignorance unable to admit it needs ideas that were "not invented here." Managers from CEO on down had to become humble enough to realize that workers they'd been bossing around for better than half a century often knew more than they did. Ford began listening to its workers. So did General Electric. Jack Welch got religion for self-directed teams and process mapping. The results spoke for themselves—not just competitive survival, but better products, greater profits, better places to work.

Now these "old-economy" corporations are listening again, extending the same attention to their markets via the Internet. This has nothing to do with facile tricks like "permission" or "viral" marketing. Instead, it's about what I have come to call *wide-area knowledge acquisition*. It's about the profound understanding that intellectual capital has little to do with ownership today, and everything to do with invitation, access and enthusiastic bottom-up community involvement. Is "open source marketing" an impossible oxymoron? Think about Linux and Napster. And reflect on how odd it is that sleepy old atomic tortoises like Ford and GE may turn out to be faster companies than digital hares like Intel, Microsoft and IBM.

In a clear reference to the infamous dictum that what's good for General Motors is good for America, Ford president and CEO Jac Nasser wrote:

> It was not so long ago that leading companies believed what was good for them was good for the world. Business leaders made decisions without scrutiny or accountability and assumed the world would accept the consequences of those choices—be they good or bad. At Ford, we believe exactly the opposite is true. What is good for the world is good for Ford Motor Company.[11]

This might easily come across as just more corporate hot air—sounds nice, means nothing—except that Ford is putting its money where its mouth is. More to the point, it is putting its many voices where its money comes from. By giving PCs and Internet connections to its entire workforce worldwide, Ford has opened itself to the marketplace as no company has ever dared. These workers will fan out online and tell their own stories, engage in their own conversations, not about Mustangs and Explorers and Tauruses, but about the kinds of things human beings tend to get excited about. You know: what kind of education their kids are getting, why government is so broken, how grandma won the chili cookoff at the state fair, where wireless technology is headed, and by the way, how much *would* it cost to start a chinchilla ranch in Tasmania?

Speak boldly and don't carry a big shtick. Most of the "thinking" in marketing these days is simply missing the boat. Mass markets have been steadily fragmenting many decades. They are being replaced by vibrant new micromarkets just now emerging from the web. These don't show up on corporate radars tuned to lock onto mass-market targets of opportunity—or the fragmented debris of former mass markets, which is what conventional market segmentation keeps desperately trying to salvage.

A Preview of the Gonzo Model

For nearly a century, companies like Ford have told workers to "check your brain at the door." Corporations broadcast work orders down a tiered bureaucracy driven by command-and-control management. Similarly, they broadcast orders to the marketplace in the form of advertising: buy our product! But imagine Ford today, releasing all those workers into a chaotic uncontrolled and uncontrollable market space. Suddenly, the company might very much like to know what's in their workers' brains—and not just the sorts of things they do on the job. Imagine the following scenario. While speculative, there is nothing preventing companies from exploring this model, and much to gain by testing its potential.

Suppose Ford discovers, through offering open web space to self-motivated employees, that one-tenth of one percent of its workforce are gung-ho organic gardeners. Why would a car company be interested in such an avocation? Two reasons. First, 350,000 people is a pretty fair sample of the population at large, so it's reasonable to guess that a similar tenth of a percent of the market might be organic gardeners. Second, Ford is also a truck company, and people who grow gardens tend to haul stuff they wouldn't want to shovel into the back seat of the family sedan. Thus, such a micromarket includes excellent prospects for pickup trucks.

Ford would first want to introduce these workers to each other, and suggest that they collaborate on building an organic gardening sub-site at ford.com—on company time of course. Imagine the enthusiasm that would result from being paid to do what you most love, instead of what you're told. Then Ford would find the best voices in this group—the most articulate, engaging and informed—

and sign them up as emissaries to the best *external* organic gardening website. Call it Organic Gardening World, OGW for short. These ambassadors would then approach this best-of-breed site bearing gifts: cash, server hardware, technical assistance, even reverse ad banners to drive traffic from ford.com's homepage to this affiliate micromarket aggregator. Say the OGW site has a regular audience of 5,000. Ford would want to increase this audience to 500,000 as quickly as possible. It would also want an exclusive relationship with respect to competitors. OGW could have other underwriters, just not from the likes of GM, Daimler-Chrysler or Toyota.

Ford's money would enable the OGW site developers to quit their day jobs in some corporate cube farm and devote full time to doing what they love best. Notice that love is a powerful attractor on both sides of the equation. And it is an equation—perhaps better, an *equator*. When organic gardeners click the banner on the OGW homepage that says "Underwritten by Ford Motor Company," they would not be transported to ford.com, but instead to ford.com/organic-gardening. And there they'd encounter Ford employees who understand and share their passion for mulch, for good rich dirt, for corn-on-the-cob served five minutes from harvest. These two groups also share an active interest in pickup trucks, automatic lift gates and power take-offs. Does this intersection of common interests hold more promise than conventional advertising? How much might it be worth to find out before competitors got the jump on the best voices emerging out there on the web right now?

Imagine taking this one step further. Say Joe Smith is Ford's primary ambassador to the OGW site, and is highly visible in posting there. It's part of his job. He doesn't write about Ford products, but about his knowledge of organic gardening. He knows a lot, and he's well respected for his advice. Now say Mary sends him private email. "Joe, I know you work at Ford. I wonder if you can help me. I bought an Explorer a while back, but the driver's side door is sprung and my dealer is giving me the run-around." Joe promotes this to the EVP Customer Service at Ford corporate, for which he has hot-line priority, and 20 minutes later Mary gets the following note. "Mary, Joe tells me you're having problems with your Explorer. Sorry to hear it. Call Bill Smith at the number below and schedule a time to have it fixed. I worked it out with Bill to take care of you at no charge." How many times would a company have to comp such service to gain word-of-mouth evangelists it couldn't buy with a $100 million ad campaign?

Welcome to gonzo marketing. As with the gonzo journalism from which it takes its name, this kind of engaged participation is the exact opposite of "objectivity" that pretends to have no perspective, no point of view. Every website worth its salt is an act of journalism, news of some passionate interest and engaged advocacy. By underwriting and participating in the life and growth of such sites, corporations can forge powerful relationships with emerging micromarkets. This is a win-win, not a zero sum, model. Everyone benefits: the corporation, its workers, external site producers, and their audiences.

Could there be problems of undue corporate influence on content? Sure. But these are no different from the problems faced today by traditional publishers, who set up "church and state" boundaries between advertising and editorial departments. A site with many underwriters will be safer from such influence—attempting which will be cause for terminating contracts. A company seeking unfair advantage would risk permanently ceding its relationship to a competitor. Not a real swift idea.

Why would a huge corporation get out of the way and enable mere workers to speak on its behalf? Workers are no longer valuable for their labor alone but also for their curiosity about the world *outside* the company—for their interests and passions and the uncontrived voices through which they express themselves. People want to talk to people, not flacks and lawyers and scripted marketing zombies with hidden and none-too-friendly subagendas.

Why would a company used to dictating to its markets via broadcast advertising suddenly switch gears and pay attention? Willie Sutton robbed banks, he said, because that's where the money was. Today, corporations must establish more intimate relationships with markets because that's where the knowledge is. Intellectual capital is no longer a strictly internal affair. Engaged conversations with relevant micromarkets will become a crucial source of insight and innovation, and the quality of this market intelligence will ultimately determine market share. Without such interactions, efforts to create competitive products and services risk taking place in a vacuum. At least one company understands this today, and many more will follow. "We need great ideas," says Nasser, "from people both inside and outside of Ford. We will listen to those ideas with respect and seriousness."

As products come to reflect genuine esteem for workers and customers instead of self-congratulatory ballyhoo and the adversarial targeting tactics that surround the concept of brand today, companies will be far better served, and so will their markets.

Gonzo marketing provides a model whereby companies can stop manipulating people as if they were abstract demographic data, and instead create genuine relationships with emergent online communities of interest: powerful new web micromarkets. The paradox is that companies can have everything they've always wanted. Greater market share. Customer loyalty. Brand equity. All those empty phrases that today make people blow coffee out their noses. But companies can actually achieve these goals. No, really. All they have to do is follow the advice my Junior High principal once shared with me. "Son," he said, shaking with anger, "you've got to get your thinking straight!"

Naturally, I didn't. Instead, I immediately began developing my notion of worst practices. Fortunately for you, the worst of the worst will not be covered here. Serious mistakes are critically necessary to the learning process. In my own case, since these mistakes have given me such a powerful competitive advantage, I'm afraid they must remain proprietary. Plus, there are certain statutes of limitation to consider. I've made more than my fair share of catastrophic errors. Make your own.

What the balance of this book does cover is a complex constellation of ideas capable of forging an entirely new kind of relationship between commercial organizations and post-colonial Internet cultural communities. Of course, they're *only* ideas. At present. But—as you may have already read somewhere—if they're any good, ideas propagate well over networks. And ideas create new markets.

The Value Proposition

> *"**Value Proposition.** The reasons why a product is of sufficient value to the customer to be well worth its price. This term is often used in ad agencies as they formulate their ultimate pitch. . .*
>
> *Values. The deeply held beliefs and attitudes of the members of a particular society."*
>
> —THE PORTABLE MBA IN MARKETING [1]

> *"The possession of wealth, which was at the outset valued simply as an evidence of efficiency, becomes, in popular apprehension, itself a meritorious act."*
>
> —THORSTEIN VEBLEN [2]

> *"Money—it's a hit."*
>
> —PINK FLOYD [3]

THE SECOND CHAPTER OF *KOTLER ON MARKETING* IS TITLED "USING Marketing to Understand, Create, Communicate, and Deliver Value."[4] Maybe this will help me, I think. Maybe I'll get what I'm missing if I read this bit. Yet out of 18 pages, there is no mention of *value* until the 16th page, where all it says is: "The full positioning of the brand is called the brand's value proposition. It is the answer to the customer's question, 'Why should I buy your brand?'" Maybe it's just me, but whether marketing was used or not, I have to say that value—the core concept this chapter promises to unpack—was not understood. Neither was it communicated or delivered. If it was created, it was created somewhere else. And that's my point. I'm not picking on Kotler, particularly. In fact, I like the guy. But this failure to communicate is not at all atypical. Business in general, and marketing in particular, seem to assume we know what they mean when they sling around terms like *value, brand* and *positioning,* and equate the resulting blur of vague ideas to something we might actually care about. This notion of value *was* created somewhere else—in some wish-fulfillment fantasy world where what is valuable to business maps seamlessly and unquestionably onto what is valuable to me. Value is value. It's obvious, isn't it? What if I said no?

It feels like spring, yet it's almost solstice, mid-winter coming in. Catching the light, a flock of pigeons turns through the sky over the highway and I remember. I couldn't have been more than 10 or 11, the age my daughter Selene is now. I raised pigeons, and every morning I would watch them fly out over the tilled adobe bean field, the huge fig tree at its center, the dairy where other, wild pigeons slept at night in the cow barn. We would go there with flashlights to try to catch them without waking the farmer, who was rumored to have a shotgun. This was California, the heart of Silicon Valley, though there wasn't any silicon there back then in the late 1950's. My heart would sing to see my flock tilt and wheel in the sun. I would feel something I couldn't describe, and still can't, to see them coming home at nightfall. I am driving and remembering and feeling how much is lost, how precious this life.

"I will survive" sang Jerry Garcia a year after nearly dying and eight years before he actually did.[5] Trying to explain The Grateful Dead is like trying to tell a stranger about rock and roll. No, it's like trying to tell the ungrateful, walking dead about life—that value has something to do with gratitude. Gratitude for the mystery of the world and the heart to feel into it. Diamonds in the dust. Value as treasure unrecognized. The story has it that Garcia found "grateful dead" in an old Funk & Wagnall's dictionary entry referring to a ballad in which a traveler takes pity and lays a wandering ghost to rest. Grateful, the dead man richly rewards the deed. Shades of "Finnegan's Wake," the traditional song on which James Joyce's sprawling novel of the same name was loosely (very loosely) based, in which Tim Finnegan's funeral gets entirely out of hand and his corpse comes back to life when some drunken reveler splashes whiskey on it. Or of the Egyptian Book of the Dead, which is purported to say: "in the land of the dark, the ship of the sun is drawn by the grateful dead." Or of Dylan Thomas, who sang in another key, "After the first death there is no other."[6] Or of *El Dia de los Muertos*, the day of the dead, when roses bloom in skeletal eye sockets and the people dance in the streets to a grim fandango celebrating life.

Among other things you may imagine at this juncture (and thanks for keeping them to yourself), this exercise smacks of what anthropologist Clifford Geertz calls "thick description."[7] Using a complicated tale about sheep and thieves and justice and the lack of it in colonial North Africa in 1912, he demonstrates that any time we attempt to describe "a particular event, ritual, custom, idea, or whatever," we end up spinning stories about other people's stories about yet other people's stories, and sorting it all out becomes next to impossible. It's a rich tapestry, and thick description, while it may seem confusing, often comes closer to what's actually going on than would "thin description"—the kind of succinct clear-cut abstraction that appears perfectly plausible, but totally distorts reality. Not that I'm claiming any methodological rigor in these musings, but the thickness I'm attempting to suggest is what music and painting and literature—what we roughly call The Arts—typically point to. And what the specialized languages of logic and science and business typically do not. It's a Zen sort of thing you could say. *I* could say; who's to stop me? Finger indicating moon-illuminated finger. The thickness of life as life is lived between the inexorable poles of birth and death. "Man is an animal suspended," says Geertz, "in webs of significance he himself has spun."[8]

Webs, yes. And although the Big Daddy web did not exist when that was written, that's why the choice of quote. That's where we're headed. It's where we already are. But wait. Though we have these words for our current situation—words like Internet and World Wide Web—it seems to me they obscure at least as much as they reveal. Because networks are inherently social realities, any attempt to definitively say what they are becomes immediately suspect. It depends on where you're standing when you look at them, and what sort of baggage you've brought along to the observation deck. "Meaning is use," said Ludwig Wittgenstein, meaning things mean what you make of them. But he also said, *"Die Welt ist Alles was der Fall ist"*—the world is everything that is the case. And really, how far does that get us? Except that "Case" is the main character in William Gibson's *Neuromancer*, which, when it was published in 1984, was the first entry in a then-hot new literary genre called cyberpunk. And in German, "neu Roman" means "new novel." The novelist then the new romancer. Sure, it's a stretch, but who knows what these creative types are capable of? Everything has at least two meanings.

Because it's expected, I guess, business tends to be way too serious. Tends to take language far too literally. "A thing *is* what it is called, and it could not be called anything else," writes Peter Berger in *The Social Construction of Reality*, explaining how children perceive the world. But the following shoe may fit much larger feet: "All institutions appear in the same way, as given, unalterable and self-evident."[9] His point being that they're anything but. As you may have already picked up from the book title, his point is that reality is socially constructed. And institutions are hardly exempt from such construction: the Church, the State, Fortune 500 corporations, the Internet, the World Wide Web. When you get online, as Gibson wrote, reality is a consensual hallucination. If you're lucky.[10]

Evidently, Friedrich Nietzsche liked to say "there are no facts, only interpretations."[11] Unlike myself, Geertz and Berger and Wittgenstein probably actually read the guy. He supposedly says this in *The Will to Power: Attempt at a Revaluation of all Values*, which sounds way too heavy for my head, and which, anyway, was patched together by his sister, who was married to a Nazi and took, shall we say, certain liberties with dearly departed Friedrich's notebooks, thus giving him a much worse rap than he might have had otherwise. Talk about your thick description. Admittedly, the rap was already pretty bad, because he's also the guy who lobbed the "God is dead" grenade into the middle of the Enlightenment garden party. To say the least, this did not ingratiate him with the God-fearing—though if they were really all that afraid, you'd think at least some of them might have taken this as good news of another sort. After all, a few hundred million Buddhists do. At any rate, what I think he meant, among other things I can imagine (which I am keeping to myself), is that divine authority was no longer what you might call a highly credible source in the working out of what certain things signified or what signified certain things. Like value, for instance, to loop back around to our theme, about which, at this point, *nothing* is certain. Well, good then. That means it's working.

As Nietzsche bought the farm in 1900, you can see that this sort of general shakiness about the meaning of things has been floating around for quite some time. Hell, you could go back to the classical philosophers. Say you're walking in Memphis, home of Elvis and the ancient Greeks.[12] Is what you think a thing to be what everyone else understands it as? Is the world as it appears to you, or does it look completely different to someone who *didn't* grow up in Darien, Connecticut, and get an MBA from Wharton? Of course, Plato and Aristotle and that lot wouldn't have been able to tell an MBA from a banana fish. And anyway, who cares? Who cares, especially, because such questions verge on dangerous ground, on terra incognita. Business prides itself on hard-nosed practicality and pragmatism, even if it gets all dewy-eyed wondering where its pragmatism came from. Philosophy, anthropology, sociology, linguistics? Leave that stuff to the longhairs. We got a business plan to write!

OK, so you write the plan. For a killer B2B e-commerce portal. And you structure the plan around the Holy of Holies, the infamous 4 Ps of marketing: product, promotion, place and price.[13] Of the four, only the last generates revenue; the others represent costs. Price is what you can charge based on some proposed value. If you're a consulting group, maybe you write a meta-plan, something for clients to chew on, if not perhaps entirely digest. If you're working at the Ernst & Young "Thought Center"—*From Thought to Finish*—you write this:

Moving From First Mover to First Prover:

The race for dominance in business-to-business (B2B) digital marketplaces is picking up steam....A winning business model is based on alignment of a company and its industry with how the company will achieve competitive advantage in each of four areas: the company's *unique value proposition; delivery chain management; functionality;* and *profit mechanisms.*[14]

Cool! And not only that, Ernst & Young also promises to "stress test" your business model. After they've created it, naturally (imagine something here about the fox guarding the henhouse). For this important work, the company has assembled a team with a "unique set of skills"—uniqueness having ultrahigh cachet at the moment—consisting of "investment bankers with top tier wall street experience, and academics and economists with diverse backgrounds including Harvard Business School."[15] Wow, huh? And probably cheap too. How could you go wrong? Except maybe by buying into the odd notion that a degree from Harvard ever qualified anyone for the diversity category.

Look, I have no particular animus toward Ernst & Young. I've spoken with some very smart people there over the years. But the fact is, you will find this sort of nonsensical no-nonsense cut-to-the-chase business rhetoric on thousands of corporate web pages today. Locating an example took me about two minutes on Alta Vista. Here's the search string; try it yourself:

+B2B +"e-commerce" +"value proposition"

More substantively, you could go wrong with any number of customers, prospects, partners or suppliers by creating a "value proposition" with zero idea of what value means to a couple-three billion people, each of whom is genuinely unique, and who, taken together, are a hell of lot more diverse—you can take this one to the bank—than a bunch of fucking academic economists. Assuming that its world is *the* world, choosing to be naïve about language to the point of volunteer autism, business ends up looking a lot less hard-nosed than soft-headed.

However, having thus blinded itself like Oedipus (what did it see that it couldn't bear to see?), business is reduced to common-sense dictionary definitions of value—though this "common sense," as we'll soon see, has nothing in common with the commons as construed to mean the people, the great seething mass of humanity that has been in these latter days transformed, as if by magic, into the miracle of global markets. That is to say, these definitions were largely created by business itself (more about the fox guarding the lexicon below). The *American Heritage Dictionary* includes the following definitions of *"value"*:

1. An amount, as of goods, services, or money, considered to be a fair and suitable equivalent for something else. . .
2. Monetary or material worth. . .
3. Worth in usefulness or importance to the possessor; utility or merit. . . .
4. A principle, standard, or quality considered worthwhile or desirable. . . [16]

It seems reasonable to assume that considerations of what is worthwhile or desirable might have some bearing on price. You'd think, right? Business certainly thinks so. But the same dictionary defines *"price"* as follows:

1. The amount as of money or goods, asked for or given in exchange for something else.
2. The cost at which something is obtained. . . .
3. The cost of bribing someone. . .
4. A reward offered for the capture or killing of a person. . .
5. *Archaic.* Value or worth.

Though numbers three and four throw a bit of a curve—"every person has a price" and "a felon with a price on his head," the respective entries go on to explain—at least one and two are pretty much what you'd expect. The real zinger is the last item. Archaic? But wasn't value just explained in terms of cost? In fact it was: "an amount, as of goods, services, or money, considered to be a fair and suitable equivalent for something else . . ." And that, as the saying has it, is the price you pay.

Maybe it's some lexicographer's little joke, an Easter Egg like the ones Microsoft coders sneak into Office apps. Maybe the intent is to suggest that price *used to* reflect value, but that was then. Ha ha. Or maybe it means something far more ominous: that an older sense of value has been supplanted. For while Nietzsche never achieved his goal of revaluing all values, business has done precisely that. While nobody was looking.

In business, value determines price, or at least sometimes suggests it. Price is then a function of value—what something costs bears some relationship, we suppose, to what it's worth. But what about value in a larger framework than cost? What is the value of something to our lives? Without needing any fancy equations, we all know the value of oxygen even though it doesn't have an explicit price tag (yet). Aside from price, the larger value of products and services is connoted by a mystical constellation of values that are ideally supposed to be captured and represented by the concept of *brand*. The most successful branding campaign ever carried out was the branding of brand itself—getting human beings to accept the implicit assumption that all value is monetary, that everything has a price in dollars and cents (or currency of your choice). This largely unconscious theory of value is what defines and drives consumerism, in which identity is determined by what you have and can get instead of by who you discover you are or may become.

Because value is subjective and perceived differently by different cultures and communities, it cannot be reduced to fit neatly into a single systematic and comprehensive conceptual framework. However, this cultural relativity, this diversity of perspective and interpretation creates very large practical problems—especially for corporations committed to growth at any cost, especially for companies willing to let others bet, via the financial markets, on whether such growth is sustainable beyond, say, next Thursday. By revaluing all values in monetary terms and throwing out anything that didn't have an obvious rate of exchange, a sort of tacit universal metaphysics was born by default. God is dead, but business is alive and well. Long live McDonald's! Would you like fries with that? Long live Disney! It's a small world after all. Long live the Global Economy! Tagline pending.

In *Jihad vs. McWorld,* Benjamin Barber describes what he calls McWorld as a set of "onrushing economic, technological, and ecological forces that demand integration and uniformity and that mesmerize peoples everywhere with fast music, fast computers, and fast food. . . pressing nations into one homogenous global theme park, one McWorld tied together by communications, information, entertainment, and commerce."[17] Later, contrasting Americans' choice of multiple automobile brands with the non-choice of public vs. private transportation—a choice that was never explicitly offered—he writes: "This politics of commodity offers a superficial expansion of options within a determined frame in return for surrendering the right to determine the frame. It offers the feel of freedom while diminishing the range of options and the power to affect the larger world. Is this really liberty?"[18]

Freedom as nothing left to lose—Benjamin Barber, meet Bobby McGee.[19] All values have been revalued. The frame has been hijacked. And as untold numbers of e-commerce pundits announce with messianic fanfare and not a trace of irony: "Brand is everything!"[20]

It's Alive! It's Alive!

Love is not love
Which alters when it alteration finds. . .

—WILLIAM SHAKESPEARE[21]

Love is love and not fade away. . .

—CHARLES HARDIN AND NORMAN PETTY[22]

Entropy is the outward and visible sign of the second law of thermodynamics. In layman's terms, it means the house always wins, but place your bets anyway ladies and gentlemen; there's one born every minute. It means there's no free lunch and perpetual motion devices make exceedingly bad investments. It means the transitoriness of the composite.[23] Because friction—there's the rub—is always slowing things down, taxing energy transactions until there's nothing left to tax. And there's nothing left because, when things slow down *enough*, they disappear. Ice Nine, if you've read Vonnegut, or the fine print on those Dead albums: at absolute zero there's nothing doing. Entropy means that, once wound by the Big Bang, the cosmic clock is always running. Running down.

The directional vector of this process is the gradient, the slippery slope on which we build our hopes and dreams, technologies, empires, civilizations. Steep grade ahead; test your brakes. Not much of a toehold really in the greater scheme of things. A fool's errand you might say. And yet, if all that's true, and things always move from a greater to a lesser degree of order and cohesion, then how is it that a point of no dimension whatsoever, one day before there were days to count, erupted with a violence so far beyond all measure that it's still red-shifting galaxies back to the beginning of what we lamely conceive of as time? Or that a handful of hydrogen comes to look around itself one day, at the world, the stars, the blackest, deepest night and says: "What a gas!"

That's the reversal.

We are dealing today with levels of complexity at which the immutable second law kicks in bigtime and begins to manifest as something tangible in our lives. The effect we feel is a kind of chaos in which things fall apart more readily than they come together. This downhill slide means more thankless work for everyone—desperately trying to manage the inherently unmanageable, with increasingly small returns on the investment. Despite the 1000-megawatt euphoria of ubiquitous technology cheerleaders, the answer is not faster chips and logic-gate flips, more FLOPS or more bandwidth. It isn't "enterprise-wide knowledge management" or whatever foolproof fad is circulating at the moment. The answer is that there is no answer.

We are drowning in complexity and the more we try to simplify things, the more complex we make things in the process. It's hopeless. There is no way out.

No *obvious* way, that is. And perhaps no permanent way. But there is one thing that seems to contradict the iron law of entropy. Life. Strangely opposite to the way we tend ourselves, the thermodynamic gradient is hell-bent for ultimate simplicity. And that simplicity is death. Simple atomic structures, perfectly equalized distribution, zero Kelvin. In contrast, life is complicated, as you may have noticed. Left to itself for billions of years, with no engineers in evidence and no management consultants, our planet suddenly became extremely complex as the result of contracting a virus. A billion years later, this viral anomaly developed into bipedal hominids with big brains and bigger plans. And we've been groping around ever since, blind, stumbling in the dark.

Sometimes a great wind comes out of space and shifts the points of the compass completely, revises longheld notions of what's valuable, what's worth spending life on. That's what happened to me in the course of writing this book. I fell in love. And how does something like that fit into the context of a business book? I ask you. I ask myself. Business books are boring. They're supposed to be boring. Dispassionate and objective, detached from personal concerns. The world of business is a world unto itself. Whatever insight business books may deliver, they must do so within a strictly circumscribed set of boundaries, within a framework that validates and reinforces their core subject. Which is of course: business. The tautology is so neat it's seamless. The business of business is business. Not even daylight can slip through the cracks.

But last time I checked, there was no world of business somehow separate from the world as a whole. There was no reality to the separation we speak so easily about between work life and private life—a.k.a. "real life." These are artificial distinctions, convenient fictions. But whose convenience do they serve? Yours, gentle reader? Mine? I don't think so. Something is desperately wrong here, I think. Then I think, well. . . maybe it's just me. Maybe I got bored with the power and majesty of commerce, with its challenges, obstacles, impact and opportunities. Got bored with its limits and limiting definitions of value. Got bored because I looked into my own heart and found something far more valuable there. I ask myself if I'm alone in this. And again, I don't think so. I think I've got company.

Hmmm, "company." Now there's a business word if there ever was one. But how does the company I've got in my boredom with business differ from the kind of company a business creates? Language is funny stuff, mixing us up at every turn. Or perhaps, since I love a good conspiracy theory as much as the next poor sod, being *used* to mix us up. *Webster's Third* provides help in the form of linguistic archeology. The word *"company,"* it tells us, comes from the word *"companion,"* which originally meant someone with whom you shared food—specifically, with whom you broke bread (*panis* in Latin).[24] That's strange. Gets sort of Biblical there, doesn't it? But maybe this is leading us further away from the inherent nature of value. Maybe I'm just tripping here, reaching for a rationalization for

why I'm so bored with business. Me and all that company I suspect
I've got.

But it gets even stranger. How does a company, a corporation,
come into being? Not a trick question: it incorporates. But it is a trick
answer. Back to the archeology, *corpus* in Latin means body. So to
incorporate means to become embodied—to be made flesh. Is it just
me, I ask myself, or are there linguistic clues here that business first
sought legitimacy in the deepest mysteries of Christian theology?
Maybe so. Legitimacy was certainly a problem for early business,
dealing as it did with sublunary matters. There's a word you're not
likely to find in your *Wall Street Journal*. And for good reason. The
Oxford English Dictionary defines *"sublunary"* as:

> Existing or situated beneath the moon; lying between the orbit of
> the moon and the earth; hence, subject to the moon's influence. b.
> Inferior, subordinate (to). *Obsolete*
>   Of or belonging to this world; earthly, terrestrial.
>   Characteristic of this world and its affairs; mundane; material,
> gross; temporal, ephemeral.[25]

The sense comes through that the affairs of this world—perhaps
business especially—were not terribly well thought of at one time.
The Church, back when there was just one in Western Christendom,
denigrated such involvement, to say the least. The whole idea of
money was deeply suspect. We still speak of "filthy lucre," even if
the modern use of the phrase is usually jocular. At one time, lend-
ing money at interest constituted the sin of usury. This explains why
many more Jews than Christians went into banking—and also explains much of the resulting racial bias that has persisted to this day.
Jews were not only the infidel, they became a sort of untouchable
caste, performing necessary services for which they were, at the
same time, deeply resented.

There was another community of practice whose concern with
the sublunary sphere formed a counterbalance to the otherworldli-
ness of the Church and its focus on the afterlife. To the alchemists,
the material world was *prima materia*—the source of the earths and
metals their art sought to transform. They were not just proto-
chemists. They were philosophers working out a worldview that

was heretical in the eyes of Rome. They immersed themselves in the material plane, the world of here and now—and out of this immersion came a powerfully legitimizing analogy for commerce.

In *The Business of Alchemy,* Pamela Smith writes that in the 17th century, commerce was considered an unproductive practice. Merchants were seen as taking without returning anything to the communities in which they lived. They did not produce anything themselves, but acted as parasites, feeding off the exchange between the people who made things and the people who bought them. "The unnatural offspring of this unnatural activity," writes Smith, "was money. Money was considered unnatural because it was a means of exchange that did not contain the seeds of its own regeneration."

Despite this strong prejudice, the paradox became obvious to many: money did seem to produce an increase in material well-being. It clearly created something valuable, but no one could quite figure out how. There was no model in nature—which, there being no venture capitalists at the time, is where you went to find business models in those days. This quandary had people scratching their heads and the merchant class hopping up and down on hot coals. Business desperately wanted to be accepted as legitimate, but in keeping with the perception of all things sublunary as inferior, subordinate, mundane, ephemeral and generally gross, the whole proposition smelled fishy.[26]

Enter the alchemist Johann Joachim Becher, who, as official physician and mathematician to the court of some now-long-since-deceased German dude (the precise historical details need not concern us here) supplied the missing link. Long story short:

Alchemy...became the vehicle by which Becher spoke to the court about production and material increase. The language of alchemy was particularly well suited to the discussion of commerce, for alchemical transmutation—the ennoblement of metals—provided an example of fabulous material increase and the production of surplus. This was especially true in Becher's theory of alchemical transmutation, which postulated that the multiplication of precious metals took place by means of consumption. Alchemy was thus a natural, virtuous activity within the compass of human art. . . .[27]

It's hard to imagine today, when commerce has become the life blood—some would say the death knell—of the planet, that there was once a time when business had to stoop to higher authority. Clearly, it got what it wanted in the end, and it accomplished this largely the way it gets things done today: by influence peddling. Political lobbying not having yet been invented, the moneychangers went to the temple. Metaphorically speaking, of course. Max Weber's classic study *The Protestant Ethic and the Spirit of Capitalism* (1904) has been criticized as overly simplistic. Some argued that he put too much stock in the Calvinist notion of predestination and of wealth as an outward manifestation that the possessor was among the elect, i.e., those white, male Bürgermeisters lucky enough to be holding automatic get-out-of-jail cards and who were therefore and inevitably Bound for Glory, no thanks to Woody Guthrie. The book nonetheless brought much attention to the complex relationships that developed between ecclesiastical and earthly powers. This work was somewhat more successfully continued by Weber's student, R. H. Tawney, in *Religion and the Rise of Capitalism* (1926). Specifics of the Calvin-for-Capital controversy aside, it's clear that business went from cap in hand to calling the shots, and it did so through accommodation. Commerce went looking for, and found, strong support from religion.

So, could "*incorporation*" have been playing off the Christian mystery of transubstantiation—Word become flesh? Whatever the answer, the fact remains that this term we use every day, along with its shortened form, *corporation,* hides an anthropomorphic metaphor that has no basis in reality. No corporation has ever become embodied. But however mistaken, this metaphor has great power—more so because it is perceived subliminally. On the other hand, ad agencies apply a variation of it quite consciously in the process of product branding. Citing the Jolly Green Giant, the Michelin Man and the Pillsbury Doughboy, a book titled *Brand Spirit* states: "While there are many executional typologies in advertising, some of the most prevalent and successful are those which exploit brand anthropomorphy to the full."[28] The authors are associated with the advertising firm of Saatchi & Saatchi.

The embodied-corporation metaphor allows corporations to mimic human beings. To act as if. But the corporation has no heart.

The cries will go up at this one, I know. But the reaction is based on another misplaced metaphor. Forget how much your business gave to charity or how it's planting trees or teaching ghetto kids to use computers (so you can hire them later at minimum wage). I mean, the corporation lacks the physical organ we call the heart. That thing in your chest that goes thump-thump. Here, I'll make it easier for you: the corporation has no sex. Those who protest even at this obvious truth need to be reminded: it can only screw you *metaphorically*. But this is serious. This is important. Embodiment is a very big deal. Bodies don't come into being through mergers and acquisitions. They are born of woman, as King James put it. Bodies don't file for protection under Chapter 11. They die.

No corporation has ever fallen in love. Reflect on that a moment. Roll it around on your tongue, in the back of your mind. Does it seem a non sequitur, irrelevant? It's not.

Companies don't fall in love. But people do. And whether we speak about it publicly or not, as a species we tend to place great importance on this fact, this entry into a larger more connected world. Easy to ignore, forget, but this is vital. Love opens our hearts to each other, to people other than ourselves, and to the space we share as human beings cast into life without a manual, without a hardwired set of instructions. If, in our 100,000 years or so, we have made catastrophic mistakes, fought devastating wars, pillaged and raped and killed, we have also created complex cultures, built societies, created fabulous art out of nothing but imagination. Drawn on by the longing in our hearts, we have survived. Error but also Eros. Love has shaped and informed and colored our world as much as power. More. But we forget. We get embarrassed. Why? There is a reason, and that reason will unfold as we explore. This time of change is not any time. This world not any world. It is ours and we are here today, as never before, to chronicle and celebrate its wonders. To take it back.

When *The Cluetrain Manifesto* was published, a particular bit seems to have gotten left out. Perhaps someone got embarrassed. Because it's been on the website all along, it took me months to realize that what I'd written had mysteriously gone missing from the book. So, never having recanted anything, let me rectify the omission right now, in a place where it seems to me. . . ahem, appropriate. Whether or not it puts me in dire straits, let me step right up to the microphone. . . [29]

PEOPLE OF EARTH

*The sky is open to the stars. Clouds roll over us night
and day. Oceans rise and fall. Whatever you may have
heard, this is our world, our place to be. Whatever
you've been told, our flags fly free. Our heart goes on
forever. People of Earth, remember.*

Who are we? Look around you. Open your heart. Remember what you have forgotten.

"But what does this have to do with business?" business asks. The question itself reflects the problem. Blind to the central experience of our reality, business never thinks to wonder. Is never awed, inspired, never enthusiastic, curious, ecstatic. Business has *never* wondered—for the same reason that business has never fallen in love. Yet all these capabilities and qualities are intrinsic to the human character. They make us what we are. Corporations say, "We love our customers! You bet!" They say, "We love our workers! It's the people!" But these are lies. Corporations are incapable of love. This is not a moral condemnation, but a simple truth. They aren't equipped for it. Corporations have no heart. If you cut them, they do not bleed. If they die, no children mourn their passing. When they say "we love . . ." they are using words as counters in a game, as they count out money.

There is a conjurer's trick of language here, and at first it seems trivial, a mere convenience. Since companies are populated by people, the anthropomorphic projection sets off no alarms. As a result, we have gradually forgotten that "the company" is in many respects a reverse metonym—a figure of speech in which the whole takes on the qualities of its parts. It is not a reality. Companies produce goods, sell products, manage inventory. So far, so good; no problem. But later, closer to the present, companies begin to want our loyalty, our trust. They want us to be happy. Suddenly, big problem. The metaphor has gotten up off Dr. Frankenstein's table and is walking on its own. *It's alive! It's alive!*

But it's important to remember that it's not alive. The corporation pretends to subscribe to values it does not and cannot understand. Human values. Like love, like trust, like camaraderie and joy. These are things we genuinely value, but they have been devalued and denatured to advance the very different interests of the company. In the process, we are not only losing our language, we are losing our lives.

In the beginning was the Word, moving silent and unspoken upon the face of the deep.[30] But the word has been incorporated and co-opted into the service of another power, whose force is not grounded in the same spirit. We break bread in the company of strangers and it is as ashes in our mouths, giving no strength, no sustenance. Spirit, once sacred, has become an apparition, a ghost in the machine, and we are haunted by it. The historical journey from *Heilige Geist* to Zeitgeist moves from churchly dogma of the Holy Spirit to the secular and desacralized soul of a new machine.[31] And the word became dreck and the marketing communicators moved among us.

"Research on excellence and peak performance," writes Barry Heermann in *Building Team Spirit*, "confirms that high-performing teams and organizations consistently feel the spirit of the organization in their work, and that this feeling is an essential part of the meaning and value that members and observers place on their work."[32] And what precisely is this spirit? What *is* its meaning? What *is* its value? We cannot translate such terms into organizational "equivalents" without doing violence to what we once recognized as both most wholly other and most deeply human.

While religion staked out this territory long before business, neither has any rights of ownership. These feelings and meanings and values predate any institutional claim. "The spirit does but mean the breath," says Tennyson, and etymologically, he is correct. In the Vulgate Bible, the Latin *spiritus* was used to translate the Greek word for soul: *pneuma*, which means to breathe—the same word from which English gets *"pneumatic"*; the same concept from which we draw *"inspiration."* The first entry for *"spirit"* in *The Oxford English*

Dictionary reads: "The animating or vital principle in man (and animals); that which gives life to the physical organism, in contrast to its purely material elements; the breath of life."[33] Despite the preponderance of scriptural—and more recently, sports and business—uses, spirit does not depend on devotion to either eclesiastical or organizational objectives, and neither piety nor gung-ho are needed to understand the sentence: "The horse's spirit was broken."

Something animated and vital looks out from our children's eyes. Whatever it is, we recognize it and know it is precious. Yet except in rare cases today, that spirit is broken early and irreparably. The light goes out all too soon. We know, because at some inarticulate and dimly conscious level, we are those children. We feel the wind of spirit move us at odd moments, but put it down to nostalgia or temporary possession by some impractical flight of fancy. We shake it off and get back to work. Robbed of a voice to speak of these things, something animated and vital looks out from our own eyes, but only in rare, unguarded moments—and even then, wary, circumspect, suspicious. We let no one see what we fear no one will understand.

Where is the value in this, I wonder? What is the cost? Catching the light, a flock of pigeons turns through the sky over the highway. I am driving and remembering and feeling how much is lost, how precious this life.

There is an ever-present danger in such talk of authenticity and heart and wondrous awe—that it will come across like so much New Age trash. Naïve. Idealistic. Out of touch with economic realities and the challenges of global competition. Don't bet on it. The Internet has brought hundreds of millions of human beings together in an entirely new way, and we are using it to explore the things we truly value, genuinely care about. We are using the net to talk about the things that turn us on, about what and whom we love. It may not seem so from the outside, but we are sharing our hearts' desires in a way that could never have been imagined by business command and control or the stentorian voice of broadcast.

And as for Mr. and Mrs. America and all the ships at sea, I got your value proposition right here. Take a chance. Take a trip. Take a leap of faith. Incorporate for real. Take a walk on the wild side.[34]

The Red Queen Is Talking Backwards [35]

"Sing, O goddess, the anger of Achilles . . ." [36]

"Tell me, O muse, of that ingenious hero who traveled far and wide after he had sacked the famous town of Troy." [37]

Respectively, these two invocations launched the *Iliad* and the *Odyssey,* epic works that signal the dawn of Western civilization. But what does poetry have to do with business? In the era of the Internet, a lot. Paradoxically, the highest of high tech has created a doorway through which magic is re-entering the world.

The naive history books we read in school celebrated the triumph of science over ignorance and superstition. Experimentation based on empirical evidence gave us proven facts, not flights of fancy. Data won out over conjecture, and many times, knowledge over wisdom. Despite the miracles since wrought by science, the victim of this victory has often been imagination.

Today we want the cold, hard facts, the definitive word. We can't be bothered with perspective and opinion, hunches. We want to manage knowledge and make it "actionable." We want to "operationalize" intellectual capital. This is understandable given a view of the world as cold and hard, as a place where things can be known unequivocally, without a shadow of doubt. But this view born of scientific and technological tradition is just one way of seeing things. There are others.

"Content is King," the cliché tells us. [38] While the proposition has been widely debated, its obvious male bias has been ignored. Historically, science and technology have indeed been masculine pursuits. Both have shaped our world so long we can't remember anything that came before. And notice that both are about prediction and control. Cause and effect, action and reaction. Pull this lever, watch that plane incline. Provable. Repeatable. Powerful. Neat. [39]

But the world is not always neat. Most of it is extremely messy and, despite our erudition, still mysterious. The abstractions and reductions of rational logic try to explain the world, but they mainly explain what is already visible. Their built-in assumptions—for instance, that everything has a "scientific" explanation—blind this view to much of life. And literal, biological life is not a theory. We are inextricably embedded in it. Think about what really happens in a virgin forest. Think about what happens in the human heart.

These are deep waters with uncertain maps. Dark, hidden, flowing, oceanic, orgasmic, this is the realm of birth and death, of sex and passion, sleep and dream, of myth and intuition. Feeling not calculating. Yielding not controlling. This is the realm of the feminine.

Forget the sexual politics of gender. Yielding does not mean weak. Feminine doesn't even necessarily mean female. This is older knowledge. Much older. The ancient Chinese sages thought of Heaven as masculine, Earth feminine. Yin and Yang. Darkness and light. Complements, not polar opposites. Harmony comes from balance, not from victory of one over the other.

Yet in our culture today, science has won hands down, and its offspring, technology, has beaten all other views into submission. Technology begat big business and big business begat mass media. The intertwined histories of science, technology and commerce have left a legacy of domination and control—from the geographic colonialism of the so-called major powers to the more psychic forms of colonialism represented by media empires such as Yahoo and AOL, Disney and Rupert Murdoch's News Corporation.

In the marketplace, the mouthpiece of this colonialist impulse is broadcast. In the workplace, it is command-and-control management. Both are about imposing power top down. And both deliver the cold, hard facts in definitive, no-nonsense terms: work orders, database records, stock prices, sports scores, dispassionate and supposedly "objective" news reports.

This way of framing the world has collided head-on with the Internet. People have come to this medium by the tens of millions with other interests and concerns, high among them body-based emotions far from the mechanistic inclinations of the Business-Technology complex. The Internet has given everyone a voice. But *vox populi*—the voice of the people—is vastly more vital than the sterile pronouncements of corporations and media conglomerates.

The most fundamental quality of the feminine is mystery, not certain knowledge. Suggestion and connotation, not exhaustive description. Poetry and parable, not news analysis. As a culture, we are moving from cold hard facts to warm and fluid narratives. Warm as in body temperature, not chill robotics. Fluid as in organic forms, not rectilinear wire frames. And these human stories exert tremendous attraction. The god breathes into us and we are made alive. That is the etymology of *"enthusiasm."* The goddess lends breath to voice and we are literally *"inspired."*

Who is creating such stories today? Whose voices will draw new listeners the way Druids drew down the moon, the way Greeks drew a wooden horse to the gates of Troy? Tell me, O muse, of *those* ingenious heroes. Sing to me, goddess, of anger and estrangement. I'm a motherfucker, baby, your mind my sky, your eyes my fire. This world, this life so intricate, delicate, complex. Precious beyond measure. I'm slamming my head against the walls of empire, the habits of power, enraged. Blasting and burning for your love. Imagining the network finally connected. Imagining joy. A wall of horns and drums and dangerous magical noise. I'm bending over my Fender, working the circuits, incendiary, incandescent. Rocking in the free world, serving notice on Babylon. Ain't in for a dollar, ain't in for a dime. Ain't going down for no two-bit dream. Armed only with imagination, I'm back in your spiral arms tonight. Everything has at least two meanings. But one thing girl that I want to say, love is love and not fade away.

CHAPTER 3

Code Blue in the Marketing Ward

"The propagandist's purpose is to make one set of people forget that certain other sets of people are human."

—ALDOUS HUXLEY[1]

"The broad mass of a nation . . . will more easily fall victim to a big lie than to a small one."

—ADOLF HITLER[2]

"This little piggy went to market."

—ANONYMOUS

WHEN *ADVERTISING AGE* ANNOUNCED ITS 1999 MARKETING 100 AWARDS ceremony—the magazine's eighth annual tribute to the people behind that year's hottest brands—some copywriter wrote: "The most important element of a successful marketing plan is not the budget or media selection, but the idea."[3] Roger Shiffman took home a top-100 slot for marketing Furby, and Kenn Viselman won for promoting the Teletubbies. The event was sponsored by Comedy Central. No lie. It may put things in perspective to realize that, among its Top 10 Jingles of the Century, *Ad Age* lists "I wish I was an Oscar Meyer Wiener."[4] Remember: it's the *idea* that's important.

If you're not laughing, you're in deeper shit than you thought. Chances are good that you *are* laughing, though. Or crying. Or saying, hot damn, that's right, or that's wrong, or that's utterly beside the point. Whatever form they may take, the sum of such reactions, added to constant analysis and endless talk, constitute the global conversation I wrote about in *The Cluetrain Manifesto.* "Through the Internet, people are discovering and inventing new ways to share relevant knowledge with blinding speed. As a direct result, markets are getting smarter—and getting smarter faster than most companies." (Hang onto that thought for a minute and see if you don't pick up an echo.)

Now I can imagine some dyspeptic critic writing, "In what sense can it be said that these random views amount to '*relevant knowledge*'? Haven't we heard enough from these stridently opinionated web-heads like Locke and his ilk? Not one of these people has ever had to grapple with the daunting management challenges facing a Fortune 500 company or brought in a billion dollars in revenue. Who do they think they are to question the *genuinely* relevant knowledge hard-won from a century of hands-on marketing experience?" Something like that.

Or something like the assessment of *Cluetrain* that appeared in *The New York Times Book Review.* While granting that "the general thrust is on the mark," the reviewer accused the book of sloganeering. "What the Slogan Era's 'business revolution' is really about is not borrowed from politics; instead, it's a phenomenon that offers middle-aged managers a second chance to sound a barbaric yawp and imagine a new significance to their lives."[5] Not content to compare my deathless prose to Holden Caulfield's outpourings of teenage angst, *The Times* came back a few weeks later for a second round of recreational ass kicking. This article implied that certain aspects of the net are reminiscent of the '60s. One got the feeling this was not intended as a compliment. "The web, in Mr. Locke's view, brings the revolution against the sonorous all-knowing corporate voice to its inevitable climax and resolution in favor of the plebeians. 'The Internet enables people to talk directly to each other and to corporations,' he said. 'It is something businesses ignore at their own peril.'" The piece ends with a sneer: "Heavy, man, heavy."[6]

The point is not to complain of mediocre reviews—hey, if you piss on somebody's parade, you have to expect return fire—nor is it to out myself as a dope-smoking brimstone-hurling web-whacked anti-business middle-aged adolescent sloganeer. Rather, the point is to introduce someone who is none of those things—except possibly middle aged; it can happen to the best of us—but who has nonetheless been making some pretty radical pronouncements of late. "The bottom line is that *markets* are changing a lot faster than *marketing*," he writes in a book published 12 months after *Cluetrain*. And there's the echo you've been waiting for so patiently. "Today," he says, "most company marketing strategies are obsolete!" Emphasis and exclamation in original. And why is this so? Because, as he writes, "With the World Wide Web, we are moving into a new marketing era."[7]

Who is this masked man? And what gives *him* the right to yawp so barbarically? Let's just say he is to marketing what Werner Heisenberg was to quantum mechanics, or Jerry Lee Lewis to rockabilly. If marketing had a Godfather, a *capo di tutti capi*, Philip Kotler would be it. Since 1962, he has taught at Northwestern University's Kellogg Graduate School of Management, defined the field of marketing to generations of corporate vice presidents—his textbooks on the subject have long been required reading in MBA programs worldwide—and consulted to companies such as IBM, Apple, GE, Ford, AT&T, Motorola, Bank of America, Merck, Ciba Geigy, JP Morgan, Dupont, Westinghouse and Merrill Lynch. So when this guy says marketing is fucked, you best believe it. Though he didn't put it quite that way. Unlike myself, Kotler comes across as a gentleman.

I opened the last chapter by hacking on one of his books, but that came out in 1999, and a lot can happen in a couple years. Especially these days. We'll encounter him again below, and in another chapter for the seminal role he played in establishing the concept and practice of social marketing. For now, let's see what he's been saying about antisocial marketing. In the latest word on the profession, *Kellogg on Marketing*, he writes:

Industrial-Age marketing thinking is rooted in the metaphor of marketing as hunting. The marketplace is seen as a jungle. Marketers have to scope out the jungle (market research) and define the prey that they want to capture (target marketing). Marketers must study the prey's habits and habitats (consumer behavior). Marketers have to build a better mousetrap (product differentiation), lay traps and bait (advertising, direct mail, sales promotions), and secure the prey and prevent it from escaping (customer retention, relationship marketing).

The hunters/marketers assume that the prey is not as smart or well informed as they are. The prey acts on emotion (positioning), is easily seduced by trinkets (promotions), and wanders unwittingly into the danger zone (retail stores, salespeople). The hunter has extensive information about the whereabouts of the prey, and knows how to aim the rifle (value proposition) at the prey's soft spot.[8]

So let's cut the counterculture crap, OK? If people in general don't trust business, if they find it insulting and demeaning to be so cynically manipulated—and people do feel this way, in numbers far greater than corporate denial allows for[9]—it doesn't necessarily mean they're stoned. Or stupid. It might just mean they're not drinking the KOOL-AID® anymore.

"Discover the Kraft Family of Brands" the web page taunts me.[10] I am driven to kraftfoods.com in a masochistic fugue of documentary due diligence. As a responsible author, I must definitively determine who owns the KOOL-AID® trademark. But once there, I serendipitously discover this surreal exhortation: "Let the WIENERMOBILE™ take you to the OSCAR MAYER Virtual Lunchbox!" It's gotta be synchronicity. Even as I realize *Ad Age* got the spelling wrong, I start humming their Top 10 Jingle of the Century. "Oooooh I wish I was an Oscar Meyer Wiener . . ." And for some reason that will remain forever shrouded in the deep recesses of my tortured psyche, this causes me to suddenly recall the most frightening conspiracy theory ever circulated on the Internet. "What if," the message speculated darkly, "the Hokey-Pokey really *is* what it's all about?"

The Real Thing: Stories, Brands and Lies

"my heart is where it's always been. . . "

U2[11]

Richard Earle advised Johnson & Johnson during the Tylenol poisoning scare—an impressive credential indeed, as that company's public response was both fast and forthright. In *The Art of Cause*

Marketing, he explains why "art" figures in his book's title. Conventional advertising can be artful on occasion, he says, but seldom can it be called art. "True art is something that moves people in important emotional and personal ways," he writes, "something that stays with them and possibly affects their lives." Social marketing and cause marketing are themes we'll explore more deeply in a later chapter. For now, let's just say that the difference between traditional marketing and social marketing is critical. The first is focused on selling products; the second is aimed at raising awareness of issues that have high relevance to society as a whole. In the case of social marketing, Earle writes, "because the consequences are so far-reaching and because the objective is *always* to move people and affect their lives, it is very important that *every* piece of cause marketing be crafted as carefully as a serious work of art!"[12]

Though it was surely not the author's intent, this observation speaks volumes about conventional, non-cause marketing, correctly implying that most advertising does *not* move people in personal ways or intrinsically affect their lives, no matter how much companies try to convince us—and themselves—that their product pitches have such persuasive power.

Marketing has always been a black art—and it's getting blacker by the minute. In the sense of shrouded, invisible, unknown. In a fit of Amazon.com one-click-purchase possession, I recently bought 20 volumes of the *Harvard Business Review* Paperback Series. This collection covers more angles of business than you can shake a stick at (future stick-shaking was in fact my motivation for buying them): management, leadership, governance, performance measurement, information technology, you name it. However, in none of the book titles—nor in the titles of the 162 included *HBR* articles—does the word "*marketing*" appear. Not once. I find this curious.[13] It's there in the indices, of course. But the listings say things like: "Marketing strategy. See also brand building; mass media advertising; sales promotions; sponsorships." So if I do those things, then I'll be marketing, right? And to help me, the series does include a volume on *Brand Management*.

Almost en passant, Randall Rothenberg writes in *Advertising Age* that "it goes without saying branding has been exposed as a hoax." I like this guy—and not just because he sends email crammed with pointers to wonderfully germane books like Paul Lazarsfeld's *On Social Research and its Language* and James W. Carey's *Communication and Culture* (we got talking after he reviewed *Cluetrain*). I like him more because of the stuff he throws straight in the face of marketing's inner sanctum. "Brands are promises," he continues, "of service, quality, values and substance—made by a company to its own people, and thereon to its customers. To believe such a promise, which normally takes years to build, can be short-circuited by a multi-million-dollar network dump, in an economy where employees have the loyalty of rutting gerbils, strains credulity."[14]

Still, marketers invoke brand as if it were the Holy Grail. They speak of its power in hushed and reverential tones. The rest of us think they're barking mad. If marketing is only fully and completely understood by some elite priesthood of MBA-equipped professionals, then why should the market give a damn? If they haven't explained it to me—and they haven't—then something is very wrong here. There has been, to quote from *Cool Hand Luke*, a failure to communicate. The Big-M Marketing department behaves as if it isn't performing in front of a live audience. On the Internet, however, if there is no audience, neither is there a market.

But let's back up for a second to when we were all working without a net. I met Theodore Levitt in Pittsburgh in 1987. Cool guy. After his talk, I handed him a paper about the work I then did, called "Corporate Communications: Telling Stories That Transmit Vision." I was surprised to get a handwritten note a few days later saying he'd like to publish it in *Harvard Business Review*, of which he was then editor-in-chief. I'd just need to make a couple fairly simple changes, he said. Like a jerk, I never made them, and it never ran. Levitt had also written an important book called *The Marketing Imagination*—what a curious juxtaposition of words. Oxymoronic, you could almost say. Much earlier, in 1960, he had published a seminal article in *HBR* titled "Marketing Myopia," where he said: "Marketing is a stepchild. I do not mean that selling is ignored. Far from it. But selling . . . is not marketing. . . . selling concerns itself with the tricks and techniques of getting people to exchange their cash for your product. It is not concerned with the values that the exchange is all about."[15]

There's that maddeningly amorphous notion of value again. In 1975, *HBR* re-published this article along with Levitt's "Retrospective Commentary," in which he speculated as to why the piece had been so successful. At that date it had sold well over a quarter million reprints. And in this speculation he points to a dimension of value rarely if ever raised in marketing literature.

> Is it that concrete examples, joined to illustrate a simple idea and presented with some attention to literacy, communicate better than massive analytical reasoning that reads as though it were translated from the German? Is it that provocative assertions are more memorable and more persuasive than restrained and balanced explanations, no matter who the audience? Is it that the character of the message is as much the message as its content?[16]

Here, one of the greatest names in marketing returns the focus to the story and how it's told—and why it might *matter* how it's told. How provocative and persuasive are the stories marketing tells today? What is the character of the message?

In its first issue of 2000, *Fast Company* ran a piece of corporate puffery indistinguishable from advertising.[17] "Experience the Real Thing" the title beckoned. With no distracting hint of critical editorial distance, the text extolled in breathless prose "the Coca-Cola branding experience in Las Vegas, where nostalgia, storytelling, and technology create a magic formula." Storytelling seems to have achieved a certain cachet in corporate circles, though as an eviscerated, bankrupt concept. It's amazing to listen in on marketers trying to imagine what a story might be—almost like having a front row seat at a cargo cult ceremony. "We wanted to bring the brand to life, to tell the stories of Coca-Cola, and to express Coca-Cola's core values: fun, refreshment, and specialness in people's lives," says Deborah MacCarthy, manager of Coke's College Channel. Yeah, I can relate. I don't know about you readers out there, but for me, Specialness comes right after Truth, Justice and The American Way on *my* list of core values. Specialness? *Specialness?* What the hell are these people talking about? I'm getting spontaneous flashbacks of the Talking Heads movie *True Stories* intercut with *The Gods Must*

Be Crazy.[18] Ladies and gentlemen, please return your tray tables to the fully upright and locked position, suspend your disbelief and put on your tinfoil pyramid hats. We are now entering. . . [cue lights, cue music] the *Brand Dimension!*

> "Any presentation has to have a dramatic arc," [some brainless Coca-Cola flack] explains. "We wanted to create the sense of a journey, with a call to action at the end. If I give a presentation that's intended to sell, I tell a story whose call to action is 'Purchase my product.' In Las Vegas, our goal is to get people emotionally involved in the brand—so much so that they're ready to spend big bucks in the retail store downstairs."[19]

I can report that after reading this *Fast Company* article, I did get emotionally involved in the brand. I broke all the furniture in the office and swore a mighty oath to deconstruct such idiotic notions of "story" every chance I got. No time like the present, I figure.

Twice head marketing honcho at The Coca-Cola Company, Sergio Zyman, describes why, under his guidance, things went better with Coke: "We were successful because we never forgot that our goal was to get more people to buy more stuff more often so the company could make more money."[20] Stirring words, to be sure. But who cares? Really. While this is certainly what every company hopes to accomplish, do a company's atavistic wish-fulfillment fantasies constitute a story? Such empty and self-serving statements are not only insufficient today, they generate outright hostility. Once upon a time, such discussions took place in ultra-private mahogany-paneled board rooms, where it was safe to talk about how your marketing program pivoted on a devious remote-control trip to trick more demographic abstractions into buying more stuff. Today, such heretofore sensitive matters as "eyeball acquisition cost" are openly bandied about in the public Internet *agora*, where such talk has helped make it painfully obvious that companies seldom give a damn about what real people want or care about.

Even Zyman's own product—his book in this case—is now open to assessment in the networked marketplace, an assessment over which he as producer has no control. On Amazon.com, reader-reviewer Byron Menides, adjunct professor at Worcester Polytechnic

Institute's School of Industrial Management, writes: "I was disappointed after reading Sergio Zyman's book with the provocative title, *The End of Marketing as We Know It.* Old marketing based on mass merchandising with little attention to customer needs was dead years ago . . . I am surprised that a book published in 1999 says so little about the impact and influence of the Internet in business to business and consumer marketing."[21]

But the fact that the Internet is missing from the discussion comes as no real surprise. This is marketing as it was canonized in the age of mass-market broadcast media, the dynamics of which differ deeply from those of the online world. The problem is not that marketing as Sergio Zyman knows it—manipulative, intrusive, gimmick-ridden and inherently dishonest—has come to an end. The problem is that this view of marketing remains unquestioned in most corporations and that its techniques are now being deployed in a new medium to which they have only negative relevance.

As Coca-Cola has been around for a long time, it may be tempting to think that its notions of marketing are typical of older, well-established companies, or of companies that offer commodity consumer products like fizzy brown sugar water. But much younger high-tech companies are prone to the same mentality and make the same mistakes. In an article titled "Legends in Their Own Minds," *Salon* looked at two business bestsellers: *High St@kes, No Prisoners* and *Renegades of the Empire.* Reviewer Thomas Scoville called them:

> . . . particularly juicy specimens of the prevailing business rhetoric of the dot-com era. There is a kind of language—an amalgam of hyperbole, geek-speak, and pop-media code phrases, delivered in a perverse, super-desiccated and emotionally bankrupt tone—to be found in both of these books, and it is this contemporary mutation of language, rather than the stories themselves, that may ultimately communicate the Zeitgeist most effectively.[22]

To offer more than the facile business pitch, stories alone are not sufficient. What is critical is the intent with which they are told. The best stories arouse curiosity; they invite us to wonder. They may be captivating, but they aren't about capture and control. John Borthwick, a VP at AOL's Development Studio in New York, wrote to me after reading *The Cluetrain Manifesto*: "You talk about the importance of storytelling within organizations, and how stories humanize information. One reason I think this works is that telling stories encourages speaking from personal experience instead of talk based on corporate abstractions. Even when they're fictional, stories resonate because the back button is shared experience." While business rhetoric so often reflects the soulless quality of mass marketing, stories have a palpable heartbeat. Where the pitch seeks to isolate, reduce, to make us small and fearful, the story includes, expands, encourages. Imagination makes us larger.

At the end of the year 2000, *Context* magazine invited Sergio Zyman and Jerry Della Femina to interview each other about marketing online.[23] Della Femina has played an enormously influential role in the history of advertising, having first achieved notoriety in 1970 with his best-selling book, *From Those Wonderful Folks Who Gave You Pearl Harbor.* The title was a slogan he suggested to the Japanese electronics firm, Panasonic. It cost him his job, but the book hit the charts. Della Femina leads off by saying, "I don't know any advertising agency that has mastered the Internet yet. Being able to understand it and sell products on it through advertising seem almost impossible." He says that most online advertising creates resentment, working to shut down attention rather than elicit interest. And Zyman concurs: "I agree that banner ads are a joke."

It's refreshing to hear such overt skepticism about Internet advertising voiced by those wonderful folks who gave us so much vacuous handwaving in the first place. It's interesting, however, that adman Della Femina comes across more convincing than Zyman, the corporate marketeer. The latter, like so many of his brethren in The Craft (connotations of witchcraft fully intended), still invokes the concept of brand with all the crypto-mystical implications corporations insist on attaching to it. Zyman says: "The trick is to find ways of creating content that can actually communicate the benefits of a brand to consumers." And what "benefits" would those be? If there is any use at all in the litany of wondrous qualities a brand purportedly embodies, the advantage is to the company that creates such a mystique, not to the consumer. So Zyman is right. It is indeed a trick.

One turned far too often by corporations—and the reason emerging web markets are now turning the tables on the tricksters.

Zyman also provides unintended humor when he notes that "sometimes consumers can get manipulated." No! Do you think? And his comments on the opportunities for companies using the Internet "to grow bigger by building more powerful brands" are oddly anachronistic, if not just plain out to lunch. Leave it to a dyed-in-the-wool mass marketer to see economies of scale lurking in the wings just as one-size-fits-all "scaling"—going after larger and larger, but more mythical markets—is precisely the problem the Internet is best suited to solving.

In contrast, Della Femina doesn't use the word *brand* once, except in an almost opposite context. Where Zyman alludes to the mysterious *magic of brand*, Della Femina says: "We saw movies like *The Hucksters*, and we thought the ad executive did a particular *brand of magic*" [italics mine]. I couldn't help wondering if the subtly inverted trope was a conscious hack on the Big Guy from Coke. If so, score one for Jerry.

Della Femina says, "We're going to have to be clever and figure out different ways to reach people. But we're not going to reach them through advertising on the Internet." I think he's right, though I would shift the emphasis slightly. It's entirely possible to reach people through the Internet—just not through Internet *advertising*. This sort of neurotic attachment to labels is preventing business from realizing the genuine potential of the net. The typical syllogism runs like this. Marketing must be annoying, so if we're not annoying anyone, we must not be marketing, and therefore can't possibly make a profit. Ergo, the sky is falling.

At the end of the piece, Della Femina touches on an alternative to such turkey-in-the-rain stupidity, noting that companies are "trying to talk to people without the direct sell." Smart companies would do this, yes, though it seems that, on average, corporate IQs are still not breaking any records in this respect. I'd be a lot happier with this approach, if instead of leveraging what Della Femina rather loftily labels "truth-based communication," companies would just stop lying so damn much.

One form such lying takes is sucking up to particular demographic sectors that marketers drool over but don't even remotely begin to comprehend. A perennial favorite for these ministrations is the so-called youth market. On May 16, 2000, rock star Courtney Love ranted to the Digital Hollywood online entertainment conference in New York, among other things, about the time she entered into a sponsor relationship with a company that makes a popular brand of soda pop. She didn't mention whether it was Pepsi or that other one. And most likely, no one cared. What's the difference?

"It was really dumb," she said. "You had to buy the cola. You had to dial a number. You had to press a bunch of buttons. You had to do all this crap that nobody wanted to do." But that was just for starters. She also said she felt embarrassed to be shilling for a product she had no particular use for. And she didn't much like the marketers she was forced to deal with. "They treated me like I was an ungrateful little bitch who should be groveling for the experience to play for their damn soda. I ended up playing without my shirt on and ordering a six-pack of the rival cola onstage. Also, lots of unwholesome cursing and nudity occurred. This way I knew that no matter how tempting the cash was, they'd never do business with me again."[24]

Slice and Dice

A website accompanies Philip Kotler's textbook on *Marketing Management*, now in its tenth edition. In discussing chapter nine— "Identifying Market Segments and Selecting Target Markets"—the site says "To remain effective and profitable, marketers must strike the delicate balance between the ineffectiveness of trying to be 'all things to all people' through mass marketing products to everyone; and the cost prohibitive extreme of completely customizing a marketing mix to each individual."[25]

Like most marketing today, this logic admits—in principle—that mass marketing is a thing of the past. Mass markets, though once a huge source of profits, were in many respects a side effect of marketing inefficiency. As marketing adopted more sophisticated research tools, it became obvious that one size did not fit all. At first, divvying up mass markets into subcategories was a rough science, and the resulting segments were still very large. However, the process has become increasingly refined, to the point that, as the

Kotler site says, "segmentation becomes critical in the marketing process. Segmentation enables marketers to divide prospective customer groups into 'segments' that consist of people with similar demographic, psychographic or usage patterns."[26] Demographic slice-and-dice techniques are described in books such as *Divide and Conquer: Targeting Your Customers Through Market Segmentation*—the title as telling as the contents—and the far more technical and detailed exposition of *The Clustered World*.[27]

However, the admission-in-principle that mass marketing is no longer effective, or even particularly workable, hasn't changed the fundamental mindset that underlies it. The mass marketing mentality is well expressed by Zyman's "get more people to buy more stuff more often" mantra. Perhaps this is understandable coming from a marketer whose aim was to sell what is perhaps the archetype of commodity products. Despite trying to mind-meld it with phantasmagoric images of fun, refreshment, and let's not forget *specialness*, Coke is still just sugar-water in a can. In the grand taxonomy of product categories, cola is perhaps one evolutionary notch above coal and pork bellies.

Savvier marketers have grappled with the obstacles and opportunities attaching to segmentation in a more rigorous manner. Regis McKenna understood and articulated the value of niche markets and highly targeted marketing. In his 1986 book, *The Regis Touch*, he counseled a rifle-shot over a shotgun approach, saying that companies that tried to satisfy more than one niche were courting Chapter 11.[28] This advice was primarily aimed at startups such as Apple, with which he had worked from the earliest days. However, successful startups sometimes end up as Fortune 500 companies, as Apple did despite many missteps, and at that point the allure of mass marketing comes back with a vengeance. By 1991, McKenna was thinking out loud—in *Relationship Marketing*[29]—about a more generalized approach to market niches. This spawned an entire industry subcategory known as Customer Relationship Management or CRM (not to be confused with Cause Related Marketing, which we've touched on already and will encounter again soon enough).

At roughly the same time, Joe Pine was preaching a related new wrinkle in mass production and mass marketing in *Mass Cus-*

tomization: The New Frontier in Business Competition and a series of articles in *Harvard Business Review* that were eventually published in 2000 as *Markets of One: Creating Customer-Unique Value Through Mass Customization.*[30] The trajectory of these developments moved from focusing on undifferentiated mass markets to targeting highly selective niches, and culminating in "personalization" techniques such as the one-to-one marketing of Don Peppers and Martha Rogers.[31] Along this trajectory, these approaches increasingly acknowledge the importance of the Internet and electronic commerce. This new medium enabled marketers to reach individuals much more directly than, say, direct (snail) mail. However, the quotes around "personalization" are necessary because all these methods are still driven by database technologies. It is critical to remember the contribution of mass customization to this chain of development, because what "personalization" invariably boils down to is marketing to a mass of niches. In other words, and make no mistake, these purportedly "personalized" approaches to customers remain a form of mass marketing.[32]

An advanced personalization technique called *"collaborative filtering"*—which has been put to especially interesting use by Amazon.com—constitutes a potentially powerful exception. It's easy to forget that one of the primary uses of hypertext—the tangled web of stuff the web is based on—is to enable learning, which begins with establishing meaningful categories, connecting like to like. When I go to Amazon and see what other people found interesting enough to buy, I often gain valuable insight from a much larger social network than I could hope to connect with by any other means. Also, note that since Amazon's also-bought links are backed by nontrivial outlays of cold hard cash, they probably represent a more honest evaluation than the off-the-cuff opinions of friends and colleagues—or publishers' advertisements.[33] Collaborative filtering is the technology that enables the boundaries of such communities of interest to be determined. Malcolm Gladwell, author of *The Tipping Point*, wrote what is perhaps the best overview of this technology and its true significance—in *The New Yorker*, of all places. In "The Science of the Sleeper: How the Information Age could blow away the blockbuster," he says:

Collaborative filtering underscores a lesson that . . . humans have been stubbornly resistant to learning: if you want to understand what one person thinks or feels or likes or does it isn't enough to draw inferences from the general social or demographic category to which he belongs. You cannot tell, with any reasonable degree of certainty, whether someone will like "The Girl's Guide to Hunting and Fishing" by knowing that the person is a single twenty-eight-year-old woman who lives in Manhattan, any more than you can tell whether somebody will commit a crime knowing only that he's a twenty-eight-year-old African-American male who lives in the Bronx. . . . None of this means that standard demographic data is useless. . . . But the central claim of the collaborative-filtering movement is that, head to head, the old demographic and 'psycho-graphic' data cannot compete with preference data. This is a potentially revolutionary argument.[34]

Meanwhile, back to the present point, which bears repeating in any case: *most* "personalization" is still a form of mass marketing. Historically, market segmentation has always been a top-down proposition, targeting groups of prospects according to the sales objectives of the company. But people are connecting with each other on the Internet bottom-up according to their own passions and interests, which seldom map directly to products. This bottom-up emergence of new markets is not an anomaly, but the continuation of a trend already well established before the net became a commercial force. It is hugely significant and will eventually become the primary source of corporate revenue. And here's the kicker: this entire phenomenon is invisible to current market research based on segmentation. Attached to their tried-and-true methods, corporations are literally running on empty, running blind.

Let's turn to Levitt again. In "Marketing Myopia," he said: "Industries that assume themselves to be riding some automatic growth escalator invariably descend into stagnation. The history of every dead and dying 'growth' industry shows a self-deceiving cycle of bountiful expansion and undetected decay." And even in 1960, he equated this blindness to a fixation on the economies of scale associated with mass production. "The tantalizing profit possibilities of low unit production costs may be the most seriously self-deceiving attitude that can afflict a company. . . . The usual result of this narrow preoccupation. . . is that instead of growing, the industry declines. . . . The industry has its eyes so firmly on its own specific product that it does not see how it is being made obsolete."[35] He follows this with a brief synopsis of the buggy whip industry.

In his 1975 retrospective commentary on Marketing Myopia, Levitt blames the continuation of this trend on the sudden influx of "operating or financial executives" into industry. Today we would probably not be wrong to lump them into the general category of bean counters. "Executives with such backgrounds," he writes, "have an almost trained incapacity to see that getting 'volume' may require understanding and serving many discrete and sometimes small market segments rather than going after a perhaps mythical batch of big or homogeneous customers."[36] Levitt's use of "may require" here should be read as high facetiousness. His point is that without *understanding and serving* no amount of *going after* is going to do much good.

Yet this is precisely what most data-based marketing technologies offer—deeper penetration and higher margins with only the *simulacrum* of understanding and the improved service capabilities such understanding might enable. But perhaps that's too abstract. Try this: do you feel all warm and fuzzy inside when you get email addressed "Dear Bill" or "Dear Mary"? Assuming, of course, that one of those is actually your name. (Not taking anything for granted here. This is the remedial paragraph.) Do you feel that the company thus addressing you understands you and is therefore in a better position to serve your deepest and most existential consumer whims? If so—and I'd really like to be more gentle about this, believe me, but—you are a fool.

The basic problem with this approach is that, in sharp contrast to television, the Internet has failed to produce sufficient fools. The dependable old mass-media trick—ramming canned commercial "messages" down a one-way broadcast pipe—just doesn't get networked audiences to sit up and beg. It doesn't even get them to roll over. On TV, repeated pitches may create brand awareness. On the web, they create brand annoyance. This isn't the way we're communicating with each other online. We argue, cajole, we joke, we talk. We tell each other stories. On television, a company has 30 seconds to be clever. But on the web, it has unlimited gigabytes to say what it's all about and why anyone should give a damn. This isn't a preview, like a TV ad. It's the main feature. If you advertise to us on your site once you've gotten us there, you've lost a prime opportunity to engage us, to converse with us, to tell us a story. You've blown it and we won't be back, no matter how big your banner budget.

The net has influenced the style of some broadcast advertising, but Internet audiences are hipper than many suspect. We see a knock-out ad on the tube and we're rolling on the floor laughing. At the same time, we know full well that we're unlikely to encounter the same mentality if we go to the website or call the customer service line. We'll get business as usual. When we appreciate certain ads, we're usually cheering for the agency creatives who conceived them. When I see a great spot for IBM, I immediately think "Man, somebody at Ogilvy is sure having fun!" I know from experience that no one is having fun logging trouble tickets at IBM's call center. It's a high-tech sweatshop.[37]

So what now? If a) the we-really-know-you-and-love-you-why-look-your-name-is-right-here-in-our-database gambit plays only with sub morons on the net, and b) it turns out that the Internet is far less efficient than television in turning out sub-morons. . . then oh dear! What's a marketer to do? As we'll see next, some have gone off and thought about this problem deeply.

OverSimplicity®

Perhaps the real problem is that all that razzle-dazzle brand manipulation has consumers plumb tuckered out. Maybe the real problem is that it got too goshdarn *complicated*. In a nutshell, that is the underlying premise of *Simplicity Marketing: Relieving Customer Stress in the Digital Age*, by Steven M. Cristol and Peter Sealey.[38]

The fundamental axioms of business are precipitously red-shifting, receding at the speed of light from the power and relevance they once had with respect to pre-Internet commerce. "The Digital Age" is invoked in this book's subtitle for good reason: corporations are feeling—if not fully understanding—the enormity of this shift. It's good business these days to question core business assumptions.

One way of questioning the tried and true is to find a new lens through which to reassess long-established business practices. Deming's lens is a good example. By looking at the whole organization from the perspective of Quality, companies began to understand and accept the wrenching changes they would have to undertake to remain competitive in newly globalized markets.

Cristol and Sealey attempt to present Simplicity as an equally powerful explanatory and predictive lens for marketing. Markets are faced with a daunting array of product and service choices that have proliferated to the point of becoming counterproductive, driving customers away rather than attracting them. The authors emphasize stress as a major factor in contemporary consumer psychology, and stress reduction as a concomitant opportunity for business. They warn of the dangers of incrementally extending products and creating new brands. Instead they propose consolidating product and service functions via their "4 R's" approach to Simplicity Marketing—replace, repackage, reposition and replenish. All are aimed at alleviating customer anxiety.

But is Simplicity thus defined as powerful a lens as Quality proved to be? Paradoxically, the answer is yes only if we discount the real impact and ramifications of the digital age, and agree with the tacit but strongly implied message of *Simplicity Marketing*: that the Internet does not constitute a radical rite of passage into a truly new economy, and requires of business no dark night of soul searching.

The authors cite Seth Godin's book *Permission Marketing*, which holds out a similar promise to companies: that they can retain, or more accurately regain, some measure of control over their markets. However, the comfort this brings to marketers comes at the cost of self-delusion. Since the advent of the commercial Internet, markets are in control. And the First Step in any effective 12-step program of recovery has to be: get used to it. Business as usual is not alive and well. It's dying. The net has called code blue on the marketing department, and it's flatlining, monitors screaming that the patient's pulse is gone. When open heart surgery is the only recourse, suggesting a simplified lifestyle, or a please-and-thank-you rationale for the same old high-cholesterol spam, comes a day late and a couple trillion dollars short.

"As with the segmentation process, traditional approaches to prioritizing segments for targeting are not meant to be thrown out," *Simplicity Marketing* assures. "They are meant to be enhanced by considering customer stress as another important variable . . . "[39] But the dynamics the Internet brings to bear on market interactions raise fundamental questions about the viability of conventional segmentation and targeting. By freighting old concepts with new parameters, the authors seem to be suffering from their own denigrated incrementalism.

While the authors acknowledge debate about whether the "4 P's" of conventional marketing remain valid in a digital economy, they choose not to engage the issue, instead positioning their own "4 R's" as complementary to existing practice. "Regardless of which side of the debate you're on, the 4 P's are still the foundation learned and used by most marketing managers for planning and execution."[40] And with that weak disclaimer—the familiar Everybody's-Doing-It defense—far more challenging and potentially enlightening questions about how marketing fits into an altogether new kind of electronically mediated commerce are neatly swept aside.

The same kind of slippery trope appears at the beginning of the book. "How," the authors rhetorically inquire, "did we get to a consumer world of 40,000 products in a supermarket, hundreds of long distance and cellular calling plans, 52 versions of Crest toothpaste . . . ?"[41] But the crucial question of how we got into this mess is ignored. Historically, the explosion of consumer choice resulted from competition for unprotected niche market sectors, first from smaller domestic producers and later from large international companies seeking to penetrate lucrative U.S. markets. These competitors were effective because the companies whose share they went after were often arrogant and complacent, believing they were impervious to attack. Think Honda Civic. Think Sony Walkman.

While the global economy and the economies of scope it spawned may be old news, most companies are still missing the fact that the Internet hugely accelerates this same trend. In the late '60s, auto executives dismissed the VW Bug. "Only students drive those," they said. Notice that 20 years later, business missed the significance of the early Internet for the same reason. "Networked Unix workstations? But only students drive those . . . "

Today, competition is coming not from offshore, but from agile net upstarts catering to web-based micromarkets that don't yet raise a blip on the demographic oscilloscope. Even after decades of warning signals, most companies still believe they are in control of their markets, impervious to attack from below. But online, the market *is* the competition. Think Linux. Think Napster.

Through the reputation so many corporations have developed for self-serving consumer manipulation, marketers have lost credibility. Today the marketplace is connected, networked. Consumers are talking among themselves. And this changes everything. Cristol and Sealey argue that markets are stymied by too many options and must depend on vendors to make sense of their world again. For this they will be grateful, and gratitude will beget trust, trust will beget loyalty, loyalty will beget greater market share, and greater share will beget new profits. Thus runneth the prophecy. But the prophets are wrong and the profits are not forthcoming.

Markets are not stymied. They are not as confused as many companies nostalgically continue to wish they were. In the digital age, markets are rapidly becoming smarter than the companies that pretend to serve them. Faced with a broad array of choices, potential buyers are turning to the only source they trust: each other. Typical exchanges take place through email or online message boards, and they go a little like this . . .

QUESTION: I'm trying to get my head around the differences between products X, Y and Z. I'm getting a migraine from all the marketing double-talk. And the pricing schemes seem as if they were invented by Rube Goldberg. Can anyone help me sort this stuff out?

ANSWER (RECEIVED TEN MINUTES LATER): Forget any of the above. I've used them all and they all suck. Take a look at a little company a knowledgeable pal turned me on to. He thought highly of their product, and having used it for six months now, so do I. These folks got it right. Their site isn't fancy and they have no four-color brochures to send you, but there's an online demo that'll blow your mind. Also, because they haven't invested in the usual "brand" nonsense, you'll pay about 60% less than you would have for X, Y or Z—might as well pocket some of the difference in their banner ad budgets. This outfit deserves more recognition. If you're as impressed as I was, spread the word.

If X, Y or Z is your product, there goes your $10 million simplicity campaign. Because this word *will* spread. Like wildfire. This isn't "viral marketing" or "permission marketing" or "simplicity marketing." It's just real simple. Given the right vector—and the net has supplied it—people will talk about the products they hate and the ones they love. The latter will be well crafted, developed to address real needs, and backed up by friendly open straight-talking customer service. You got a problem? Well bummer, dude. And bam, it's fixed. That's simplicity.

"Entities should not be multiplied beyond necessity," said William of Ockham almost 700 years ago, a formulation that has come to be known as the law of parsimony or Ockham's razor. In non-philosophical terms it means: keep it simple, stupid. If marketing simplicity boils down to elegant, responsive product design, quality craftsmanship, a clear articulation of what the product does, and fast attentive customer service, then why inflate such a perfectly useful concept into a theory that invokes needless—and largely empty—neologisms such as *"overchoice," "brand soul," "brandscape"* and *"stressographics"*?

There's nothing simple about reducing people to databased demographic profiles, and nothing respectful about painting targets on their backs. If you really want simple, try telling the truth. But this prospect strikes abject terror into the hearts of those whose mission it is to package segments and deliver eyeballs.

A Hand Full of Gimme and a Mouth Full of Much Obliged

"Hey, baby, there ain't no easy way out. . . "

—TOM PETTY[42]

I first met Seth Godin in 1993, virtually speaking. He edited the *Information Please Business Almanac & Desk Reference* which included email addresses, something new at that time in a business publication. I contacted him. Later, I contributed to a book he put together called *E-Mail Addresses of the Rich & Famous*. When I found myself named in the acknowledgements, I emailed Seth, thanking him and expressing my surprise. "I should have dedicated the book to you," he replied. "You gave me more addresses than anyone else." We were never close pals, but we were friendly. By all accounts, he's a good guy with a working sense of humor. In *E-Mail Addresses*, he claims to have written "over 400 books, including *Valley of the Dolls*, *The Eiger Sanction*, *Catcher in the Rye*, *The Cat in the Hat*, and many others." All of which inclined me to like what he had to say. But I don't like what he's saying. I have trouble with his ideas for two reasons: 1) they've been enormously influential, and 2) they're fundamentally wrong. If not for 2, 1 would be cause for congratulation. Without 1, 2 wouldn't much matter. Together, it's a dangerous combination.

Godin is the most visible presence in online marketing today. I can't think of anyone else who comes close. And it isn't just because he was associated with Yahoo. His popularity is solely the result of his ideas. Despite the contributions of serious analysts like John Hagel (*Net Worth* and *Net Gain*), there was a perceived vacuum of solid ideas about e-commerce before Seth Godin came along. Or so anyone would have to conclude from the impact he's had. Marketers took up the banner of permission marketing with a vengeance.

"What do you consider your greatest professional achievement?" asks *The Industry Standard*, and Godin replies "I created the idea of permission marketing back when the web was all about Java, hits and push. Now, everyone from the press to key aggregators are rushing to embrace the idea that extracting attention and value from a relationship takes frequency and for that to happen online, you need Permission(TM)."[43] No kidding about the trademark. Looks like it's official then.

But the vacuum is still there. Godin does a good job on the ineffectiveness of broadcast advertising, on the annoyance of what he calls "interruption marketing," and on the way word-of-mouth works online. The problem is the service into which he presses these insights.

E-Mail Addresses of the Rich & Famous is out of print now, at which Godin breathes a sigh of relief.[44] Why? It raised quite a furor at the time about privacy and a neologism that had just come into the world: spam. Spam, as we all know today, is unsolicited commercial email. The offending item was a proposal the book tried to float.

> A simple new convention will allow easy communication without overloading the system. . . Just follow these two rules when mailing to someone you don't know: If you're sending unsolicited mail, precede your subject with a *?*. If you're sending a commercially related piece of mail, precede your subject with a *$*. This is a courtesy that will allow people to screen their mail and increases the chances that your mail will be read by someone who *wants* to read it. (italics in original) [45]

It didn't float. Nor did it just quietly sink. It caused a firestorm. Godin took a good deal of flameage for trying to rationalize a framework for sending ?$—which is to say, spam. He was obviously thinking early on about how marketers could use the Internet to reach prospects, and he's obviously been thinking about it ever since. He finally found his framework. In *Permission Marketing: Turning Strangers Into Friends and Friends Into Customers*, he calls permission marketing "the way to make advertising work again."

> Permission Marketing. . . offers the consumer an opportunity to volunteer to be marketed to. By talking only to volunteers, Permission Marketing guarantees that consumers pay more attention to the marketing message. It allows marketers to tell their story calmly and succinctly, without fear of being interrupted by competitors or Interruption Marketers. It serves both consumers and marketers in a symbiotic exchange. [46]

I have to smile at the notion of calm, succinct, fearless marketers. The image that comes to mind is the used car sales division of the Power Rangers. But hold on just a second, I'm thinking. . . I turn the page. "I know what you're thinking," Godin says. "There's a catch." *Damn*, this guy is good! He's reading my mind.

> If you have to personalize every customer message, that's prohibitive. If you're still thinking within the framework of traditional mar-

keting, you're right. But in today's information age, targeting customers individually is not as difficult as it sounds. Permission Marketing takes the cost of interrupting the consumer and spreads it
out, over not one message, but dozens of messages. And this
leverage leads to substantial competitive advantages and profits.

Actually, I'm not thinking anywhere even close to traditional marketing—reader, back me up here—but I notice that the issue of personalization expense is raised, displayed to the congregation in the
spirit of full disclosure—then neatly swept under the rug. These
rhetoricians, I tell ya (it takes one to know one). In fact, the mention of personalization here is genuflection to an empty buzzword.
The only "personal" element in the ensuing "symbiotic exchanges"
is likely to be "Dear John." Some will argue that, no, customers are
divvied up according to their expressed or demonstrated interest in
certain product categories. But that's not *personal*. It's not something some person takes personally. It's good old traditional segmentation and targeting. For those who may have forgotten, a personal communication is more like this:

> You have spaced out picking up the kids from day care for the last
> time. You're an irresponsible no-good drunk, Jim. Get help—from
> someone else. I'm leaving you forever.
>
> —ALICE

Now let's ask ourselves: how much more information does Alice
have about Jim than the typical permission marketer has about any
given random pick from its base of five jillion target prospects? Alice
may not *like* Jim a whole lot, but he knows right away on opening
this mail that it's not a form letter.

Actually, there's not just one catch. There are two. The second
gets talked about far less than the first (which doesn't get talked
about much either, such is the raw corporate enthusiasm for this
stuff), but it contains a bigger gotcha. Here it is now: and how do
you *give* consumers the "opportunity to volunteer" to be marketed
to? Well, er, ah, um, that is . . . The actual no-mumbling answer is
simple: you spam them. The companies that have jumped on this
bandwagon were already itching for a rationale to do just that—why

let the MLM bottom-feeders have all the fun?—and Godin gave it to them on a silver platter. These companies aren't starting webzines and inviting a few dozen pals to sign up. They are sitting on databases that contain tens of millions of email addresses representing people they know no better than the Man in the Moon.

But perhaps you'd like a second opinion on this. Writing in *Harvard Business Review*, Peter Sealey says "Godin. . . concedes that permission marketers also rely on interruptions to introduce themselves to a broad base of customers. But the introductory ads can be quite simple because they don't need to sell the product. All they need to do is ask permission to say more. From that point on, all participation is voluntary." [47] Allow me to translate sans murky euphemisms: it's not voluntary *at first*. So what's for lunch, Mom? *Spam!!!*

Sealey goes on to say that "Permission marketing gives consumers *some say*, but the process is still *managed by the marketer.*" In this case the italics are mine—to point out that the core program has not really changed at all. This is not about a new form of symbiotic exchange. It's about a very old form of command and control.

Godin has heard criticism like this before. To his credit, he hasn't blown it off as irrelevant, any more than he ignored the flames he fanned up with *E-Mail Addresses of the Rich & Famous*. He doesn't just listen, he takes it seriously, he thinks about it, mulls it over. Godin is trying to get it right. The question that motivated his latest book was clearly: How do you get people to give you permission to send them "exciting email offers" without having to first shotgun them with "invitations" that look like, smell like and—oh hell, why quibble—*are* in fact spam?

The opening page of *Unleashing the Ideavirus* frames the same problem in—you'll be unsurprised to learn—somewhat different language. "The #1 question people ask me after reading *Permission Marketing*: So, how do we get attention to ask for permission in the first place? This manifesto is the answer to that question." [48]

It's odd. Godin talks a lot about manifestos. Even though everyone knows those are the sorts of things that Godless communists produce. Introducing the basic concept in *Fast Company* before the book came out, Godin said: "an idea that moves, grows, and infects everyone it touches . . . that's an ideavirus. . . . It starts with an idea manifesto, a powerful, logical 'essay' that assembles a bunch of existing ideas and transforms them into a new, larger idea that's unified and compelling. . . As long as you can use your manifesto to change the way that people think, talk, and act, you create value. . . "[49] Right. As long as your "manifesto" doesn't spook companies like Procter & Gamble, Coke, Disney, Newscorp, IBM. What would companies of this towering stature make of a manifesto that said things like "Armed only with imagination, we're gonna rip the fucking lid off"?[50] Godin needed a more cleaned-up and presentable idea of what a manifesto should be. Maybe—why not?—it could be a sweepstakes or a lottery. A game. Something more *fun*. Who knows, maybe something that conveyed refreshment and specialness.

"So, is an ideavirus a form of marketing?" Godin asks. And he answers himself: "Absolutely! But today, what else is there?"[51] Well, gee, let's see . . . I can think of two things right off the top: 1) imagination and 2) ripping the fucking lid off—though I hope *Gonzo Marketing* as a whole will constitute a more rigorous and complete answer. The question itself implies everything this book deprecates, deplores and despises. To wit: that marketing has any future at all as a dressed-up tricked-out exercise in manipulating human beings, operating on the (entirely) base assumption that their only value is to consume commercial products for a price.

"But you're being unrealistic." I can hear the response already. Have heard it my whole damn life, as have we all. "That's impractical and irrelevant. Business is business and that's the way it's always been." Well guess what. That's not the way it is any more. Grow up. Get used to it. Power has shifted irreversibly while business continued to delude itself with laughable schemes, transparent lies and obsequious bullshit.

Yes, memic propagation *is* an important factor in how ideas move around online, but adding the commercial dimension is not just a minor wrinkle. It fundamentally changes the nature of the dynamic. Are marketers really naïve enough to believe that the same brain-numbing "key messages" their advertising and PR departments have been peddling all along are somehow going to magically "go viral" and capture hearts and minds?

"Contrary to what you may think," writes Godin in a moment of high levity, "the Macarena was not an organized, sinister plot; it just happened. But many other products, services, hit movies, or catchphrases are the intentional acts of smart entrepreneurs and politicians who know that launching and nurturing an ideavirus can help them accomplish their goals."[52] This is marketing as information warfare—hardly a new concept. It's the same old spin and manipulation. Yeah, it's more sophisticated, but the main tactics are still target and attack. Using a slew of slick new-economy neologisms, Seth Godin has reinvented and repackaged a very old concept: propaganda.

Godin says that "the future belongs to marketers who establish a foundation and process where interested people can market to each other. Ignite consumer networks and then get out of the way and let them talk."[53] But what exactly is a "consumer network"? People tend to join into self-selecting communities online, but unless we're talking about buying clubs, they don't typically aggregate around products. Instead, they come together around common *interests*. They may "consume" products in the process, but this consumption is a side effect. They do not network as the "consumers" business has seen them as for a century, but as new tribes of hunter/gatherers. Often enough to constitute a trend, they are not only *not* hunting for products, they are hunting the businesses that make them— as radical bricoleurs, eyeing rusted-out corporations for spare parts. Too weird, you think? Too bizarre? Some companies have discovered large collections of MP3s cached deep within their firewalled IT fortresses. Who put them there? The company will never know. It was merely a temporary host. A convenient hard disk for a roving band of cultural nomads who have since moved on. A new species some speculate. It's 11 o'clock. Do you know where your children are?

In these subtle and often alien distinctions lie a world of difference—a chasm that business-as-usual can never cross.

But buck up, it's not *all* that grim. If you take the advice of the *Rocky Horror Picture Show*, liberation from these blues is just a jump to the left. And no, it's not a political thing. It's about getting your groove back, Jack. It's about joy, remember? But mostly, it's about *DOING THE TIME WARP AGAIN!* Cue the band. . .

In 1991, on a day that will forever live in infamy, MCI launched its "Friends & Family" marketing program. The basic idea was that, in exchange for lower rates calling them, you could drop a dime on intimate acquaintances, thus causing them to be mercilessly hounded by the company either a) forever, or b) until they had to be put on powerful prescription medications, whichever came first. This initiative was hugely successful up until the inevitable moment when participating MCI customers had lost all their friends and/or been disowned by their families.

A more sanguine and approving version of this story is recounted in a chapter on viral marketing in *The Anatomy of Buzz*, where it is explained that, while such campaigns are roughly as effective as feeding d-Con to rats, they tend to be prohibitively expensive. "If you're not a marketing executive at a telephone company," says author Emanuel Rosen, "you may think, 'Okay, but what can *I* do about this?'" On first reading, I thought to myself, "Yeah, how many tons of C-4 *would* it take to permanently remove MCI from the planet?" But more careful attention to the text alerted me that this was not the response the book was really calling for. I came to see that the author's rhetorical question was meant to imply that the typical marketing reader would be thinking, "Hey, how come *I* can't do this?" In the old days, it just wouldn't have been possible, we're told. But there's good news too. Now, "with the net," says Rosen, "this type of promotion is no longer limited to telephone companies."[54] Oh, aren't you *glad?*

Nonetheless, telephone companies seem to have a special bent for this sort of thing, having taken to the whole viral/permission idea as enthusiastically as the Black Death took to Europe in the 14th century. While writing this chapter, I woke up one morning to this crap from Sprint.

From: Sprint [r15901@discounts-direct.com]
Sent: Thursday, January 18, 2001 2:17 PM
To: clocke@panix.com
Subject: Dear Christopher, Sprint requests your permission

Dear Christopher,

Everyday more and more exciting and important information is being communicated via e-mail. In the future, Sprint would like to communicate with you

via e-mail, and send you exciting and "Up to Date" information on new products and services that Internet users like yourself would have interest in.
Sprint is presently seeking your permission for the privilege to serve you efficiently and electronically via e-Mail. Thank you!

Where in the world did a freaking Telco get the idea I might like
to receive their "Up to Date" information "via e-Mail"? Who is responsible for this befuddled spew? Wait a second... I think I
know—"sceking your permission" is a big clue—and I think a little
payback is in order.

You may argue that a concept like "payback" has no more place in
a serious business book than would that beastly trope so hated and
shunned by people of good will everywhere: the *ad hominem* attack.
But, while that is certainly true in the usual case, let us reason this out
together. How many email addresses would you suppose are in
Sprint's database of targets for this letter? Come on, pick a figure. OK,
now memorize it and don't tell me. If you guessed any number
smaller than the sum of all sentient beings in the known universe having both telephones and Internet access, you would be wrong. So
now take this very large number and multiply it by the number of
companies that want to establish a direct pipeline to your VISA card—
approximately equal to the number of grains of sand in Hawaii—and
you begin to get some idea of how many times you can count on
being interrupted by some imaginative marketing oxymoron asking
your permission to "serve you efficiently and electronically." Do you
still think payback is out of line? Just as I thought. Thank you!

Gonzo Interlude in the Marketing Ward

"Your doctor has your written permission
to inject just about anything he wants into your IV bag."

—SETH GODIN, *PERMISSION MARKETING*

"You'll pay money just to see yourself
with Doctor Robert..."

—THE BEATLES, *REVOLVER*

I never should have taken the job. It was just after midnight in L.A. and I was sitting at the desk in my third-floor office drinking cheap whiskey from the bottle and watching a blood red moon rise over the City of Angels. A full moon. In Scorpio. The calendar had just ticked over to Friday the 13th. Could my luck get any worse? The phone rang.

Where do these studio execs get my unlisted number? PacBell says it values my privacy. Yeah right. It turns out to be Harvey Promoski over at Universal. What a loser. He's telling me the script writers walked out on his project today. No wonder. *Bottomliners* sounds like one of those films that should never be made. Not a lot there to distinguish it from every other POS these guys have cranked out in the last ten years, but hey, what do I know? Promoski's telling me there's big money behind the thing. Julia Roberts likes the storyboards, he says panting, all excited. Yeah? So who's she play? (Just asking. I'm not committing to anything here.) Martha Rogers, he says. He's impressed, I can tell. I can tell he wants company. And we're talking to Kiefer Sutherland and Kevin Bacon, he whispers (like it's a big secret if he's telling me), for Seth Godin and Sergio Zyman. Respectively, he says. Harvey reads the dictionary.

What are you telling me 'you never heard of them,' he yells into the line, like it's a personal affront. The actors, yeah, I say, but not the other ones. Was I supposed to? Maybe you better give me the plot. I listen. I tap my pencil on the blotter. I look at the clock. My luck has gotten worse.

Bottomliners. Whose godforsaken idea was this? I can't believe what I'm hearing. It seems a bunch of third-year grad students at the Kellogg School of Management figure out a way to experience Chapter 11 without really bellying up. They come back, he's telling me. Do you *get it?* They know what it's like to bore in, but they're still holding all their options! Wow, I say, not bothering to explain why. But get this, he says, they start having these, like, creeped-out visions, on accounta stuff they did. You know, customers they screwed, perpetrating boredom, lies. I can tell he's reading from the script. "Somehow we've brought our sins back physically. And they're pissed."

We even got the creatives working on it. *"Bottomliners*—Some lines should never be crossed." Whaddya think? Why do they call them "creatives," I'm wondering, but I know it's not worth asking. Yeah, I say, sounds hot. So what was it you wanted from me? He tells me again about the script guys taking a powder and the next thing I know I'm on a plane. They want to know what it's like to be at death's door. Background, he said, we need background. What can I say? I need the money.

I'm at the St. Vitus Dance Hospital for the Criminally Insane. I finally manage to find the staff lounge and here's my contact, Dr. Robert. Rising to shake my hand, he tells me everything's been set up. The marketing ward is right this way, he says, not wasting time, and I should follow him. He's got grand rounds, he explains, and they just got a wave of new admissions so it's pretty hectic. I can imagine, I say, looking around. I've never been in a marketing ward. How's your immune system, he asks, producing a paper mask from the pocket of his white coat. I dunno, I say, some days I get as many as 100 spams and I haven't crashed yet. That's nothing, he says. In the Level IV hot lab we've recorded over 100,000. No kidding, I say, bored already. I jot the figure in my notebook. Per minute, he says, glancing at me sideways. You don't want to go viral, believe me. I take the mask.

Good decision, he says, the place is crawling with MTDs. This is a new one on me, so I ask. Oh sorry, I forget, he says. Specialization, you know. Not fatal, usually, but they can be very nasty. Marketing Transmitted Delusions. I look at him. I don't say anything.

Dr. Robert takes the chart from the foot of the bed as he sweeps into the first room, all cheerful confidence. And how are we feeling today, Mr. Godin? I grab a look at the chart. Hey, isn't this the guy Harv mentioned? The doc looks over at me, annoyed that I'm interrupting. Form follows fiction, he says, winking, and jams a thermometer into Godin's mouth. Ooo didn ash my pamishon, he protests.[55]

The guy doesn't look good. Do they ever leave, I ask. Oh, they come and go, says the doctor, but the recidivism rate is high. Over 98 percent. This fellow's a regular, aren't you, Mr. Godin? He reads the thermometer. Frowns.

What about the ad agencies? says the guy in the bed. With so many talented people, why aren't they working to solve this problem?

There, there, the doc says, checking Godin's pupils for dilation. Don't you worry about the ad agencies. You're in good hands here.

Why's he talking about ad agencies? I ask, puzzled.

Oh, Seth here thinks a lot about advertising. It's his profession. When he's out there, that is. Got a thing about permission, though. It's odd. You should have seen it when we asked him to sign the permission forms. He smiled down at Godin as if he were a bad little boy. Took five orderlies to get this rascal into a straitjacket.

Early on at Yoyodyne, says Godin as if it just occurred to him, we discovered that we needed one full-time customer service person for every 10,000 people in the database.

And are we taking our meds like we talked about? asks Dr. Robert, ignoring him and surreptitiously rolling his eyes at the ceiling for my benefit.

Godin looks at him a minute, blank. Then says: Your doctor has your written permission to inject just about anything he wants into your IV bag.

That's correct, says Dr. Robert, approvingly. They've obviously been over this ground more than once. And are we cooperating with the staff? But Godin is counting on his fingers now, distracted. Suddenly he looks up at us as if coming to. One lucky customer could win a $100,000 shopping spree, he says.

I'll be back on Tuesday, assures the doctor. If there's anything you need, you just tell Nurse Ratshit. And he ushers me out. Yoyodyne? I ask when the door closes. What was that all about?

Dr. Robert looks concerned. He's been watching this *Buckaroo Banzai* video over and over and yelling 'Laugh-a while can, Monkey Boy!' Scares the crap out of the night desk. But look, we've got to keep moving.

Who's next, I ask as we walk down the long fluorescent hallway. The doctor checks his list. Hmmm, let's see. Today we've got Sergio Zyman, Don Peppers, Harry Beckwith, Steven Cristol, Peter Sealey, Geoffrey Moore, Al Ries, Jack Trout, Sam Hill, Glenn Rifkin . . . quite a list. He flips the page on his clipboard. Oh, and Gary Hammel.

Are they all like him?, I ask, gesturing back to the room we've just left. Are they, all, like . . . you know.

I'm afraid so, the doctor replies, stopping to look at me full on. He takes his glasses off and rubs his eyes. Suddenly he looks weary. Beat. Been at it too long, I think. Must take a special kind of person. To keep it up. To keep the cheery smile in place while listening to such demented gibberish day after day. Personally, I don't see how he does it.

Broadcast: The Meme That Wouldn't Die

Although something clearly has to give, it is enormously difficult for any one individual, group or even company to drive the kind of change that's most required. The assumptions underpinning the business status quo are distributed across many organizations and corporate cultures interwoven in a complex ecological web involving companies, market research firms, advertising and PR agencies, and mass media. The complexity of these relationships, and the cross purposes these various factions are often pursuing, work against understanding, let alone creating, new and fundamentally different relationships to audiences and markets.

This tangled complex is the result of a viral pandemic so powerful that everyone's infected. But the nature of the contagion is such that hosts don't know they have it. The name of this disease is broadcast.

Business has become a dream world of nostalgia and denial, desperately trying to hang onto a memory that is fast slipping out of control. Too many companies today are on a collision course with a networked reality that doesn't recognize old notions of control and doesn't operate according to principles that once appeared to be timeless laws of nature. E-commerce planning founded on broadcast assumptions is guaranteed to fail. Catastrophically. When fantasy and reality clash, reality always wins.[56]

Broadcast is a genuine paradigm in the sense Thomas Kuhn defined the term in *The Structure of Scientific Revolutions*—an overarching theoretical framework that makes reasonably logical sense of the world, or some large part of it.[57] The part of the world that concerns us here is business—its aims, objectives, strategies and tactics. At the most fundamental level, the primary goal of any business is to create products or services it can sell for a profit. Strategies and tactics map to marketing and sales—how the business identifies potentially interested prospects and converts them to revenue-contributing customers.

For the past 100 years or so, the broadcast paradigm has colored, shaped and informed corporations' strategic market planning and the tactical implementation of those plans via specific sales initiatives. The broadcast paradigm made sense of a confusing array of data and helped to coordinate complex organizational efforts. It provided an effective basis for achieving goals and measuring progress. In short, it worked. And because it worked so well, the broadcast paradigm is now so deeply ingrained that its principles are taken for granted—universally accepted axioms that are transparent to the point of invisibility. Business is largely unconscious of these first principles. They remain unexamined. Ask a company why it behaves as it does with respect to markets and marketing and you're likely to get the answer a five-year-old might give: because. Businesses behave as they do because, well . . . because that's just the way things are.

Wrong.

And fatally wrong today. The Internet represents a genuine paradigm shift. The broadcast model never explained "the way things are" in some eternal and unchanging way. True, it explained the way things *were* for quite a long time. And that time was a time of great productivity and burgeoning wealth, both for companies and for society at large—First-World societies at any rate. For business, the first three-quarters of the 20th century constitute a sort of golden era, and the memory of this period still casts its Midas-touch aura over business thinking today. A critical factor in this automesmerism, this attempt at self-hypnosis, is stonewall denial. That world was so good, it worked so well, so smoothly, and we understood how and why. Let's stick with that. Let's stick to our knitting, stay the course. Let's not admit that this fabled golden age is quickly fading.

But it is. The world is not fixed, immutable. It changes. Over the last several decades, two enormous forces have radically reshaped the world of business: the global economy and global networks. And these two powerful trends are linked in fundamental ways, though their linkage is still not obvious to most corporations. It is not obvious because business is blinded by nostalgia for the broadcast paradigm. Broadcast is the meme that wouldn't die.

To understand how "the way things are" has changed, it is necessary to grasp the way things were before, in those halcyon days of the broadcast era. Those days out of which the world is now passing forever. To understand and make effective use of the Internet, business must grasp how different it is from all that has gone before, and how much it has already undermined the broadcast model.

Broadcast is a media phenomenon. Specifically, it is a *mass* media phenomenon that arose in response to the needs of mass production and mass marketing. Media and business are often perceived as being separate, but this is largely a convenient fiction maintained at great cost to hide a powerful secret in plain sight: what we call "the media" today evolved and are only allowed to exist as the handmaidens of mass advertising. As soon as we call the Internet a "medium," we fall into the trap of assuming that it too must inevitably follow this pattern. If the net is a medium, then it must be an advertising medium. Right? From the perspective of business, that's what media are for—to serve its advertising needs. That's what media mediate. Otherwise, why would they exist?

To put it generously, this is a self-centered perspective. Less generously, it's a deluded perspective that explains why business has had so much trouble understanding how to work with the net. Why won't this damn thing behave itself? Why doesn't it do what it's *supposed* to do? The answer is that the "it" in this case is a different kind of it. Another animal altogether. While the Internet will eventually connect billions of people, it will never be a mass medium in the way television is a mass medium. The difference is crucial.

Mass media are "mass" because they have for so long served the core requirement of mass production: to move "excess" inventory. The more product such advertising could move, the more profit the company made, so obviously, the bigger the audience the better. Mass media are mass because they're huge. And the way such hugeness is achieved is by appealing to lowest-common-denominator tastes in terms of programming content. The program, the content, is merely bait to draw the audience. The real show, the real message, is the advertising. And advertisers want to lower the common denominator so that they can get everyone possible into the audience. The best medium is the most massive medium. The best place to place advertising is where the most eyeballs will be forced to eyeball it. This is why CNN loves Elián Gonzalez and Princess Di and OJ Simpson. This is why the cultural legacy we are creating and exporting to the rest of the world is a simpleminded sitcom with a dumbbell laugh track.

This is the broadcast model. Did somebody say MacDonald's?

People didn't come to the Internet for more of this featureless, characterless crap. They came for less. They came because they were bored silly by sterile vanilla one-size-fits-all commercial media. They came because they were hungry for something entirely else. And we found it: each other. The net enables people to speak, not just to listen. And to speak about things we're truly interested in. In 999 out of 1000 cases, we're not interested in talking or hearing about your product. This new empowerment of the audience is intrinsic to Internet technology. It's not something extra or something that can be taken away. It comes with the territory.

This is very bad news for mass producers. The good news is that there aren't many of those left. Look around. Since the advent of serious global competition, companies have not been able to rely on single products with long product cycles. Instead, they've been forced to create a wide array of options to compete with offshore producers and providers seeking to steal even tiny slices of their market share. As a result, markets that were once mass markets have exploded into a vast array of micromarkets.

Mass marketing to micromarkets is just plain stupid. And companies already know it. This insight has long been practiced in the form of demographic segmentation and target marketing. Companies that are already marketing to segments are clearly no longer marketing to the undifferentiated mass. In one sense, the web has merely put this powerful pre-Internet trend on a diet of steroids.

But there's another deeper sense in which networks are changing the fundamental nature of commerce. When companies use the techniques of demographic segmentation, they look at markets through the lens of product. "We have this thing. Who can we get to buy it?" In contrast, when online audiences look at this new medium, they look through the lens of interest. "I'm curious about this subject. Who can tell me more?"

People gravitate toward websites that feed their curiosity, that speak to their passions, their genuine interests. And in this process new micromarkets are just now emerging. Thousands of them. They are coalescing around voice: around people who are articulate, entertaining, knowledgeable and informative. These micromarkets are too small to show up on any demographic radar. To reach such micromarkets and form productive relationships with them, companies need to share the interests they represent. And to do so they must first stop speaking in the insistently demanding voice of command-and-control to which they became addicted in the days of broadcast. *Attention K-Mart shoppers!!!*

Instead of pitching products, corporate communications must seed conversations that become the basis for further community discourse. Effective communications will come not from traditional PR and marketing mouthpieces, but from employees spanning the corporation—real people with real passions, real enthusiasm. In contrast, one-way product pitches will fail to connect with genuine market interests. They will fall on deaf ears.

In the post-broadcast era, brand will become the sum of all a company has said and the *spirit* in which it has said those things— a powerful symbol of the state of the relationship between a company and *all* its stakeholders. In the best cases, brand will become a reputation for shared understanding and deep respect. Brands that do not convey these values will become embarrassing public flags signaling ignorance, arrogance and needlessly lost opportunity.

While broadcast is anything but subtle in its methods, understanding its full implications calls for a delicate touch. The dynamics of television and mass media have shaped and molded us, changed our minds in fundamental ways. But as we use those same minds to look at how media affects us, the effects can be extremely difficult to perceive. You're unlikely to see them by looking at yourself straight on. You'd probably want to change the channel after 30 seconds. You won't find them reflected in ratings statistics or in analysts' pie charts and spreadsheets. Occasionally, though, you may stumble across some odd exchange, a scrap of conversation that goes nowhere. Just words in passing. Ships in the night. It may look trivial on the surface. But look deeper. Wonder about it.

In March 1999, Brian Lamb interviewed NBC news anchor Tom Brokaw on C-SPAN's *Booknotes* program—Brokaw's book, *The Greatest Generation*, had just come out. And there's this nearly poignant moment where Lamb says, ". . . in television and radio, you almost become something other than what you are." Then he asks "Why has the business grown up that way where there's a lot of yelling and, 'We'll be right back after this!' You know, what's that come from? Because we don't talk to each other . . . "

For some reason that's not entirely clear—it's as if they're not talking to each other—Brokaw responds by reminiscing about the original broadcast announcers. "Edward R. Murrow was highly stylized," he says. "I mean, he's a reverential figure for all of us, but he couldn't get away with that now. You know, that cigarette smoke and the kind of the use of the language and how he did it and, 'the fault lies not in the stars but with us,' and that kind of thing . . . "

Lamb, evidently feeling that this response has not quite addressed the substance of his question, takes another shot. "Let me ask you again, though," he says, "why is it like in commercials, especially radio commercials, they're yelling at. . . what. . . what happened?" Brokaw digs way down deep this time. And comes up empty. "I. . . I don't know. I. . . there's this. . . it's probably the rock 'n' roll attitude about radio that it has to be louder."[58]

Sure, that's right. Blame it on rock and roll. But the fault lies not in the stars.

CHAPTER 4

Stories as Strange Attractors[1]

Control is the enemy of imagination. The two aren't just
incompatible; they are inimical. One drives out the other.
Deming, the Total Quality guy, said "drive out fear." Imagine.

DAVID WEINBERGER, GOOD FRIEND AND *CLUETRAIN* CO-AUTHOR, DEFINES
the web as "many small pieces loosely joined." This chapter will be
like that: an undone puzzle; a bit of sky here, a wisp of cloud, perhaps a shadowed face. This piece is also part of a larger piece. It's
a story about stories that start conversations. A story about how
conversations lay the groundwork for commerce—and how, sometimes, commerce grounds conversation.

But the story will not be linear. It will jump around. We expect
this of fiction, but not of business writing, which should proceed in
stately order, from one clear point to the next. However, since the
arrival of the tangled higher-order logic of the web, business has become more dependent on narrative than on explication—and the
narrative is no longer straightforward and predictable. It takes odd
turns. It turns you on, then turns on you. It leaves you stranded.
And then, just as you thought you'd reached a dead end, the road
picks up again. The plot thickens. Stories are strange attractors.

Gonzo marketing isn't really about marketing at all. At least not
the kind that mutters amnesiacally about the 4 Ps of Product, Place,
Price and Promotion. Since the web came along, place no longer
matters, the right price is often zero, and the first rule of promotion
is to never talk about the product. Maybe instead, marketing should
be about persuading people to listen, just as the goal of fiction is to

get readers to willingly suspend disbelief. Hmmm, curious thought. But if that's the point, then "*marketing*" is probably the wrong word for the program. Which is why I call it gonzo marketing—a boring, not very friendly concept turned inside out and stuffed full of yarns and fables, myths and sagas, outright fictions: stories.

If I set out to tell you about my product, I'm already hosed, right out of the gate. You're not interested. Your eyes glaze over. And I can't *make* you listen these days—not with 30 bajillion web links beckoning every second. Certainly not the way I could make you listen with a 30-bajillion-dollar advertising budget and a populace hardwired to The Tube. Mass marketing is a special case of mass production in which the product is mass-produced commercial "messages." In the pre-net heyday of broadcast advertising, these messages had to appeal to the widest possible audience. Therefore they could offend no one. They could have no real personality. They had to be one-size-fits-all, bland, vanilla, preferably humorless. So pervasive was this jargon-ridden communicational "style" that even individuals deployed it in one-to-one business letters wherein they did such things as thank each other in advance for their earliest attention to those important matters impacting mutual concerns in re their earlier communication. Many businesses still think and talk this way.

With the advent of the Internet, markets have again become open, unconstrained conversations. Free talk. And the best conversations, the ones people gravitate toward, are based on stories. Stories, like conversations, don't have targets, fixed goals, Q2 objectives. They circumambulate their subjects. They explore. They don't have mission statements. If the pitch is the epitome of broadcast, the story embodies the essential character of the web.

Open-Source Marketing

It's Spring 1999 and I'm nearly broke. I'm getting worried. My phone rings. It's Steve Larsen, who was then senior VP marketing at Net Perceptions. I've known him since 1994, when he was at Prodigy and I was at Mecklermedia exploring a concept that would soon come to be called e-commerce. Now, he tells me, he's thinking about putting together a website focusing on personalization. I have to ask what that means. "Don't worry about it," Larsen says, "You'll pick it up real quick." Oh, so he's talking about a gig. Good timing. "Anyway, we were just kicking around who we could get to help us out with this, and at the same instant several people said 'Hey! This is a job for RageBoy!' So whaddya think? Are you interested?"

The result was that, for two years, I was editor-in-chief of personalization.com, and Net Perceptions was my client.[2] The project started with Steve and I experimenting with an idea suggested by something said by Eric Raymond, president of the Open Source Initiative. The web page at opensource.org explains the basic concept as it applies to software:

> The basic idea behind open source is very simple. When programmers can read, redistribute, and modify the source code for a piece of software, the software evolves. People improve it, people adapt it, people fix bugs. And this can happen at a speed that, if one is used to the slow pace of conventional software development, seems astonishing. We in the open source community have learned that this rapid evolutionary process produces better software than the traditional closed model, in which only a very few programmers can see the source and everybody else must blindly use an opaque block of bits.[3]

When he signed the manifesto at cluetrain.com, Raymond wrote: "The cluetrain is to marketing and communications what the open-source movement is to software development—anarchic, messy, rude, and vastly more powerful than the doomed bullshit that conventionally passes for wisdom."

What a terrific sound bite! But what if I took it seriously? Was it possible that there could be such a thing as "open-source marketing"? On its face, the idea seemed absurd. The canonical model for the open source movement is Linux, the development of which has been collaborative and widely distributed, percolating good ideas from the bottom up without explicit direction from any focal control point. How could marketing—competitive, centralized and highly managed via a top-down chain of command—bear any resemblance?

But the more Steve and I talked about it, the more we realized that an open-source marketing model fit with what we already believed. On the personalization.com site, we first banned any form of product promotion. We set up a forum for anyone who wanted to talk about the subject, pro or con, and we even published several articles that basically said personalization sucks. Then we decided to invite Net Perceptions' competitors to join in.

Steve had seen an early draft of *The Cluetrain Manifesto* and was interested in answering the question: If markets are conversations, how do you go about starting and sustaining that kind of conversation? We both felt that the success of the site should be measured on the quality of the content and the diversity of its sources—the number and variety of people participating—instead of by the sales leads it generated.

When the site launched, Steve wrote a column explaining what we were up to. He told the story about how we originally met (and how I got the name RageBoy from Esther Dyson). He followed with a telling comment: "I knew Chris would provide the separation from Net Perceptions necessary to the site being accepted as a legitimate source of high-quality information on an important topic and not just propaganda from some PR machine."

Separation as critical prerequisite for legitimacy? Isn't that kind of a weird concept for a marketing guy to be entertaining? No weirder, certainly, than putting his company's core market positioning into the hands of someone who calls himself RageBoy. But the response was fantastic. Many people wrote articles for the site (without pay, so it wasn't that). About 10,000 visitors—many from major corporations—subscribed to the newsletter I started putting out. The forum immediately started filling up with substantive discussion and lively debate. Links from other pages were plentiful and personalization.com got some great write-ups. Jesse Berst of ZDnet's *AnchorDesk* told his two-million-plus subscribers about the site: "Although it is sponsored by personalization vendors, it contains thoughtful commentary and information about the pros, cons and uses of personalization." And *USA Today* quoted me on the seed of an idea that eventually turned into the book you're now holding:

"In the days of broadcast media, pre-net, everything was outbound. You had these demographers slicing and dicing the market to see who the perfect target for their ads was," says Christopher Locke, editor of Personalization.com. "What's going on online now is the complete opposite of that; it's micromarkets which are emerging out of nowhere."[4]

But it wasn't all thoughtful commentary and penetrating insight. RageBoy, my psycho online alter ego, definitely put his oar in from time to time. Announcing the first Personalization Summit conference, held November '99 in San Francisco, he managed to break out of the leg irons, get control of my terminal and write to thousands of personalization newswire subscribers:

Hear!

[this followed by a list of well-known industry speakers]

Experience!

[followed by a litany of equally well-known companies]
- Steve Larsen, vice president of marketing, Net Perceptions, droning on interminably and telling really bad jokes.
- Christopher Locke, editor of personalization.com (securely restrained in a bamboo cage for your personal protection).

See!

1000 virgins sacrificed to the Great God Baal . . .

One CEO telephoned me within minutes of this crossing the net. "I've never seen a business newsletter quite like this," he said. He was clearly perplexed. I tried to be serious. "We only live to serve," I told him. But he registered anyway, as did hundreds of others. The conference sold out early. It was a standing-room-only success, exceeding everyone's expectations. And the newsletter was the only vector we used to flog the thing—if you don't count press releases, which are basically worthless. Did something strange happen to marketing while the world was busy making other plans? Yup. The web has turned the world upside down and inside out. When paradox becomes paradigm, worst practices work best.

Only Rock and Roll

In *The Cluetrain Manifesto* I talk about the ancient marketplace, the social hub around which civilization emerged. It was a confusing place, filled with noise, with talk, with song. Nearly 20 years ago, standing at a Tokyo news kiosk, I read an interview with Keith Richards in which he said he saw Mick Jagger and himself as being in direct line of descent from antique bards and medieval troubadours.[5] In place of "Let It Bleed" and "Sympathy For the Devil," I suddenly flashed on the lyric poet-musicians of the 12th century, on Beowulf, Homer, and even further back to bones and rattles and skin drums around some Neolithic campfire.

For me, this was a moment of radical reframing. Here was this roughneck rocker junkie talking about being connected to an authentic human lineage, which in turn connected him to both his own purpose as a man, and to his audience. Quite literally, to his market. Suddenly, Richards wasn't just a London punk grabbing for money and fame. He was reenacting and embodying a ritual that has united people at a primal, atavistic level for thousands of years—however dark, a powerful communion. Reading his almost throw-away comment revised my entire outlook on popular music. And on marketing.

Is the heritage of the ancient marketplace merely a legacy of barkers hawking their wares in some B-movie commercial carnival? Or was there ever poetry to it? Was there once upon a time some deeper story? Advertising shares certain qualities with the craft of storytelling. Unfortunately, the stories advertising tells are created to please clients, not the audience. That's upside down. Only a live and fully wide-awake audience—not a "focus group"—can truly judge a story's value. But instead of asking whether the story was effective, the ad agency today asks the client whether the story sold the product.

Because broadcast is intrusive, it's possible in that model for crappy stories—another way of saying ads—to sell mediocre products. However, the Internet is not broadcast. Broadcast assumptions—especially the high value advertising places on intrusion and manipulation—immediately fall apart on the Internet. If the story bombs online, that's the *end* of the story. If nobody listens, nobody buys.

I am inordinately fond of books. And I spend a lot of money acquiring them. It's a neurosis I've learned to live with. Who gets all this ill-gotten loot? Amazon. Certainly not because they're aiming spam and banner ads at me, but because of the stories and conversations there. "Huh?" you ask. "What stories? What conversations?" Perhaps you're too old, too set in your assumptions to see what's happening. Go to the Harry Potter pages. Slowly, haltingly, the children of the world are beginning to talk to one another. *They* understand. No one had to explain it to them. Barnes & Noble and Borders may have the same books, but they haven't yet embedded them in as rich and attractive a context. Not attractive as in pretty. Attractive as in magnetizing and awakening interest. Catalogs of bare product listings rarely have that effect, whereas interactions with other people often do.

New medium or not, companies are always going to try to sell us their stuff. It's what they do. It's what we expect them to do. But the point is no longer just to capture people's attention—though that remains critical. It's to encourage their goodwill. From this point forward, companies will never achieve substantial market share without first establishing an elusive quality called *"mindshare."* Do I want to obey my thirst and glug down a Sprite? Do I want to take the Pepsi Challenge? Do I care if you got milk? No, no, and no.

But I might care a lot if some company offered to hook me up with a bunch of interesting people who think sorta like I do, and have similar or complementary tastes and interests. People who could tell me stuff I wanted to know. Or even better, people good at telling stories, sharing experiences, insights, new perspectives. There are many places where that sort of exchange is happening on the net. But most of them are zines or e-mail lists or personal sites created by talented turned-on individuals.

Very few companies offer anything even remotely close. Sure there are huge chat conglomerates like ICQ and Yahoo and AOL, but they're just providing the tools or the pipe, not the juice. To them the stories are just message traffic and page hits. What about companies that sell other things, like cars or shoes or power tools? The sites that all these trillions of dollars of e-commerce are supposed to be coming from. Maybe I'm blind and I'm missing it. But I just don't see people hanging out at corporate websites. There's nothing to do there but buy more stuff so the company can make more money. Gosh, *that's* exciting! Thanks, Sergio.

To capture the interest of online markets, where we have gotten used to talking amongst ourselves in uncontrived, unpremeditated human voices, companies need to tell human stories. Not the smarmy, cloyingly sentimental "human interest" stories businesses are so fond of leveraging in support of some arcane brand mysticism, but rather, stories that come from having actually grappled with the class of problems the product or service purports to solve. In other words, companies need to tell stories based on genuine understanding, not purposeful misdirection. However, to tell such human stories, companies need human beings—a "product" with which they've never had much success. It's not that they lack the raw materials. They start with perfectly good stock. But they consistently turn out androids that sound like Tickle Me Elmo dolls.

Marketing Myopia Revisited

In the realm of technology, the unnatural spawn of Big Science and Big Business, it's all facts and figures. It's passionless objectivity all the way down. I woke up one day and said to myself: Yeah? Well, screw that. I was at an AI conference. Artificial intelligence not artificial insemination. And all these academic research types were arguing about natural language processing. They were arguing about it as if language was their personal property, something that they'd inherited along with their degrees and official membership in The Discipline. I remember getting angry. I remember thinking about the cave paintings at Lascaux and Altamira, about dictionaries as a form of lexical archeology, about Indo-European etymologies that went back the steppes of Asia, to people who rode into battle bareback and made up words for the sounds their swords and axes made, for the sounds of love, for the sounds of the night. And I thought, who do these hosers think they are, these long-winded doctors of philosophy with their anemic propositions and their feeble proofs? I walked away and never looked back.

I love language. And not just for what it can do. For what it is. But I'm also a working stiff. Somehow, I ended up in high-tech marketing. And for years I asked myself if there might be some way to combine my interest in language with my work in marketing. Could there be some hidden connection? This is one of those questions that is so profoundly stupid, you actually blush when you finally hear yourself asking it. "Hmmm, let's see . . . language, marketing . . . language, marketing . . ." And then the light bulb went off. Duh!

Could it be just remotely possible that the articulation of a company's history, direction and focus, what it cares about and spends its time doing, how it perceives its contribution to the world beyond itself . . . that all that could have some bearing on things like management, leadership, brand, positioning, value proposition and suchlike buzzwords? Double-duh! But companies mostly want to talk about just one thing: the product. And they mostly want to say just one thing about that: buy it! If markets are conversations, this makes for one hell of a dull conversation.

Why is corporate speech so unimaginative? In "Marketing Myopia," Theodore Levitt wrote:

> The reason [the railroads] defined their industry incorrectly was that they were railroad-oriented instead of transportation oriented. . . . What the railroads lack is not an opportunity but some of the managerial imaginativeness and audacity that made them great. . . . Even an amateur like Jacques Barzun can see what is lacking when he says: "I grieve to see the most advanced physical and social organization of the last century go down in shabby disgrace for lack of the same comprehensive imagination that built it up."[6]

Note here that Levitt turns to the amateur, and the amateur gets it right. Note also the references to imagination and audacity. Where professionals are cool and analytic, beginners and dilettantes often see things more clearly—and care more deeply about what they see.

The more people care, the more they are willing to risk. Concern, passion, shock, outrage: all tend to inspire engaged, audacious, imaginative speech. And such speech has true voice, the power to compel attention because—are you ready for this?—it is grounded in love.

In an era of networked markets, the love of the amateur and the delight of the dilettante represent a critical new dimension of economic reality, a powerful new market dynamic. The common online rabble—among which I definitely count myself—has no love for commerce and its convoluted, self-deluded marketing schemes.

Gonzo marketing is about reframing and recontexualization. Re-imagining. So imagine this: gonzo marketing is marketing from the *market's* perspective. It is not a set of tricks to be used against us. Instead, it's a set of tools to achieve what *we* want for a change. At the same time, it holds great promise for business, because . . . well, because we believed it all those years when business said it wanted to know what we really wanted. And for starters, what we want is for business to leave us the hell alone!

Fortunately for me, I'm schizophrenic—a definite plus when attempting to hold such views *and* make a living in the business world. So I actually do see the value of gonzo marketing to companies. I see it as a powerful form of market advocacy, which companies sorely need. They need it because, despite all the lip service, they are incapable of imagining what is going on in the minds of their own markets. Not so fortunately, the downside of this juggling act—where the "act" is telling the truth about things as I perceive them—is that I can only work for those rare companies that really want to know what their markets are thinking, as opposed to the many that merely pretend they want to know. But this market segmentation is OK by me. It prevents me from having assholes for clients.

You think this is Internet "attitude" talking? Ironic postmodern overstatement? Forty years ago, Ted Levitt speculated in some amazement about how the auto industry could have missed the public's clear preference for smaller, more fuel-efficient cars. "The answer," he wrote, "is that Detroit never really researched customers' wants. It only researched their preferences between the kinds of things which it had already decided to offer them."[7]

Narrative Goes Online

So-called personalization technologies purport to help companies understand their customers better. And in a way, they do. When Amazon tells you that "customers who bought this book also bought . . ." and gives you a list of titles, these *collaboratively filtered* results represent the collective knowledge of widely dispersed individuals. However, as used by most companies, personalization is an oxymoron. Without knowing anything about customers as people, it merely automates "cross-selling" and "upselling" opportunities—a more sophisticated version of "Would you like fries with that?" Does this sell more fries? Yeah. But that's an extremely limited view.

Re-visioned from a higher vantage point, the view looks radically different. Collaborative filtering works bottom up by feeling out the edges of emergent micromarkets based on personal tastes and interests—in effect, defining potential online communities. This is a powerful capability, much better suited to a networked medium than the top-down demographic slicing and dicing typical of broadcast. Such techniques could enable companies to stop marketing altogether— at least in the sense of marketing *to* and marketing *at*. Instead, personalization could be used to get genuinely personal, connecting members of these emergent micromarkets *to each other*. Do that, and something different in kind results. People start talking, having conversations, telling stories.

Recall all those kids on Amazon vibing back and forth about Harry Potter. J. K. Rowling's first four *Harry Potter* books have so far elicited over 10,000 reader reviews—an incredible number. What's the commercial benefit? It's impossible to measure with scientific accuracy, but here's a clue. As I write this, the fifth volume in the series won't be published until next year—at least nine months away—yet today it's Amazon's #1 bestseller. Is that worth something in cold hard cash? You bet.

Amazon is facilitating this conversation and the resulting community of interest is far more likely to value the facilitator than if the company found a way to "message" at them more efficiently. Efficiency is not effectiveness. Talking about MyWidget—your wonderful product—is generally boring and tends to quickly turn into gushing, blatherous hype. But talking about the kinds of problems a product was created to solve, the opportunities and obstacles it was created to take advantage of or overcome—in other words, its larger market context—can often help people to decide why (and if) they should give a damn about it in the first place—a significant challenge for many companies these days.

Amazon.com's real innovation was to create a marketplace where customers, not advertisers and marketeers, could assess the value of products. For years, academic librarians built OPACs—online patron access catalogs—but to the best of my knowledge, none ever asked the reader, "so hey, did you *like* that book?" Back at the beginning of this chapter, I wrote: "sometimes, commerce grounds conversation." This is a good example. It took a commercial organization, not Yale or Stanford or the Library of Congress, to get ordinary people talking to each other about—of all things—books.

Do site visitors scanning reader reviews feel they are being advertised to? I don't think so. Especially when they encounter reviews warning off potential buyers: "This book sucks. It was a waste of money. Don't make the same mistake I did!" Is there slop in Amazon's system? Uh-huh. Are there design flaws? Definitely. Inequities? Possibly; I don't know for sure. But overall it's a great model. And it opens up rich possibilities, of which I suspect we've only seen the surface. The company is enriching its relational space—both hyperlinked knowledge and person-to-person relationships—in many ways: through its affiliates program, wish lists, member pages, reviews of reviewers, discussion boards, purchase circles, auctions, "Honor System PayPages," "Listmania" lists and so on.

The really interesting marketing action at Amazon is not how this information is being used to pitch products—"Would you like *War and Peace* with that?"—but in how it's being used to hook people up and get them talking with each other. "Hey, I just read *War and Peace*, and man, I gotta tell ya, this Tolstoy dood rulez!" So what's gonzo about that? Easy. It's anti-marketing. To be more precise, it's anti-marketing-as-usual—it's actually very *smart* marketing. Because people talking to each other don't sound like marketing droids.

Don't Examples

In 1996, Microsoft was running a thing called *Internet Magazine* on its site. The people responsible for putting it together got wind of my zine, EGR, and against all reasonable expectations, evidently liked what they saw. In fact, they said hey, write some of that gonzo stuff for us—none of this crap we get about how wonderful Microsoft's products are.

I was fascinated by the anything-but-our-product focus, so I tried to get to know the crew. One person sent me mail saying: "You wouldn't believe the background of this team: acupuncturist, MFA in poetry, mediaeval vocalist, '60s protestor for civil rights in the south, and many other secrets. Best of all, it's an ego-free-zone!" And then there was this, in response to my query about an odd quote in one of these Microsofters' sigs: "The Black Sabbath line comes from the convicted ex-journalist from S.F. He gets in every day at 7 a.m. and cranks up the volume and the writing. He also understands IE 4 better than most of the entire marketing team."

Remember: we're talking about the notorious Evil Empire here. The editor-in-chief was Emily Warn, a published poet. I bought one of her books, where I came across this: "But the haze in the hills is not fog or smoke from hermit fires. It is America breathing."[8] Wow, I thought, there is life in the trenches. Heart is still alive and beating inside the corporate monoliths. But a couple months later, Microsoft shut the project down.

Audioactive sells MP3 encoders and related sorts of things. I was impressed by the site when I first went there several years ago. It was funny and self-effacing. You could tell the crew was turned on, having fun. One page talked about the technology. This is pretty daunting stuff, it said. And it could be boring. Are you sure you want to wrap your head around the algorithms these wire-head scientists came up with?

The Audioactive site was good-looking and conveyed deep competence. I remember it a million sites later for only one reason: it had voice. I could feel there were real people on the other end. But when I went back to those pages to grab some examples, I couldn't find a single one. The site has been sterilized. The edge, the humor, the voice is gone. All the information is still there, and maybe the pages are a little slicker. But now the company sounds like every other e-bozo outfit on the web.

One day in June 1997, I hit the Microsoft website looking for some information now long forgotten. At the top of the main page was a headline about a recent deal: "Microsoft Invests $1 Billion in Comcast." Nothing very surprising there. What was memorable was the sub-slug: "We found some extra cash lying around in a sock drawer." Whoa! What was this? I ripped into the press release, hoping for more, but fell asleep at the terminal halfway through the obligatory Gates quote: "Today's announcement will enhance the integration of broadband pipes and content to expand the services offered to consumers." Zzzz . . .

I went back to the page for weeks afterwards, wondering if there'd be more inspired headlines, captions, further signs of life from whoever had produced the sock drawer line. No dice. Maybe one day I'll run into this person and hear the story of how she got demoted to Encarta shipping clerk for unauthorized cheek. Too bad. Too sad. Why do companies insist on being boring and character-free? Moreover, why do startups, those zany hackers with the wild ideas and boundless energy, insist on emulating big asleep-at-the-wheel companies as soon as they land their first-round financing? I imagine an exchange that goes something like this.

VENTURE CAPITALIST: "You fellows are bright as a pin and we like your spunk. Otherwise we wouldn't be handing you such a big wad of cash. But you have to realize this isn't a game anymore. No more goofing around. We expect to get a whopping return on this investment, and for that to happen, you're going to have to start acting and sounding like a real company."

DEVELOPER: "Gee. How does that work, exactly?"

VC: "Well, look at your Fortune 500 companies out there. You want to join them one day, right? We certainly want you to. You don't see them being funny do you? You don't see them making cracks about their products or management team. No, you don't. And you won't. Not ever. You have joined the ranks of serious business, and while you may find it a little plain, I can assure you this is how it's done."

In a medium well known for sites with names like "The Cathedral of the Hydrogenated Snack Cake," why would *any* company assume it needed to sound "businesslike"? Why would it ever write something like this unedited clip from a bona fide press release?

IBM is focused on delivering customized, flexible and scalable Internet solutions for companies of all sizes. Drawing on resources from across IBM and 90,000 IBM Business Partners, IBM's Global Net Generation Business helps Service Providers and other web-based companies (hosters, portals and born-on-the-web B2B and B2C companies) establish their businesses and become profitable in Internet time.[9]

Hey, in "Internet time" I'm snoring over here, guys. I'm cuttin' Z's again.

Rhetorical Questions

Steve Larsen periodically mails out an informal screed he calls Friends of Net Perceptions. It used to be Friends of Prodigy (which "had fewer friends" he notes), then Friends of CitySearch. He's been doing this for a long time now. In one of these he recapped the inside story of what it was *actually* like to go public. This was a hysterically irreverent look at what most company executives consider a sacred rite of passage into corporationhood. He ends thusly:

In the next bizarre iteration of this newsletter run amok, I'll clue you in on some other interesting stuff. If you are smart and value your sanity, you'll get off this list NOW! As always, getting off requires that you whirl a live chicken around your head three times on the night of a full moon while muttering lyrics from an obscure Doors tune . . .

He ripped off the chicken-whirling trope from EGR—though he tacked on the Doors bit, which I think adds a nice touch. Anyway, you get the idea. This isn't exactly your average business communiqué. It's solidly in the gonzo camp. Yet he sends it out to clients, journalists, industry analysts, even to investors. Steve doesn't hesitate to tell these readers to subscribe to my EGR ravings, where— trust me on this one—they are liable to encounter all manner of unseemly and highly unbusinesslike content. I ask him whether this isn't . . . uh, just a little risky. "Marketing is about real relationships," Larsen replies. "I tell my friends about stuff I like, no matter how off-the-wall. They don't always share my tastes, but they end up knowing me better."

Only in a world gone crazy would that be gonzo. But the business world today is not just crazy. It's headed for the rubber room. In "Fear and Loathing on the web" (gonzo ported from Las Vegas to AltaVista), I quoted David Weinberger, who said: "The dogs have it right. Customers want to take a good long whiff. But companies so lobotomized that they can't speak in a recognizably human voice build sites that smell like death." That was one thread, one shared stream of consciousness that led to the cluetrain manifesto, where later I would write:

> To speak with a human voice, companies must share the concerns of their communities. But first, they must belong to a community. Companies must ask themselves where their corporate cultures end. If their cultures end before the community begins, they will have no market. Human communities are based on discourse—on human speech about human concerns. The community of discourse is the market. Companies that do not belong to a community of discourse will die.[10]

I'm cautiously edging toward a theory of rhetoric here. The word *rhetoric* often causes eyebrows to be raised, and is sometimes even met with alarm. This reaction involves the conflict between two contradictory sets of semantics:

rhetoric, noun

1. persuasive speech or writing: speech or writing that communicates its point persuasively
2. pretentious words: complex or elaborate language that only succeeds in sounding pretentious

From ancient times to the present, the study of rhetoric has always focused on effective, persuasive communication. However, lacking a theory of rhetoric—an informing overall set of communicational principles and a sense of what they are to be used for—institutional speech has largely been reduced to the second definition.

Stories often employ figures of speech: similes, metaphors. They use these rhetorical devices to ground abstractions in the familiar—like the face of a friend emerging from an anonymous crowd. Slacking off and surfing around one day (my usual routine), I came across an article titled "Ashby's Law Revisited."

> Where before, companies could get away with making the right noises about flexibility but really remain as rigid as they want to while instead trying to pull political and other strings to control the environment, they can't any more—trying to do this in the current environment will be akin to bolting the stable door after the horse has fled and is already out there in the wild mounting many mares and making many foals.[11]

The writer's name is Olu Oni. When he wrote this, he was just some guy, one of millions of people posting pages to the web. However, when the weekend is over and he puts on his shoes and tie and business suit, he is Assistant Vice President for Global Markets Technology at Chase Manhattan Bank. When he writes like this, he isn't speaking on behalf of his company. He is very careful to say so. But when he leaves for work, does he leave the poetry at home? I doubt it. Consider the metaphor of the horse. Notice that it is drawn from the world of the living. Notice that the horse is wild, that it has broken free. Notice that its first thought is to replicate itself.

Some metaphors are so powerful they speak directly in the language of the collective unconscious. In an e-mail conversation we got into about cluetrain and his paper on Ashby's Law, Olu wrote: "Markets have strong supernatural and spiritual bearings in Yoruba culture and indeed the reason for the adage 'do not buy from strangers' is because of the belief that spirits also came to the market to transact in souls . . . Buy from a stranger and the transaction may cost you more than you bargained for."

The best stories can become myths that draw people together, create entire cultures. The people within the culture so created are not strangers to each other precisely because they know the old stories. They share and reflect on them. They remember together. This creates powerful cohesion, even identity. And sometimes the stories are warnings. They persist because they continue to protect the people, often from great harm. Is the notion of a market traffic in souls merely superstition? If it's just a metaphor, what is it a metaphor *for?* Is it possible that the engine of commerce decoupled and estranged from the concerns of any human society could actually steal people's souls? In some real sense, destroy their life force? Perhaps it's not a metaphor at all.

If you think deeply about this story, it becomes an allegory—richer, deeper, entangled with other meanings. You turn it over in your mind. You talk about it and retell it. This is how stories travel through time, as word of mouth from ancient days. This is how stories replicate themselves.

For a long time, all our lives in fact, the engine of commerce roared on, insatiably devouring the 20th century. The deafening sound it made was not only the noise of industrial factories, but also of the mass communication machines that pumped out an endless stream of mesmeric anti-myth—the empty stories that were advertising. Then along came the web and the Thorazine wore off, the hypnotic spell began to break. As networking replaces broadcasting, communication must become richer and more interesting—not just louder and more insistent. It must have character, invite participation. Must differentiate itself from the plethora of uncommunicative corporate blather, which by its sheer volume—in both senses—threatens to drown out all memory of life-before-the-brand.

For purposes of such differentiation, it's a good idea to explore styles and concepts that corporate communications are apparently incapable of even conceiving. Such radical approaches include, but are not limited to:

- being funny
- being playful
- being angry
- using big words
- using bad words
- using parody and satire
- dropping arcane literary allusions
- admitting to heavy use of illegal pharmaceuticals

And, for extra credit, most outrageous of all:

- telling the truth

The challenge today is to engage with people in something larger than yourself. Something you have in common. Something murky and ill-defined that's hovering on the edges, waiting to be discovered. Whatever that something is, it's out there on the web. Lurking. The world has changed. Fundamentally and irrevocably. The comforting certainty of the database, the fixed field, the form, is gone forever. Good. The fill-in-the-blanks approach to information and knowledge, to life, is what T.S. Kuhn—The Paradigm Guy®—called puzzle solving: the slavish, formulaic rule-following that comes between revolutions, scientific or otherwise. It's stupid, stultifying, boring. And on the Internet at least, it's over, finito, dead, kaput. Hail Eris!

Marketing has an agenda, an objective. It wants us to do something, buy something. Now! Stories aren't like that. They suggest, they explore, they imagine. They say, hey take your time. Become larger. The web is storyspace. It's its own strange attractor.

But wait. Doesn't all this reduce to some vague form of muddleheaded web mysticism? Gonzo or not, shouldn't "marketing" have something to do with making money? Absolutely. The real question is whether websites emulating the lowest-common-denominator style of mass media will be effective at bringing in new business. Today, it may seem so. But tomorrow, attempting to please everyone is likely to please no one.

Brand Id

I first heard from Brian Millar soon after the cluetrain manifesto appeared on the web. At the time, he was working at RMG International, a subsidiary of The WPP Group. WPP is arguably the world's largest advertising and public relations conglomerate—we're talking motels on Boardwalk. Brian sent me e-mail that became an article, "Modern Life is Rubbish," which I published on personalization.com. "We now benefit from economies of scale at the cost of any modicum of humanity creeping into our dealings with brands," he wrote. "But I think that it's a temporary problem, because many of these Industrial Age monoliths are pretty doomed."[12]

He has since left RMG and WPP and started a company of his own, called myrtle. The site says:

> myrtle is a new company which helps brands communicate in an accelerated culture. Yes: people are more contradictory, more aware of choice, more demanding and less ready to be talked down to or imposed upon than ever. No: they can't be bribed, they don't think your ads are entertaining any more and they resent being sneaked up on. Yes: our work starts with consumers. We find patterns in the chaos of their lives.

By the way, myrtle is also his dog's name. "In a market that's accelerating in incomprehensible ways," Millar explains in e-mail, "doing nothing is the greatest risk of all. And in a market that's a conversation, the winners are going to be the people with something to say. Our website represents our brand's id. All the sneaky little things we've always wanted to do and say are out there for everybody to see."

Sneaky little things like what, precisely? Well . . . myrtle imagines "ultranarrow ultramodern microchannels" offering endless loops of sampled video—people swearing for hours on end, for instance, or interminably strung-together car chase scenes. "It's a meaner, more lizardly attitude to our treasured media archives," Millar admits, tongue firmly in cheek. "But then, nothing's sacred." Brian tells me that myrtle is also offering "Turin Shroud duvet covers. The extraordinary deposition image, only shown in public once per generation, preserved on your comforter forever. A gift to treasure. Yes. What have Turin Shroud duvet covers got to do with running an ad agency? Frankly, nothing as far as I can work out. But I bet they'd look nifty."

And then there are a number of items such as . . .

Human Crisps: If it's okay for vegetarians to eat, say, bacon-flavour snacks because it's just "pretend" or "bacon-effect" and contains no actual animal products, then we want to eat human-flavoured crisps. It's only fair that carnivores get a share of the new fiction-food market too. So while you're thinking, hmm . . . who do I want to eat the most, please understand we don't want just any person-flavour. We crave celebrities, novelists, philosophers, stars of stage and screen, athletes, musicians and (where available) leading figures from history. In snack form. Let's be clear—there's no actual human in them, so it isn't cannibalism, just hugely similar, and about as close as we'll ever get in today's world. Yum.

The message isn't "here's how we'll help you sell." Instead, it's "here's how we think." There's an exuberance to the site that's tangible, infectious. We won't even try to describe the blipvert for "Transparent Bone-less Lions"—except to repeat the tagline claim: "They're educational!" One gets the feeling that myrtle represents a significant departure from the kind of advertising and branding Brian Millar previously did for companies like Compaq, IBM, Mercedes-Benz and British Airways. Call it a wild hunch.

So is gonzo marketing just whacked out, undisciplined indulgence run amok? Partly, yes. But that's not necessarily the point. Nor is there any point at all without some deeper substance—the dimension of character, of voice. The myrtle site, for instance, is pure voice. Uncut, undiluted. If you become their client, what you see is very likely what you're going to get. This has manifold ramifications.

For one thing, it signals: this is who we are. In the same breath, it gives fair warning: who we are is non-negotiable. If you can't dig it, just go away.

Gonzo marketing has attitude to spare, but it's not the attitude of the poseur. Gonzo is not a style that can be faked. Sophistry is not an option. We're not talking about some generic class of "free-age" nouveau-consultants here, or camouflaged faux-hip cyber-alley suits with a fast rap. Instead, what is emerging from the huge new mind-space the Internet has opened up is a new breed of professionals-turned-dilettantes—who work for delight more than dollars and value the work itself above company or client. These creative Ronin first ply their marketing skills by representing the things they passionately care about. Their websites are their resumes, attracting precisely the sorts of people they want to—and are willing to—work with. A company doesn't hire such people, it woos them. It doesn't control them—it finds the best possible fit, then takes the trip.

But why would a company brook such unconscionable independence? Why would it ever agree to such risk? The answer is simple: because the risks of continuing in status-quo mode are infinitely greater. Authentic, engaged voice is precisely what companies desperately need today. Lacking that, they're sunk. Networked markets are smart markets. To these new audiences, the broadcast pitch is a carrier wave for unadulterated boredom. The faintest hint of hucksterism triggers an inattention so profound it constitutes a form of commercial catatonia. The billions being spent on e-commerce marketing of this sort might just as well be flushed down an enormous toilet. If somebody put up a webcam and streamed the video, it might even draw as big a crowd as the one that thronged the Dancing Hamsters page. Good show. A million laughs. But what can you do for an encore?

Most companies needn't look far to find genuine voices within their ranks. All they have to do then is get out of the way. They don't need "empowerment" programs. Such paternalism is just as stifling as the control it tries to mask. What they need are nonintervention treaties. A model already exists for this in the publishing world. Without a voice, a newspaper is nothing. So newspaper companies search out voices they respect and make them editors. Then the company stays out of the editor's face. The publisher—that is, the business side of the house—doesn't tell the editorial side what to write, or how to write it. There are plenty of instances in which this arrangement is honored in the breach, but it exists and it mostly works. It's referred to metaphorically as Church and State. Given such a setup, it shouldn't come as a great surprise that gonzo first emerged in the world of journalism. But nothing inherently limits it to that world. Gonzo marketing simply represents business getting the clue about 30 years late.

Nine Maxims

OK, time to regroup, mop up and get out. Time to try to reassemble what these many small loosely joined pieces have been intimating, insinuating, hinting at, suggesting.

Marketing has become irrelevant. As practiced today, most marketing is dependent on assumptions that may still hold true with respect to broadcast media, but have little relevance to the Internet.

Best practices usually aren't. Techniques that have worked in the past tend to be misleading and even dangerous when change is extremely rapid.

Frustration is inspiration. People who work for companies *want to believe.* They want to engage with each other and with the market, but they're hobbled by functional categories and bureaucratic management that militate toward group stupidity.

Gonzo is a terminal response. Adopting worst practices is an extreme response to frustration with existing practice. People finally engage because they care. Better engaged than enraged—though gonzo marketing is often both.

Permission is the critical hurdle. Frustration is not enough. There has to come a moment in which people give themselves permission to speak—just as gonzo journalism offered new freedom of speech to a whole generation of writers. Inspiration must pass through rationalization and fear. Only then can voice emerge and true words go forth. Such words pass the same permission on to others. Things ignite.

Storytelling is the path. True voice is the articulation of craft, and craft cares about quality. That's what defines it as craft, as art— "good enough" is not good enough. Storytelling is the path and primary tool of gonzo marketing. It's pragmatic, it's opportunistic, it's about what works. Even if what works breaks all the rules. And it will.

Gonzo marketing is market advocacy. The goal of gonzo marketing is not to better "penetrate" markets, but to better represent the market's interests—in every possible sense.

Companies aren't real enough to speak. Gonzo speech is what companies need right now, but they can't produce it. By nature, they have no personality, no character, no subjective take, idiosyncratically engaged or otherwise. Plus, they can't relinquish control, can't loosen up, let go. They are bound by the paranoia they have created.

Only individuals can be gonzo. Only people can convey enthusiasm through their stories. The marketing department doesn't have a story. Neither does the company. The discovery of worst practices is imagination replacing control. Worst practices tend to be radically anti-corporate, anti-marketing—but only because they are unconditionally human.

I opened this chapter by quoting W. Edwards Deming's dictum: "drive out fear." Deming also said if you want quality, shut down the Quality Control department. Make quality everybody's job. Companies that need marketing that actually works could take a tip from Deming. Shut down the marketing department. Then get out of the way. We'll take it from there. Hell, we'll take it anyway. What's happening in this medium is crucial, epochal. But what is unique and most consequential about the net is not what most companies are pursuing. At best, their bread-and-circus sideshows are temporary holding actions. Temporary insanity.

Today we need anthems more than analysis. We need to tell new and deeper, larger stories. Stories about ourselves—the kind of creatures who invent them, and why their creation is so important. Stories about why we can't afford to lose such a precious human legacy in a din of charlatanism and slobbering artless venality. The promise of the net is the promise of humanity coming together, seeing it-self for the first time, as we saw ourselves from the moon more than three decades ago, saw the breathtaking blue planet spinning out there. Out *here*. This time it's much more intimate. Maybe we can't see the faces yet, but we can read the words and begin to sense the lives behind them.

CHAPTER 5

Social Marketing and Public Journalism

"Social capital is about networks,
and the Net is the network to end all networks."

—ROBERT D. PUTNAM IN *BOWLING ALONE* [1]

ON THE SURFACE, SOCIAL MARKETING AND PUBLIC JOURNALISM MAY
seem only vaguely related to gonzo marketing. But they're highly
germane to where we're headed. For two reasons. First, both represent significant attempts to get closer to audiences, to become
more relevant and credible to smaller, more focused niches. The Internet is a more intimate medium than broadcast or mass publishing ever was. Whether with respect to markets or readerships, both
social marketing and public journalism are attempts to establish
more intimate relationships. Second, both developed before the Internet became a big deal, and therefore do not depend on hyper-
active tub-thumping about the wonderful new world of e-commerce. Too much thinking about business today relies on a highly
questionable form of pretzel logic that did not exist before 1995.
The Internet can make companies a lot of money. Money is good.
Therefore the Internet is good. Or . . . the Internet cannot make
companies a lot of money. Therefore it is bad. Either way, *quod erat
demonstrandum*. Such fatuous syllogisms aside, I wanted to find evidence of trends that were already underway when the net and business began to intersect, and thus had at least an outside chance of

being based on something more substantive than the promise of instant e-riches—or the pall of e-poverty.

I am not proposing social marketing and public journalism as models in the usual sense—as templates on which to build further. Instead, I find social marketing and public journalism interesting for what they say about the limitations of broadcast marketing. Both are direct responses to those limitations—detached, impersonal, bland and humorless one-size-fits-all mass communications. These movements make an appearance here because they deal with fundamental issues—both problems and potential—that have a large bearing on the alternatives this book does propose.

Neither social marketing or public journalism is likely to continue very long in its present form. Though they will continue for a time, the dynamics of the net will ultimately cause a definitive interruption of these courses, just as they will for mass marketing and broadcast. They will not survive because both seek to salvage the conventional institutions in which they are embedded—in one case broadcast advertising, in the other mass-media journalism. This point is crucial, but involves a longer story—one that I hope will make better sense when we return to it at the end of the chapter. For now, let's just say that both rely on business as usual continuing essentially unchanged. Does the expression "fat chance" mean anything to you?

Despite these caveats and disclaimers, social marketing and public journalism constitute instructive precursors—call them foreshadowings, intimations—of what I'm calling, for better or worse, the gonzo model.

Social Marketing

Everyone has experienced social marketing in some form—media campaigns to raise awareness about the dangers of cigarettes, illegal drugs, sexually transmitted diseases and various other health and environmental hazards. Social marketing was first defined in 1971 by Philip Kotler and Gerald Zaltman.[2] Eighteen years later, in 1989, Kotler and Eduardo Roberto wrote *Social Marketing: Strategies for Changing Public Behavior*, the subtitle underscoring the cultural dimension. They describe the scope of the discipline as follows: "Social marketing is a strategy for changing behavior. It combines the best elements of the traditional approaches to social change in an integrated planning and action framework and utilizes advances in communication technology and marketing skills."[3]

The goal of social marketing is to change minds—values, beliefs and behavior—not to promote products with price tags attached. If a campaign is successful, the only "product" is the effect produced: revised attitudes about some issue thought to be of high relevance to society as a whole.

But thought to be relevant by whom? Because it does not attempt to get people to buy products, social marketing is often perceived as more credible than commercial advertising. However, it also risks creating resentment. "Who are 'they' to tell me to quit smoking?" While many public service campaigns are created by major advertising agencies and delivered through conventional mass media channels, bottom-up local programs are usually more effective. When members of a particular group use marketing tools in their own behalf, the message is less likely to be perceived as coming from some paternalistic outsider whose intentions may be suspect.

Fostering Sustainable Behavior: An Introduction to Community-Based Social Marketing makes the point that attempting to change people's behavior works best when you talk to people directly. "The emergence of community-based social marketing," the authors write, "can be traced to a growing understanding that conventional social marketing, which often relies heavily on media advertising, can be effective in creating public awareness and understanding of issues . . . but is limited in its ability to foster behavior change."[4] It's limited because people tend to blow it off. The distance that broadcast inevitably creates is, well . . . distancing. The message seems to be aimed at someone else. It isn't immediate, doesn't apply to my life here and now.

At first, some big issue (say cancer awareness) is socially marketed by a big non-profit org (say the American Cancer Society) using the resources of a big advertising agency (say Ogilvy & Mather). But then, smaller organizations, even neighborhoods, realize they can do something similar—set up a block watch program, for instance. In such cases, word of mouth works much better than mass marketing. And note that, on the Internet, "community-based" need not imply geographic proximity. Online communities can be globally distributed, yet still act as communities with respect to shared interests, values and objectives.

Social marketing has been extensively deployed in the third world, especially in public health programs. *Social Mobilization & Social Marketing in Developing Communities* notes that "little success has been achieved in developing countries using a strictly mass media model." AIDs education is a case in point. Author Neill McKee writes that "mass media is seldom sufficient to bring about behavior change. Networks and peer counseling are needed, involving those most at risk."[5] While community involvement is crucial to the effectiveness of such initiatives, it is not easily accomplished, nor is this an area in which traditional marketing has much experience—or much interest. Traditional marketing is designed and delivered from the top down. It does not usually elicit input and involvement from its targeted markets.

This criticism of mass marketing echoes the feelings of many in the general online population. Because Internet audiences self-organize around common interests, and therefore tend to form natural communities, people are generally much more interested in each other than in intrusive marketing messages. In this respect, the net world begins to look a lot like the Third World.

Participatory Development Communication: A West African Agenda recaps the history of many "modernization" programs in which wealthy Western countries attempted to help less fortunate global neighbors. "Such modernization was planned in the national capitals under the guidance and direction of experts brought in from developed countries," writes Chin Saik Yoon. "Often, the people in the villages who are the 'objects' of these plans would first learn that 'development' was on the way when strangers from the city turned-up, frequently unannounced, to survey land or look at project sites."[6]

Programs like this are modeled on the top-down methods of mainstream marketing and mass media. A central organization determines what is in the best interests of their "backward" beneficiaries, then goes about implementing its "altruistic" plans without bothering to consult with the targets of their largesse. Such paternalism smacks of Rudyard Kipling's infamous "White Man's Burden," a phrase that Microsoft defines via its *Encarta World English Dictionary* as "the supposed responsibility of Europeans and their descendants to impose their allegedly advanced civilization on the non-Caucasian original inhabitants of the territories they colonized," adding that the phrase is often considered offensive.[7] No shit, Sherlock.

> *Take up the White Man's burden—*
> *Send forth the best ye breed—*
> *Go, bind your sons to exile*
> *To serve your captives' need;*
> *To wait, in heavy harness,*
> *On fluttered folk and wild—*
> *Your new-caught sullen peoples,*
> *Half devil and half child.*[8]

The white man's burden trope was an important ideological component of a much larger agenda called colonialism. This agenda is hardly an artifact of yesteryear. The attitude of large corporations coming onto the Internet has all the same earmarks. Call it e-colonialism. Here we were, all these wild and sullen half-devil children fooling around with the net, engaging in bizarre rituals and idolizing false gods. Then along came the Fortune 500 to civilize our heathen asses and get us all to worship at the Church of the One True Disney.[9] Wow, thanks.

Practitioners of participatory communication take an altogether different approach, not just teaching, but also learning from the people with whom they work. The impetus for the participatory approach grew out of anthropological field work, in which it became obvious that researchers often brought their own biased cultural assumptions to their description of non-Western societies. Recall here anthropologist Clifford Geertz's notion of thick description, which was an important step in the attempt to cure this sort of transcultural arrogance. But ultimately, there is no cure, for the simple reason that there is no ultimate authority to appeal to on questions of whose culture is better, more advanced, more civilized. These are inherently judgments of value, which cannot be decided by scientific method, no matter how rigorously applied. In response to these issues, Elaine Lawless developed the concept of reciprocal ethnography, in which the people she is observing are invited to observe her in the same manner, and to question her own assumptions, biases and beliefs. "My work is 'reciprocal,'" she writes, "in that we [herself and the people she is studying] . . . have established a working dialogue about the material, a reciprocal give and take."[10]

It is precisely this kind of give-and-take that is noticeably absent from traditional marketing. Most conventional marketers don't even seem to notice its absence, having apparently forgotten that it was ever important to speak with real customers—except perhaps in the context of focus groups. In heterogeneous societies, however—whether we're talking about the vastly varied nations of Africa or the global Internet—focus groups can be extremely misleading, as outside marketers are thrust into an unfamiliar constellation of cultural beliefs. Social marketers in developing countries focus on participation, both because they are highly sensitive to the colonialist impulse, and because they have a different set of objectives from those of commercial marketing. These differences are reflected in the following passage from *Participatory Development Communication*:

> Commercial stations which are caught-up in "rating-wars" and competition for the advertising dollar probably do more elegant audience research than participatory media managers. But there is a very fundamental ideological difference . . . Commercial stations aim to capture "market segments" which they can then sell to advertisers for a profit. Their loyalty in business is to the advertiser. Participatory media's loyalty is to the people.[11]

Among the techniques used to foster participatory communication, the author includes listening, negotiation, sensitivity to local language, appreciation of traditional customs and folklore, facilitating the sharing of knowledge, understanding acceptable methods of entering the community, knowing when and how to leave it, and keeping in touch afterwards. To say the least, these are not matters that conventional marketing pays much attention to. But ignoring them can result in ugly charges of cultural manipulation. And here—let me say it again—the net world begins to look a lot like the Third World.

Of course, conventional marketing has refined manipulation to an art form. And on that note, complicating the issue of credibility even further, we come to the closely allied notion of *"cause-related marketing,"* or often simply *"cause marketing."* But hold that thought. We'll come back to it in just a second. This is pretty dense stuff, so let's take a little break.

Intermission

Got your popcorn right here. There you go. What's that? You want a Coke? Sorry, no Coke. Pepsi.

In *The Blues Brothers* movie, Dan Aykroyd, in his character as Elwood Blues, repeatedly repeats: "We're on a mission from God." He is dead serious, which is why it's funny. The mission is to put the band back together and save the orphanage. You get the picture. Consider how many people who build personal websites feel they're on a mission from God. Some might even use the expression to denote a kind of ironic self-awareness of their own obsessive focus on something that's so tiny and trivially insignificant compared to all the Big Deal doings of E-Commerce, from Amazon to Yahoo. Now consider that a mission is a kind of *cause*. It may not be Cancer Prevention or World Peace. It could be anything that generates the same kind of hell-bent mania with which the Blues Brothers brought Chicago to a screeching halt. It could be day trading or javascript programming, home schooling, quantum physics or amateur pornography. It could be chinchilla ranching. Whatever it is, it could also be hugely effective in bringing people together who share that particular passion. Finally, consider that—without any commercial product being involved—Napster was on such a mission and had such a cause. Working bottom-up, using a community-based approach, it fostered social behavior change on a global scale. It got millions of kids to stop buying music from large multinational entertainment cartels. I'm not saying this is good or bad, mind you. It's just so. As Elwood says: "It's 106 miles to Chicago, we've got a full tank of gas, half a pack of cigarettes, it's dark and we're wearing sunglasses." And without missing a beat, Jake replies, "Hit it!"[12]

Don't ask. It's just so. The net is just like that. But we're getting ahead of ourselves.

Cause for Concern

Back to the difference between social and cause marketing. A few examples of the latter include Ben & Jerry's promoting peace with popsicles and American Express sharing its spare change with the homeless. It was in fact AmEx that first coined the *cause-related marketing* usage in 1983, when it agreed to donate a penny to the Statue of Liberty restoration project every time anyone used their card, and a buck for each new account. What they meant by the term was "the marketing of a product or service by using commercial exchanges to trigger donations, thereby raising money and visibility for a cause."[13] *Cause Related Marketing: Who Cares Wins* defines cause marketing in pretty much the same terms: "a commercial activity by which a business with a product, service or image to market builds a relationship with a cause or a number or causes for mutual benefit."[14]

In February 2001, *New York* magazine began running an ad for Absolut vodka that was created by the advertising firm TBWA/Chiat/Day. As in all the entries in this long-running campaign, it features the distinctive Absolut bottle, this time representing the logo of GLADD, the Gay and Lesbian Alliance Against Defamation. In his *New York Times* advertising column, Stuart Elliott writes that the ad "is indicative of two trends that are helping to reshape how advertisers appeal to consumers." The first is cause-related marketing, "which seeks potential customers by supporting causes they themselves support." The second is niche marketing, "which seeks potential customers among narrow demographic segments rather than the general population." The article notes that these interrelated approaches have also been adopted by much larger companies such as American Express, General Motors and Procter & Gamble.[15]

There is fast-growing interest in cause marketing, and no lack of enthusiastic proponents on both sides of the corporate/cause equation. Among the most eloquent is Bill Shore, founder and executive director of Share Our Strength. SOS describes itself as "one of the nation's leading anti-hunger and anti-poverty organizations." It has raised over $65 million for such causes since 1984. Among the many partners SOS has attracted are America Online, American Express, Barnes & Noble, Bloomingdale's, Coors Brewing, KitchenAid, Kraft Foods, Macy's, The Home Shopping Network, Williams-Sonoma, and Yahoo. SOS speaks in uncharacteristically entrepreneurial language for a non-profit. "Share Our Strength understands the return on investment these relationships provide for our partners and our work to end hunger."[16] Shore argues that people have a deep-seated desire to contribute to society, and that organizations like SOS provide an opportunity to do so. In *The Cathedral Within: Transforming Your Life by Giving Something Back,* he writes about doing something that counts:

> All of us have strengths we need to share. . . It's not just about volunteering or trying to be a better person. It's not about making your community a better place. It's not about service being good for your soul. It is more fundamental, almost primal. It is what the species instinctively wants to do: to perpetuate itself by leaving something behind; to make a mark that lasts; to make ourselves count.[17]

The corporate world finds strong appeal in such ideas. Businesses are tired of being perceived as heartless. There's only one catch: they *are* heartless. No incorporation for the corporation. No body, no heart. Remember? Or did you skip that chapter? While it's true that many *individuals* involved in business enterprises might love to feel they were giving something back—or perhaps just leaving a legacy to a monumentally engorged ego—they can only do so within the corporate framework if they can prove the ROI on such gifts.

There is no doubt cause marketing can do real good. But no matter how good the concept sounds, we're still talking about companies aligning themselves with sympathetic social causes primarily so they can move more product. The terms *"social marketing"* and *"cause-related marketing"* are often used interchangeably, which is seriously misleading. An otherwise excellent book on the subject, *The Art of Cause Marketing*, unfortunately perpetuates this confusion. "Cause marketing informs about and creates action on behalf of a cause," writes author Richard Earle. So far so good. But he then says, "Advertising which does that is also widely classified as 'social marketing.'"[18]

This conflation of labels glosses over a critical distinction. Kotler and Andreason define cause-related marketing as "any effort by a corporation to increase its own sales by contributing to the objectives of one or more non-profit organizations."[19] They also define social marketing: "Social marketing seeks to influence *social behaviors* not to benefit the marketer but *to benefit the target audience and the general society.*"[20] The italics are in the original, indicating that the authors thought it was important whether a product was being sold or not. And they say this multiple times in various different wordings. For instance, the goal of social marketing "is not to market a product or service *per se* but to influence a social behavior . . . Its sponsors simply wish to make the society a better place, not merely benefit themselves or their organization."

Why all this emphasis? Why is it so important to distinguish social marketing from cause marketing, which often adopts the same terminology? "There is . . . a legitimate concern," write Kotler and Andreason—and remember, these are dyed-in-the-wool mainstream marketing guys, not flaming Marxists—"that, without careful training and monitoring, those adopting social marketing will employ some of the more unsavory persuasive strategies that have helped create economic successes of a number of socially dubious products and services." And then they go even further: ". . . in stating that social marketing involves customer behavior that the marketer thinks is socially desirable, we make no judgments about whether in any given circumstances they are right. Sound marketing approaches and techniques can be used as easily by a Hitler or a Charles Manson as by a Mother Theresa or a Pope John Paul."[21]

Contrast these powerfully cautionary notes with the following statement which appears in the foreword to *Brand Spirit*, a book on cause marketing by two writers associated with the advertising firm of Saatchi & Saatchi. Here, Edward de Bono both acknowledges serious flak and in the same breath discounts it.

> Some might think that Cause Related Marketing is simply a cynical exploitation of public sympathy for the sake of profits. There will always be people who take it upon themselves to make these sorts of judgments on behalf of others. However, consumers always have the power of the final choice and if most of them felt it was cynical, then CRM would cease to exist.[22]

To be generous, this is an extremely weak argument. It is not only legitimate, but a thoroughly excellent idea to question the implications and effects of corporate sponsorship—on *anything*, cause-related or otherwise. The disparity in knowledge resulting from huge differences in power and financial resources between corporations and de Bono's trusting "consumers" makes the asking and answering of questions about exploitation far more than a rhetorical parlor game. The operative concern is a little item called corporate influence. If consumers didn't like nuclear power plants so much, we wouldn't be spending billions of dollars to clean up the poisonous shit they dumped into our world, right? Point being, powerful corporate interests sold consumers on the wonders of having a plutonium breeder in their very own back yard. Speaking of poisonous shit, has the intellectual caliber of television *really* been degraded by commercial sponsors? We all pretty much know the answer to that one without having to launch another study. And while we're at it, are kids adversely affected by companies sponsoring school events? Many reasonable parents find the implications seriously upsetting. This doesn't make them cynics.

By whatever name they call it—social or cause marketing—corporations are allying themselves with social issues as a way to better position their products. And what they're up to isn't always crystal clear from a quick scan. For instance, Novartis has mounted several extensive "social marketing" campaigns targeting diseases such as leprosy and epilepsy in third-world countries. While such programs may deliver solid, dependable information, their overall credibility cannot help but be colored by the fact that Novartis is a

Global 500 pharmaceutical firm that makes drugs specifically indicated for these illnesses.

In *"A Short Course in Social Marketing,"* Novartis blurs the distinction between social and cause marketing when it says that in social marketing "demand has to be created for the idea or product concept, such as family planning, as well as for the tools or *product itself*, such as condoms."[23] (My italics.) The Ciba-Geigy Leprosy Fund described in the report hinges on drugs that are manufactured by Novartis. Is the company profiting from leprosy? Not a nice thought. As it turns out, Novartis has suspended commercial sale of these products, and has committed to donate them to the World Health Organization in sufficient quantities to cure everyone suffering from the disease. This obviously makes a huge difference in assessing the company's motivation. Because the tangible products are not for sale, it is legitimate to call this program social marketing. On the other hand, Novartis does sell its anti-epileptic product, which, as the company explains in "Social Marketing for Epilepsy," has been on the market for many years. "The commercial objectives are to expand the anti-epileptics market by closing the treatment gap and to maintain or increase the market share of Tegretol® in a growing market."[24]

Such ambiguities of intent have generated skepticism and even overt hostility. The December/January 2001 issue of *Ms.* magazine featured an article about cause-related marketing, noting that between 1990 and 1998 corporate investment in such programs leaped from $125 million to $545 million—an increase of over 400 percent. Unlike many glowing words written on the subject by participating companies and marketing consultants, this spike in cause marketing was not reported as cause for joy. "Doubts about the motives behind these campaigns are being raised by consumers, charities, and cause-related marketers themselves," the article says, sharply criticizing campaigns by Philip Morris, American Express, the Internet-based Hunger Site, and Benetton.[25]

The United Weirdness of Benetton

Ah, Benetton, certainly the most controversial practitioner of cause marketing. For a $2+ billion company selling clothing, fashion accessories and sporting goods, the company sure has some strange ideas—and an attitude that never quits. Of all the cause-related sources I looked at, only Kotler and Andreason mention the company at all, and then only to say that "Benetton produces shocking ads designed to energize consumers to care about AIDs."[26] Kotler also puts founder Luciano Benetton on his list of 30 "marketing visionaries."[27] However, most cause-marketing aficionados seem to want to distance themselves from Benetton's bad example. Personally, I find myself drawn to the company's approach—precisely because it's so outré. It looks a lot more authentic from where I'm sitting than the squeaky-clean go-team boosterism that characterizes so much of this kind of marketing.

Benetton's $15 million "We on Death Row" ad campaign ran full-page photographs of condemned U.S. felons along with the company logo. This brought howls of protest and several lawsuits. But the company held its ground. "When we talk about death row or AIDS or war or peace, it's not a contrived topic," said Mark Major, director of communications for Benetton USA. "It's definitely something that people at Benetton feel very strongly about. We don't apologize for the fact that dual purposes can be achieved. We can raise brand awareness that we are a company that cares about capital punishment and we can get people engaged in the topic."[28] The *Ms.* article charges that Benetton made no financial contribution to the fight against capital punishment, but fails to acknowledge how much this kind of publicity would normally cost. On the other hand, many felt it was negative publicity. Much to its credit, in my opinion, Benetton doesn't seem to give a damn. If brand meant what the *people* in a company actually believe in—beyond the sheer wonderfulness of the company's products—I might take the concept of branding more seriously. Typically, brand has nothing to do with what anyone believes, unless a belief means something you trick someone else into.

"Benetton likes to shock," writes *The Economist* in a burst of reserved British understatement. "The company has a history of running provocative advertising campaigns that seem quite unrelated to the buying of T-shirts and jeans."[29] These have included images of neon condoms, a war cemetery, horses copulating in a field, a very raw-looking newborn infant with umbilicus still attached, and dying AIDS patients. They are the work of Oliviero Toscani, acclaimed photographer and advertising *enfant terrible*. Both Toscani and

Benetton have been accused of ruthlessly exploiting social issues to enhance the company's appeal to the "youth market." But while their advertising has generated enormous outcry, I think these guys are not so easy to dismiss as blatant hucksters.

"We're more interested in discovering people than in selling them dreams," said company founder Luciano Benetton, who once posed nude to raise money for the homeless. "Here is the discovery of beauty without stereotypes; here is diversity highlighted by uniqueness."[30] Are such sentiments genuine, or do they simply represent a higher order of cynical market manipulation? To my own ear, Toscani comes across as pretty credible. In an interview on the *Salon* website, he says, "I hate to make advertising by saying that it goes to charity." And he brutally mocks companies that publicly pat themselves on the back for giving to the poor. "Oh, we're doing an eight-course charity dinner," he mimics in scathing parody of such self-congratulation. Then, "Fuck you!" he explodes. "I hope your eight-course dinner is poisoned!"[31]

This may be as close to genuine gonzo as an advertiser has ever come. If it's a staged posture intended to improve his company's positioning, the subterfuge sets a whole new standard in rhetorical sophistication. But it doesn't appear to be fake. "Media is just a bunch of bullshit," says Toscani. "Media is the real advertising. And they belong to big companies. There are some newspapers and TV companies that can't talk about certain things because they belong to General Electric or some big gas company."[32] This isn't the kind of talk you're real likely to overhear in a hallway at, oh say, American Express or AOL.

But is such an outspoken, against-the-grain approach to marketing viable? Can it last? *Business Week* reported that this style of advertising was over. "Now, though, Luciano [Benetton] says 'shock' images are a thing of the past."[33] That was obviously wrong, however. The article was written in 1995, and since then, Toscani's work for Benetton became even more outrageous.

In April 2000, Benetton and Toscani finally did part ways. Was the company displeased with the controversy he had created? It's impossible to know for certain, but the company explicitly thanked Toscani for his "fundamental contribution to a new advertising concept" that supported the company's "brand communication requirements." Toscani appeared to be undaunted. "Fortunately, nothing lasts forever," he said.[34] He is now creative director at *Talk* magazine, working with equally controversial editor Tina Brown, formerly of *The New Yorker*.[35] We'll see how long that lasts. The venture is backed by Miramax Films and Hearst.[36]

Meanwhile, even with Toscani gone, the madness continues at Benetton. Drawing on ten years of images that appeared in its magazine, *Colors*, the company has created an exhibition in the Leopolda train station in Florence. The press release called Colors Extra/Ordinary Objects "an anthropological report on our world." There's also a website, but of course. The first item there reads: "Fatherly love—More than 850 million Roman Catholics worldwide regard the Pope as the 'earthly representative of Jesus Christ.' They also believe that he's infallible when speaking on moral matters." Pictured alongside this entry is the Official Pope John Paul all-day lollipop. There is also a Pope John Paul II bottle opener. The text reads in part: "'Does the Pope use this opener?' we asked the Vatican Press Office. 'That is a ridiculous question,' they snapped and promptly hung up." Rounding out the Western religious paraphernalia category is this: "Nun bra—Nuns of the convent of St. Rita . . . shop for their underwear at religious underwear suppliers in Rome. St. Rita's nuns prefer the Cross Your Heart model from Playtex in beige. It's unlikely St. Rita herself was so well supported during her lifetime—she's the saint of desperate causes."

But it's not just all anti-clerical fun. Also included in the collection is a land mine, which the site calls "a favorite toy of generations of Afghan children. . . Children just love the bright green color and wings of the 'butterfly,' as it's nicknamed." The introduction to the show was written by rocker Peter Gabriel. Book by—who else?—Oliviero Toscani.[37]

This form of marketing begs many questions, and many are radically unsure of Benetton's motives—at least among those who haven't already decided they despise the company. To me, Benetton's brand of drive-by semiotics has more credibility than the safe, please-all-the-people-all-the-time approach of most cause marketing. Benetton positions itself by actually taking positions, even though its stance is liable to alienate as many customers as it attracts. Somehow, I don't get the impression of marketing committees behind these acts. Rather, I sense something quite rare and wonderful in the commercial world: intelligent, quirky human beings possessed of genuine character and a thoroughly gonzo sense of humor.

Segue: Social Capital and The Common Good

Let's pull back a bit from the close-up view of how any one company connects with any particular social issue. If we look at the phenomenon in broader perspective, it becomes clear that cause marketing is part of a larger, deeper trend. "A big new idea is emerging in America," writes Harvard Business School's Rosabeth Moss Kanter. "Everywhere I look, businesses are discovering social values, and social purpose organizations are discovering business principles. And both are finding that they can create new benefits for their stakeholders by reaching out to the other."[38] Sounds terrific. In fact, we're exploring these matters in such depth because gonzo marketing sees similar potential in the intersection of community and commercial interests. For our purposes, these communities are indeed "social purpose organizations"—passionate, highly voiced websites and the new audiences coming together around them.

The Kanter quote is from a book titled *Common Interest, Common Good: Creating Value Through Business and Social Sector Partnerships,* which includes a chapter on cause-related marketing. However, common interests aside, business has often been perceived not as the friend, but as the enemy of the common good. While business obviously doesn't like this perception, it has become a lot harder to dodge as communications have become faster, more efficient and more global. It is no longer possible for companies to quietly clear-cut ancient forests or to pollute a thousand miles of pristine coastline with impunity. People care, and people are talking—across previous cultural and geographic boundaries, across obsolete demographic sectors. Across the Internet. It is no longer possible to run a sweetly profitable sweatshop operation in Southeast Asia without having dozens of websites spring up including photos and firsthand interviews with exploited women and children workers.[39]

Companies that are charged with such offenses usually question the interpretation of the events on which they are supposedly based. Do such allegations, they ask, reflect objective reality? And then we're thrown back into the ontological soup and the endless morass of philosophy. Because the real question is, whose reality trumps whose? We'll soon return to the vexing issue of objectivity. For now let's agree that many corporations want to align themselves with the common good. It's just none too clear to whom this "common good" is common.

Related is the notion of the *commons,* "a tract of land, usually in a centrally located spot, belonging to or used by a community as a whole," says *The American Heritage Dictionary.* This has become extended to mean any place where people gather to converse about issues that affect their collective well-being. In 1968, an influential paper on this subject appeared: "The Tragedy of the Commons."[40] The central metaphor involves a common grazing area, large enough that each farmer can raise a single sheep on this communal tract. However, without enforcement of who does what, various farmers—thinking what the hell, more for me—begin to add two sheep, then three, and soon the commons becomes overgrazed and worthless to all. Bummer. Perhaps the modern commons is our collective attention. Every media outlet, advertiser and politician wants to put another sheep on our cognitive pasture. The attention we need to pay to public matters is thereby rapidly depleted. Whatever the cause, something has certainly made people—Americans anyway—pull back from public involvement.

Robert Putnam is one of the prime purveyors of the concept of social capital. In *Bowling Alone: The Collapse and Revival of American Community,* he argues that sociability has taken a steep downturn in American society. The title refers to significant attrition in previously popular social involvements, such as league bowling. He voluminously documents many other examples. The cost of this downturn in community engagement is a critical measure of the social cohesion necessary to maintain a healthy democracy. What is being lost is social capital. "The core idea of social capital theory," writes Putnam, "is that social networks have value . . . social contacts affect the productivity of individuals and groups." He defines social capital as "connections among individuals—social networks and the norms of reciprocity and trustworthiness that arise from them."[41] While individuals gain from these networks, so does the larger community in which they are embedded—the public sphere. "Social capital can thus be simultaneously a 'private good' and a 'public good,'" Putnam says. "Some of the benefit from an investment in social capital goes to bystanders, while some of the benefit redounds to the immediate interest of the person making the investment."

But what precisely is this benefit? What accrues to the public good? Simple. "A society characterized by generalized reciprocity is more efficient than a distrustful society," says Putnam. "Trustworthiness lubricates social life."

Business Week criticized what it took to be the pessimism of *Bowling Alone*. "The Internet is creating new networks and communities," wrote By Farrell. "Putnam ends up documenting the decline of a particular type of social capital tied to an industrial economy—even as more heterogeneous, eclectic forms of social capital emerge in the Information Age."[42] However, Putnam makes much the same point:

> Community, communion, and communication are intimately as well as etymologically related. Communication is a fundamental prerequisite for social and emotional connections. Telecommunications in general and the Internet in particular substantially enhance our ability to communicate; thus it seems reasonable to assume that their net effect will be to enhance communication, perhaps even dramatically. Social capital is about networks, and the net is the network to end all networks.[43]

The Internet is the most powerful means we have today for building social cohesion, yet it is being used by business without regard for the larger interests of society. Gonzo marketing involves a more integrated approach, whereby corporations and markets can genuinely collaborate in the creation of social capital.

In *Knowledge and Social Capital*, Eric Lesser extends the concept of social capital into the workings of business organizations.[44] While many companies are beginning to see the advantages, they generally want to leverage, own and manage these benefits for themselves. This could be a showstopper with something called *social* capital, unless you believe that the organization constitutes a society unto itself. It's true that social networks exist within companies, and that understanding how they operate is valuable to the organization. But companies exist within a social context larger than themselves, and while they may greatly influence and shape this context, they do not control it. Lesser's book has much to say about reciprocity as it affects organizational dynamics, but includes little discussion of reciprocity between the organization and the wider community—a.k.a. the market. It is mysterious behavior, yet entirely typical of business-as-usual, to exclude the market as an integral part of the organization's social network, context and reason for existing. This should come as no real surprise, however, as Lesser is (and I quote) "an Executive Consultant with the IBM Institute for Knowledge Management and a member of IBM's Global Knowledge Management and Solutions Practice." But maybe that's just me. When I hear the word "*solutions,*" I reach for my revolver.

Having thus savaged the guy, let me praise his other book, *Knowledge and Communities.*[45] This collection reprints the brilliant paper by John Seely Brown and Paul Duguid on "Organizational Learning and Communities of Practice."[46] This was the foundation for the authors' critically acclaimed 2000 book *The Social Life of Information.*[47] There's that word again: *social.* It sure is getting popular in business circles these days. Had you noticed? If not, notice.

But business tends to talk about communities of practice the same way it talks about social capital: in terms of the internal workings of the organization, and not so much in terms of interaction with the marketplace. This is odd, since customers often have more collective knowledge about a company's products or services than the company itself. Networked communities of practice—and of plain old garden-variety *interest*—are certainly crucial. But to be genuinely useful to a corporation, they must extend beyond the corporate borders and include a much larger external audience—present and potential markets.

Gonzo marketing is a way for companies to create genuine relationships with external web-based markets. One important difference from traditional marketing—and a crucial prerequisite for success—is that the company will not *own* or *manage* the knowledge developed in these communities. It will be outside the corporate sphere of influence—at least where influence is construed to mean control.

Such border jumping has an interesting precedent. *"Benchmarking"*—the search for best practices—not only cuts across internal functional boundaries, it also gets people talking across companies, or even across entirely different industries. But there's always a trade-off in such exchanges, especially where direct competitors are involved. How much do you share relative to the knowledge advantage you expect to receive in return? If you keep the kimono closed, you get nothing. If you open it too far, you could lose it all. In fact, the whole tit-for-tat best practices gambit is based on paranoia symptomatic of closed systems knowing that they must become open systems or die, but kicking and screaming a lot in the process. Under such trying conditions—i.e., constant kimono checking—best practices become dysfunctional. It takes so long to reach consensus about anything important, that the results are either trivial or patently wrong.

Nonetheless, given the internetworking of markets, opening up closed systems has become more critical than ever—getting outside the box, outside the beltway, outside the insular frame of mind that has kept the audience "safely" removed from business decisions about strategy and tactics. The same pressures apply to the media business, though—being a very different sort of business—they apply in a different way.

The Case and Cause of
Public Journalism

The aims of social marketing are in many ways congruent with those of public journalism, a ten-year-old movement started by journalists who feel that reporting is too top-down, too much shaped by national polls, veiled political agendas and corporate press releases. They have sought to become more engaged in local civic concerns and tend to take positions on issues rather than pretend to a remote and questionable "objectivity." Recall here Hunter Thompson's definition of gonzo as engagement. We'll soon be hearing more from him and others on how such engagement—and the engagement called for by public journalism—is impossible under traditional media standards of objectivity.

Public journalism could be seen as a form of cause marketing, where the cause is democracy and the associated product is the local paper. Trying to resurrect democracy within the context of a media business's profit mandate is a tricky proposition. Trickier still, the ills that public journalism seeks to cure are not merely tactical mistakes, but inherent qualities of mass media. It does little good to ameliorate symptoms without acknowledging the disease that causes them. However, the goals of public journalism are laudable, even if they seem Quixotic in the context of conventional media. Jay Rosen chronicles the ups and downs of the movement in *What Are Journalists For?* On Amazon, he posted an overview, from which the following is excerpted.

Countering spin, hype and entertainment with real news of public import is tougher than ever, especially when the company that owns your operation pushes it onto a more commercial grid. . . . What happens in the public arena still matters to people, even if a game show does better in the ratings. . . . journalists need democracy if their work is to make a difference. But were they doing enough to make democracy work? And what could they do differently? We can reduce some of our engrained [sic] cynicism, they answered, because it distorts our outlook, and the audience can sense it. We can try to provide a better forum for discussion, and connect the talk there to problems in real life. We can lend our reporting talent not only to problems, but to possible solutions where they might exist. Going further, we can attempt to engage people in civic life, and give them more help when they take that step. At times, we can be a convener or catalyst in local communities just as we are, at times, a watchdog and critic. And we can do all this without abandoning our role as truthteller and information source.[48]

The New York Times review charges that public journalism's "most ardent supporters have taken on the trappings of evangelists." Note that evangelists is used here as a code word. The implications are not good, as Real Journalists are supposed to be "unbiased," which means they would never dream of evangelizing. Too engaged. Too *involved.* "Its detractors have denounced it as a fad, a gimmick, a commercial ploy or an idea that was not new at all," the review continues. Then interestingly, the paper invokes its own views. How much more unbiased can you get? "Influential journalists from *The New York Times* have been more scathing. In a signed Editorial Notebook article, Howell Raines, *The Times*'s editorial page editor, said James Fallows's much-discussed 1996 book, *Breaking the News*, posed an 'insidious danger, and that is that reporters and editors become public policy missionaries with a puritanical contempt for horse-race politics.'"[49]

Much of this debate centers on the slippery concept of "objectivity." What Fallows actually said, among many other juicy provocations, was this: "One of public journalism's basic claims is that journalists should stop kidding themselves about their ability to remain detached from and objective about public life. . . . They inescapably change the reality of whatever they are observing by whether and how they chose to write about it."[50] He's surely going to hell for that one. Imagine the nerve. Disrupting the profound majesty of those scintillating horse races.

From the perspective of the Internet, which—in case you've somehow missed it—is my perspective in this book, this debate is absurd. We don't need press credentials to have a point of view, and in expressing such views we don't pretend to be omniscient or impartial. For better or worse, we call em like we see em. But the debate is extremely serious from the perspective of conventional media, which either a) have not grasped the true significance of the net, or b) having grasped it just fine, are terrified by the implications. All of which could be ignored as insignificant inside-the-metaphorical-media-beltway navel-gazing except for one critical fact: old media is where business gets its news about new media. The irony here is that, in defending its high standards of objectivity, traditional media have betrayed a bias that is tantamount to a news blackout. The real Internet—the net as it is, as it actually operates—doesn't fit traditional models of media *or* business. Ergo, that Internet doesn't exist. The media has created an image of the net that appeals to business and what business already knows—which is television. But this view is a complete fiction. When the net fails to "live up" to this projection, it is judged anarchic, wild, untamable—or simply a failure. Things were simpler in the old days. All you had to do was shoot all the buffalo and the Indians.

Nearly all the controversy surrounding public journalism has come from the establishment press, which has lobbed charges of "advocacy journalism." For traditionalists, expressing a point of view breaks the first commandment of reporting: thou shalt remain impartial. These complaints would have greater moral weight if many of the mass media publications from which they come were not themselves open to charges of corporate and government influence. The principle of "Church and State," which is supposed to insulate news reporting and editorial opinion from the potential sway of advertising dollars, is often honored more in the breach than the observance. Because such bias is hidden and benefits the highest bidder, it is far more pernicious than journalists actively engaging in civic debates whose outcome they honestly care about.

The most biased and unbalanced claim the mainstream press ever made is that it is objective. Is there anyone stupid enough to believe that what is presented is "the facts and nothing but the facts," or even "all the news that's fit to print"? The press itself certainly doesn't have any illusions about the illusions it projects. Yet it wants us to take them as an undistorted reflection of "reality." This represents either towering arrogance or a degree of uncritical ignorance that should disqualify the media from reporting on anything more complex than Johnny's birthday party.

Writing about the role of the press as defender of the republic, Rosen writes

> the litany of government lying during Vietnam, the showdown with the White House over the Pentagon Papers, and the triumph of the *Washington Post* during Watergate convinced a generation of journalists that official authority was not to be trusted. From there it was a short step to concluding that their own authority rested on rituals of mistrust. Any criticism of those rituals could be seen as a demand to "soften" the news, a deadly epithet, for to go soft was to lose your commitment to truth and thus all your credentials.[51]

And, Rosen adds, "This was not an irrational fear." The pressure on journalists to keep things crisp and snappy and not too intellectually challenging came from many quarters, notably, strong competition from *USA Today* and concurrent demands from the business side to staunch the bleeding that newspapers were experiencing as a result of dwindling subscriptions. In an interview discussing his book, *Deadlines & Datelines: Essays at the Turn of the Century*, Dan Rather says this. Can you see him making the air-quotation-marks? Sort of like air-guitar, but with just two fingers.

> I think the audience says, "Well, listen, the evening news has sort of gone into," quote, "News Lite," as some evening news broadcasts have. I consider it part of my job to keep the *CBS Evening News* hard news, as hard as we possibly can, but I wouldn't kid anybody that there are great pressures to make it more entertainment, quote, "soften it up" because the belief runs strong if you do that, you attract a larger audience.[52]

A larger audience equals a mass market—and the "editorial content" is only advertising bait. Howard Kurtz, press critic for the *Washington Post*, is considerably more forthcoming. In *Media Circus: The Trouble with America's Newspapers*, he tells this delightful little story.

> "Look at the front page," Mike Barnicle says. "More often than not it's full of what I call made-up stories, ideas they cook up at these cluster-fuck meetings: 'Go out and do left-handed teenagers who are thinking of becoming gay.' They do trends, they don't do news. There's a burnt fuse, a lack of connection between people in the business and a large number of people who read newspapers."
>
> Our efforts to repair this burnt fuse are rather awkward. We hire teenagers to review movies for other teens and pretend that we've plugged into the youth culture. We assign reporters to cover shopping malls. We ballyhoo the local football team on the front page. We serve up modest portions of News Lite, congratulating ourselves for not overtaxing the poor reader.[53]

Media critic Jon Katz, discussing his book *Virtuous Reality* on *Booknotes,* says that if Thomas Paine were alive today, he'd be writing on the Internet. "He couldn't get a job at any newspaper in America," observes Katz. "He certainly did not believe in objectivity and he was far too outspoken and independent-minded to work in a news-room. And he would not have liked corporate media in the least." He speculates that if Paine had followed the dictates of objective journalism, *Common Sense* would have begun "A spokesperson for the British says the colonies should remain attached, and a spokesperson for the colonists says it shouldn't." And the American Revolution would still be the subject of the world's longest filibuster.[54]

In *Custodians of Conscience: Investigative Journalism and Private Virtue* the authors open a chapter called "The Paradox of the Disengaged Conscience," as follows:

> If investigative reporting is American journalism at its most rigorous, it is also American journalism at its most paradoxical. The essential energy of investigative reporting is still best characterized as "righteous indignation," a term coined by Ida Tarbell a century ago as the anthem of the muckrakers. . . But this unmistakable tone of moral engagement stands in apparent opposition to the presumed objectivity of news. How can journalists function as the custodians of conscience and at the same time claim to be mere observers of fact? That is, how can they expose wrongdoing without making moral judgments?[55]

The reprehensible advocacy public journalism is accused of, in fact, takes its place in a long tradition of investigative reporting. If engagement and advocacy are perceived as impediments to the media, then something is inherently wrong with the media, not with the basic human inclination to engage and advocate. Trying to suppress these inclinations artificially for the sake of some elusive notion of balance is not only futile but psychologically dysfunctional. People care. They are not simply cameras passively recording random events with no emotional valence. The pretense of such "objectivity" not only damages the pretender, but also deeply unravels the social fabric (or capital, if you prefer) of the society that depends on observant, informed, articulate and *engaged* reporters to better understand and appreciate itself.

But the truth is that "objectivity" is a McGuffin here, a diversionary tactic. The real objective is to gather the largest possible audi-

ence for advertisers. The pretense of detachment is merely camou-
flage for media whose prime directive is to serve the mass marketing requirements of business.[56]

Tom Wolfe's 1973 book, *The New Journalism*,[57] took the impulse
to engage a step further than social muckraking. Journalists are really frustrated novelists, said Wolfe, and what they really want to do
is what novelists do: make stuff up. One branch of this genre turns
into literary journalism, which claims such practitioners as Tracy
Kidder *(Soul of a New Machine, House)*, Joan Didion *(The White
Album, Miami)*, John McPhee *(The Curve of Binding Energy, Annals
of the Former World)* and Wolfe himself *(The Electric Kool-Aid Acid
Test, Bonfire of the Vanities)*.[58] These authors brought to the reporting of fact an attention to detail and a style of writing more generally associated with fiction. Another, smaller and much stranger
branch turns into gonzo journalism and claims one king-hell king-
pin, Hunter S. Thompson *(Fear and Loathing in Las Vegas, Generation of Swine)*.

"The 'new journalism' attracted attention," writes Jack Fuller in
News Values, "especially when it ran in newspapers or was written
by people whose names were identified with newspapers, by its
fundamental violation of the old traditions of the craft, beginning
with the tradition of colorlessness of expression."[59] Thompson is
colorful all right. In this mode of writing, it would be unusual to
read about the Justice Department deciding to break up Microsoft.
Instead, you might get a detailed description of how giant vampire
bats ate Bill Gates' brain. And what it tasted like. Thompson not
only used novelistic techniques, he made real events seem stranger
than fiction. Which, as we all know, they often are. And he's still
doing it. In a recent screed on *ESPN*, he wrote about the night of
the 2000 U.S. national election. On hearing that CNN had awarded
Florida to Gore, he says "My own immediate reaction was baffle-
ment and surprise. . . I was troubled by waves of Queasiness &
shudders of Gnawing Doubt. I felt nervous & vaguely confused, as
if I had just heard a dog speak perfect English . . . That will get your
attention, for sure."[60] Thompson gets people's attention. For sure.
And ESPN knows it. In another column there he writes about the
Oakland Raiders football team, bemoaning their currently kinder,
gentler ways. "The Raiders of yore had no mercy on anything they

could get their hands on," he says. "They strangled cops and ate their own babies." It must be true. I read it on the web. Yeah, it's a little weird, but that's OK by me—and a few million others. It sure beats reading marginally rewritten press releases and the Sunday *Parade* supplement.

David Mindich opens *Just the Facts: How "Objectivity" Came to Define American Journalism* by stating that "if American journalism were a religion. . . it's supreme deity would be 'objectivity.'" No other book explores this article of faith in such historical depth. Calling the phenomenon naïve empiricism, Mindich writes: "It is no less than remarkable that years after consciousness was complicated by Freud, observation was problematized by Einstein, perspective was challenged by Picasso, writing was deconstructed by Derrida, and 'objectivity' was abandoned by practically everyone outside newsrooms, 'objectivity' is still the style of journalism that our newspaper articles and broadcast reports are written in, or against." Most relevant to our purpose here, the book—which mostly focuses on the 19th century—concludes by talking about the Internet. ". . . [A]n explosion in new media has again threatened the elite, 'objective' journalists. With so many storytellers (each of the thousands of homepages, for example, is a separate news source), and with so many departing from the 'information model' of 'objective' news, journalists are called on once again to define themselves."[61] It is no surprise, Mindich says, that the issue of objectivity should arise at this critical juncture. What is a surprise are the very real alternatives the web presents to getting past the current denial about the function of journalism. Telling stories that make sense of the world is something human beings have always done, and will continue to—not within the confines of a conflicted media industry, but within the context of a diverse and vibrant global culture.

Shallow Babble and the Shock of Recognition

In a review of Rosen's *What Are Journalists For?*, *The American Prospect* notes that public journalism continues a much earlier debate between the journalist Walter Lippmann and the philosopher

John Dewey. "Lippmann had questioned the ability of ordinary citizens to be objective enough to exercise their democratic responsibilities," writes the reviewer, while "Dewey had more faith in their collective judgment and insisted that democracy can't be left to the elites."[62] Uh-huh. And in support of public journalism's position, Rosen also quotes from *The Structural Transformation of the Public Sphere* by Jürgen Habermas. It is no accident that Habermas would later go on to write *The Legitimation Crisis*, attempting to read which book made my head hurt.[63] However, from an intensive five-minute scan, I can summarize its findings as follows: "Says who?" This basic uncertainty at the heart of our culture was explored in depth by continental thinkers such as Jacques Derrida and Michel Foucault and the fundamental query was expanded into a larger challenge to the entire Western intellectual tradition: "You and what army?"

Steve Martin liked to say that he studied just enough philosophy in college to fuck him up for the rest of his life. We can all sympathize, I'm sure. But look, it's really simpler than all that. Leaving out certain American politicians, most of us have gotten past the notion of the divine right of kings. That was once the font from which legitimacy issued. We got past it with the alternative—if admittedly radical—notion of democracy. But there are holdouts and throwbacks hidden in plain sight today. One of them is "objectivity," of which some purport to have more than others. If this means being fair and balanced and trying to understand complex debates by taking both sides fully into account, then cool. But it often means something that's at the same time a lot larger and a lot less explicit—that some group has privileged access to The Truth, and you're not part of it. Hey, don't you know anything? Read your newspaper!

The Internet and the web have quietly but inexorably undermined our willingness to cop to this implied elitism. Why write a letter to the editor when you can start your own web site? If it's good, you could get more traffic than the paper has subscribers. Love him or hate him, Matt Drudge did exactly that. But is news on the web dependable? Is it true, is it *trustworthy?* Is it legitimate, the way the "legitimate press" is supposed to be legitimate?

Jay T. Harris is chairman and publisher of the *San Jose Mercury News*. In April 2000, he delivered the keynote address to the 36th annual Scripps dinner at the Reynolds School of Journalism and Center for Advanced Media Studies. That certainly has an insider ring to it, eh? But just wait. In his talk, "New Media in the New Millennium," Harris warned that since the Internet enables almost anyone to publish whatever they please, readers will have a hard time telling the difference between the output of bona fide journalists and the ravings of "plain old crackpots." Personally, I think the latter will be pretty easy to spot, as they're generally a lot funnier. Brilliantly clarifying the distinction between net-based communications and journalism—they "are not the same thing," he said. "More often than not, they are different."—Harris further explained that journalism is "a profession committed to informing the public about public issues and significant events," which mission is to be carefully distinguished from the "the shallow babble of the masses."[64] After all, without the special secret decoder rings issued to Official and Authorized members of the Legitimate Press, how could shallow babblers like ourselves possibly determine the deep significance of historic public figures such as O.J. Simpson, Princess Di, and "Little Elián Gonzalez"?

Journalism is a noble profession and my intent is not to vilify its practitioners. Why, some of my best friends are journalists! (And of course, book reviewers are not included in this critique.) However, the notion that journalism brings to the reporting of events a magical "objectivity" that is somehow sacrosanct or received from a higher authority is clearly crap. Nonetheless, the net has come in for plenty of abuse from such defenders of the purportedly privileged relationship the press has with its various audiences. More various than it cares to admit. *The San Jose Merc*'s Jay T. Harris is hardly an isolated example; there are plenty like him. First, such guardians of the public good ignored the Internet. Then they got seriously spooked by the attrition of their readerships to online alternatives. Then they pandered to "the New Media," and pontificated about its impact as if they'd actually spent time on the web, which most clearly had not. Much of the mainstream media reaction to net journalism has been either violently negative or pedantically patronizing.

The news media have been on the defensive for a lot longer than the net has been around, and it has often made of the net a convenient whipping boy for what public journalism's Jay Rosen calls "the troubles in the press." Cataloguing its problems in detail would be an exhaustive undertaking, which, fortunately for us, has already been undertaken by others. A brief scan of the titles of a handful of books on the subject tells a tale that can't credibly be pinned on the Internet: *Uncertain Guardians: The News Media as a Political Institution*; *Unreliable Sources: A Guide to Detecting Bias in News Media*; *Rich Media, Poor Democracy: Communication Politics in Dubious Times*; *Republic of Denial: Press, Politics and Public Life*; *When MBAs Rule the Newsroom*; *The Control Room: How Television Calls the Shots in Presidential Elections*; *Media Circus: The Trouble with America's Newspapers*; and a book by James Fallows that *really* pissed off a lot of publishers, *Breaking the News: How the Media Undermine American Democracy*.[65] The list could go on. And does. But we should trust established media and distrust voices from the net. Maybe I need to have this explained to me again. I don't get it.

In many respects, the press has itself to thank for the outpouring of public discourse on the Internet. People came to the net in droves (a drove representing roughly ten million souls) and responded with enormous enthusiasm to anything *different* from the bland and boring fare they'd been force fed for so long by broadcast journalism. Who created this audience? In many ways, mainstream media did. As Frank Zappa once remarked (at rather high volume), "Do you love it? Do you hate it? There it is the way you made it." This was on the album *Absolutely Free*. And freedom is the issue here. Not as in the problem, but as in the result. We may not be able to say with much certainty what the ultimate "objective" truth about the world is, but on the Internet we've given ourselves and each other an increasing measure of liberty to say what it feels like to be living in whatever version of this world we can manage— the freedom, in fact, to say whatever comes into our heads. Inevitably, this horrifies the self-appointed arbiters of taste and the elite interpreters of what is good and real. So what? Freedom is *not* just another word for nothing left to lose. Freedom is wild in the litany of senses Gary Snyder enumerated, one of which was "far out," if you recall.[66] The web is not a definitive history or a map of the stable reality so many seem to long for. The web is a non-stop planet-spanning celebration. And we ain't goin' back in the box.

The box being "objectivity," of course, which implies accepting the idea that someone else, someone "well placed," some "credible informant," some unnamed and faceless source close to the president (whether of the country or the corporation), will speak to us, channeled through some official interpreter, and tell us how it is. Hey, don't you know anything? Turn on your radio and listen to the rap that Tipper Gore and her ilk have taken such pains to label offensive—and that will get more offensive the more it's so labeled. Turn on your web browser and your email client and your MP3 player. Listen. *There's* the news that didn't fit. *That's* the way it is, Walter. And it ain't goin' back in the box. Baby.

Democracy would be a lot easier to buy if it weren't for the free speech addendum. And democracy is still a highly tentative experiment. There are plenty who feel we'd be better off if we had just the true stuff. The real stuff. The official version. Then everyone would know what was going on. Only problem is, this is called fascism. If not for the Internet, we might already be there. But even before the net—yes, kids, it's true, this stuff goes way back—there were people who didn't give a flying fuck about the official version. Artists, they're sometimes called.

Seen in historical context, gonzo journalism continues a long tradition of highly unofficial chroniclers, writers whose take on the world offended popes and kings and even commoners, their tastes attenuated to a hot-house frailty that suited the refined and elevated sensibilities of their betters. Take another look at literature. At the nasty bits of Ovid, Chaucer and Boccaccio, Rabelais. At Cervantes, Voltaire and Jonathan Swift, Lewis Carroll, Charles Dickens. At Thomas Paine and Thomas Jefferson. At Upton Sinclair and Sinclair Lewis. At Pasternak, Solzhenitsyn, Nelson Mandela. At John Steinbeck, Henry Miller, Kurt Vonnegut, Salman Rushdie. All these authors were censored or suppressed at one time. And that's the short list. While *The Canterbury Tales* were first published at the end of the 14th century, none of this is ancient history. Chaucer was challenged in a 1988 court case in Florida, the initial complaint citing sexual references, vulgarity and "the promotion of women's lib."

More specifically, the plaintiff objected to the use of the words *"ass"* and "fart" in The Miller's Tale.[67] Today, one suspects this individual has probably not availed his family of the rich resources the Internet provides. The Alta Vista search engine returns 76,095 hits for the query term "fart." Google returns 173,000. See, for instance—offered in the spirit of social commentary on such censorship—the interactive audio permutations on this theme at www.createafart.com.

While gonzo journalism is in good company with respect to its disrespect for normative social strictures, it cares deeply about the "objectivity" debate. In his acid-tongued (and -headed) obituary for Richard Nixon, Hunter Thompson says Nixon's casket should have been "launched into one of those open-sewage canals that empty into the ocean just south of Los Angeles" and that "his body should have been burned in a trash bin." It seems fair to say that Thompson was not terribly fond of this particular president, calling him many vile and terrible names.

> Some people will say that words like *scum* and *rotten* are wrong for Objective Journalism—which is true, but they miss the point. It was the built-in blind spots of the Objective rules and dogma that allowed Nixon to slither into the White House in the first place. He looked so good on paper that you could almost vote for him sight unseen. He seemed so all-American, so much like Horatio Alger, that he was able to slip through the cracks of Objective Journalism. You had to get Subjective to see Nixon clearly, and the shock of recognition was often painful.[68]

Politics aside, the gonzo turn was a crucially important response to the notion that, to be "legitimate," journalism had to be distanced from personal perspective, that it had to be cool, impartial and detached. That it had to be everything, in other words, that the net is not.

Getting Subjective

While worlds apart in many respects, social marketing and public journalism share a desire to get closer to audiences than was possible with mass media broadcast techniques. They also raise deep issues of motivation and credibility. Who is seeking to engage our attention, and why? Who can we believe? Both also deal with relevance and interest as determined by audiences themselves, bottom-up, rather than being predetermined top-down by publishers and media conglomerates. Public journalists ask their readerships what issues are important to *them*, irrespective of Gallup and CNN polls. Social marketers speak of participatory communication in which the values and beliefs of the audience are considered from the outset.

The corporate appetite for cause marketing runs headlong into the law of diminishing returns. Companies use a mass marketing metric in determining the appeal of such causes. AIDS is good, for instance. Lots of upscale youth market pull. Arthritis, on the other hand, is far less sexy. Though many more people may feel its effects, a) it is not fatal—critical to establishing deep empathy—and b) it does not target the bloated belly-of-the-bell-curve demographic that broadcast aims to reach. As more companies graze their products on the pastures of our civic concern, that concern is proportionally diminished. The tragedy of the commons is inevitably repeated when our attention to the public sphere is attenuated by too many profit-driven appeals to the common good.

The gonzo approach of a Thompson or a Toscani strikes me as much more intrinsically interesting than the earnest exhortations of the public journalists, even though their intent can easily be made to look more thoughtful and serious. I mean, who's going to dis democracy? But the paradox is that by taking on the role of guardian of democracy, public journalism risks a higher-order public paternalism. And in this it looks not a lot different from the attitudes of mainstream media. The charge of "advocacy" has never carried more weight than it does in the following gonzo critique by America's foremost sociologist and culture critic. I'm referring of course to Dave Barry. In his first work of fiction, *Big Trouble*—called out on the cover as "an actual novel by Dave Barry"—he describes the frustration of a journalist whose newspaper management wants him to write articles that, he believes in his heart, nobody wants to read:

They preferred issues stories, which were dense wads of facts, written by committees, running in five or six parts under some title that usually had the word "crisis" in it, like "Families in Crisis," "Crisis in Our Schools," "The Coming Water Crisis," et cetera. These series, which were heavily promoted and often won journalism contests, were commonly referred to in the newsroom as "megaturds." But the honchos loved them. Advocacy journalism, it was called. It was the hot trend in the newspaper business. Making a difference! Connecting with the readers![69]

Barry's character resolves this plot conflict by putting his foot through his managing editor's computer screen. The author comments laconically: "He'd burned a bridge there." Perhaps relevant to our current cogitations, the guy ends up doing advertising and PR.

Noam Chomsky is a very different sort of thinker. Unlike Dave Barry, very few have ever accused him of being funny. But while humor is a powerful weapon, there are more serious charges to be laid at the door of the press than its inability to entertain. In *Manufacturing Consent: The Political Economy of the Mass Media*, authors Herman and Chomsky write:

> . . . the democratic postulate is that the media are independent and committed to discovering and reporting the truth, and that they do not merely reflect the world as powerful groups wish it to be perceived. Leaders of the media claim that their news choices rest on unbiased professional and objective criteria. . . . If, however, the powerful are able to fix the premises of discourse, to decide what the general populace is allowed to see, hear, and think about, and to "manage" public opinion by regular propaganda campaigns, the standard view of how the system works is at serious odds with reality.[70]

This is also a reality that public journalism sidesteps no less than the traditional press. Public journalism is nothing more than a naïvely optimistic band-aid if it assumes that its audience-driven agenda will not run into headlong conflict with the powerful corporate interests that own or control an overwhelming share of conventional (i.e., non-Internet) media. And this is not an oh-by-the-way observation. It represents a crucial and defining factor in the options that will be available—or not—to any form of future journalism. We should care about this, as one of those options involves the continuance or termination of a free and open society.

The challenges faced by social marketing and public journalism stem largely from the institutional dimension of both: the institution of corporate advertising, the institution of the press as it is currently constituted. If the attempt to hew to these old models is removed from the equation, many "problems" of credibility and objectivity disappear. Much hand wringing about these matters represents a last-ditch effort to preserve Big-A Advertising or Big-J Journalism at all costs.

But Internet audiences don't care about saving these institutions. They may care a lot about preserving "a free press." But that concern doesn't map to GE, Viacom, Disney, Bertelsmann, Time Warner/AOL or News Corp—the six companies that basically own global media today.[71] Net audiences want information that's relevant, credible and engaging. If those criteria are met—contrary to the esoteric brand cabalism of mass media empires—they don't much care where it comes from. Given that many web sites are overt acts of passionate advocacy journalism, companies need to find a way to underwrite the best of breed without expecting to own them, control them or otherwise influence their independent editorial perspective. And there is a way—surprisingly simple and sane—for companies to do just that. We'll soon be exploring this alternative: the gonzo model.

This is not to say I don't care about the quality of journalism or the press as it exists today. I value the press. I hope it gets better. And it will—to compete with thousands of new voices percolating up from the nether regions of the net. If it can't compete, whether for economic or journalistic reasons, I don't think any amount of civic concern will bail it out. I'd join in thinking such an eventuality was tragic if I didn't believe that at least some of the new voices coming from the bottom up won't be as good as anything we've seen from journalism so far. And they won't need "the media" as it exists today in order to survive.

At the end of his book, *Deciding What's News: A Case Study of CBS Evening News, NBC Nightly News, Newsweek and Time*, sociologist Herbert Gans proposed something he called "multiperspectival news."[72] It would be bottom-up, he said, not top-down like traditional broadcast media. "For example," he wrote, news about Federal (and corporate) policies would "be accompanied by reactions not just from high officials, but from citizens in various walks of life who would be affected by these policies." This sounds very much like the agenda of public journalism, though Gans was writing in 1979, at least a decade before that initiative began. Multiperspectival news would also include what Gans calls "subcultural programming," content created to satisfy a broad and heterogeneous array of "taste cultures"—audiences having distinct shared aesthetic values and standards. Unfortunately, this increased coverage would also require many more delivery channels than existed at the beginning of the '80s, so it seemed wildly impractical.[73]

Who knew then that the web was on the way?

CHAPTER 6

From Micromedia to Micromarkets

"The prevalence of mass marketing has obscured the fact that for centuries consumers were served as individuals."

—ARMSTRONG AND KOTLER, *MARKETING: AN INTRODUCTION*[1]

OVER THE LAST SEVERAL DECADES, NEWS, INFORMATION AND ENTERTAINMENT have come to be controlled by a rapidly conglomerating collection of corporate media empires. When Ben Bagdikian wrote *The Media Monopoly* in 1983, 50 firms dominated U.S. media. By the second edition, the number had shrunk to 29; by the third, 23; by the fourth, 14; by the fifth, 10. The sixth edition, published in 2000, lists only six companies that together control the vast majority of journalism that Americans see and hear—news and information that also colors and shapes, if not defines, what the rest of the world believes about itself. The Big Six are General Electric, Viacom, Disney, Bertelsmann, Time Warner/AOL and Rupert Murdoch's News Corporation.[2]

At the end of January 2001, the Walt Disney Company announced it was deep-sixing its Internet portal site, Go.com. Where were *you* when the news came? I'm sure we all shed a silent tear. *The New York Times* quoted Disney CEO Michael Eisner as saying the company would "refocus its efforts on the web sites related to its broad-

cast and entertainment brands." Disney decided on the move because "the advertising community has lost faith in the Internet and
specifically in portals," according to Eisner, who reported that the
future of the Internet is—now here's a surprise—"interactive television and pay-per-view."[3]

This story is a classic. We got brands, we got broadcast, we got
tee-vee. Who was it said, "What else *is* there?" We even got lost faith
and redemption. You gotta love the way these guys talk. But listen,
can we, like, refocus our efforts on reality for just a second? Com-
plaining that the Internet fails as a mass medium for broadcast advertising is like being disappointed that a BMW makes a lousy trac-
tor. "That's right, Farmer Bill, the damn thing keeps getting stuck
between the furrows. Hell, Ol' Bessie never useta get stuck!"

Motley Fool noted a number of factors working against Go.com,
not least of which was "the questionable idea of creating an um-
brella site for an in-house family of brands, no matter how individually strong those brands may be." The article mentions that, rely-
ing on essentially the same strategy, "Time Warner's Pathfinder, a
pioneering online newsstand for Time Inc. magazines, had already
been through several failed incarnations by the time plans for
Go.com were being hatched."[4] Being kinder than I, the author does
not emphasize the obvious: that *it's not like those failures were exactly a big secret at the time.* Why is it that we all remember the bit
about the pain in the dinosaur's tail taking so long to get to the dinosaur's brain? It must be one of them Jungian archetype things.

The truth is, the net takes to advertising the way fish take to bi-
cycles. Search engines—a de-buzzed synonym for *"portals"*—are a
great idea, sure. People use them all the time, which is why they always rank highest in the Whopper Site Sweepstakes, the mine-is-
bigger-than-yours measurements of who's going where most. In
every respect that counts—and there's really only one: where deep-
pocket advertisers will plunk down their media-buy megabucks—
these metrics are indistinguishable from Nielsen ratings as applied
to TV sitcoms. While considerably less amusing, the portals are a lot
more efficient in delivering audience stats. And who doesn't love a
pie chart?

"According to Media Metrix (December 2000), Walt Disney Internet Group's combined web sites collectively represent the eighth

largest web property, attracting more than 20 million unique visitors representing 25% of the web universe per month."[5]

That's massive. But not massive enough for true King-of-the-Hill mass media players. Michael Wolff, duly infamous author of *Burn Rate*, writes about Eisner in *New York Magazine*, saying there are really two Eisners, one good, one bad. "The good Michael is the no-Hollywood-jive, drooping-sock Michael, the faithful-to-his-wife Michael, the decent, goofy, puppy-dog Michael. The Michael played by Tom Hanks." That doesn't sound so good to me, actually, but then Wolff has never been much noted for sucking up. It gets worse, of course. "And then there's the bad Michael: controlling, vindictive, dissembling Michael. The avaricious Disney-is-too-small-and-no-company-is-too-big-for-Michael-Eisner Michael."[6]

This is not just a passing observation. The operative concern here is scale, as in "economies of." We are observing a game of monster-media hubris that would make Caligula blush, played out by titanic egos risking everything— going for broke as if the world were coming to an end. And it is. Their world anyway. Accompanying its story on Disney's no-Go, *The Financial Times* ran a timeline showing that in June 2000, General Electric's NBC Internet dumped several web offerings and a month later Viacom changed its mind about launching its online MTVi music network. By January 2001, AltaVista had announced layoffs for the third time, NBC Internet and CNN had made deep staff cuts, and News Corp had decided to can its Fox internet division. All for the same reasons: audiences declining and advertisers taking a hike as a direct result.[7]

But Internet audiences are not really declining. There are more people online than ever. They've just found better ways to spend their time. People do go to portal sites, in droves. But they go there to search for somewhere *else* to go. Could be why Disney named it GO.com, eh? They don't go to click on banner ads. They don't go to "interact"—at least not in the sense Eisner means when he talks about interactive TV. As I was writing this chapter, an item arrived from *Wired News*, titled "Placing Product Before Art."

Game shows and advertisers have been quick to embrace interactive programming . . . But independent filmmakers at the Digital Independence conference said the real money to be made doesn't come from creating interactive programming for sitcoms and hour-long dramas; it's in product placements similar to those seen in *The Truman Show*. . . . the founder of the first 24-hour television-shopping network . . . encouraged directors to build that product inter-activity directly into films and television . . . "Interactive television gives . . . viewers the opportunity to drill down and find out more about the products they might want."[8]

Right. In the big love scene, what we really want to do is mouse on the lipstick and get some hot makeup tips. We want to click on the tires in the hair-raising car chase. "Honey, wouldn't those look great on the SUV?" And she says, "You touch that remote, Frank, it's over. I mean it."

Since the mid-'90s, the topic of "interactive media" has been the focus of innumerable articles in the popular press. But most of these have looked at the phenomenon through a mass-media lens, with "interactivity" reduced to advertising links and "Buy It" buttons. At base, however, the Internet is a *publishing* medium, allowing indi-viduals to express views, opinions and perspectives in a way that was never possible before its arrival. "Freedom of the press," wrote A. J. Liebling in 1960, "is guaranteed only to those who own one."[9] His witticism has taken on a double irony today, as the Internet and World Wide Web have in fact reduced the cost of owning one by orders of magnitude.

The barriers to entry are lower in this medium than in any that preceded it. The net has given writers, artists, musicians, hackers and other creative defectors from the homogenized wasteland of mass media a place to express themselves. These expressions are not uniformly compelling, to be sure—many are godawful by con-ventional standards. But their worth is not determined by conven-tional standards. That is to say, it is not determined by the expecta-tions of media conglomerates bent on appealing to the lowest common denominator and therefore, by the inexorable and inflexi-ble logic of broadcast, to the largest possible collection of passive ad receivers. In contrast, these network-mediated communications are valuable to whatever degree they can draw an audience, be it two or two million. They are valued by whomever comes back.

The Internet is still young. Very young. But people have already learned to use the search engines and all the nifty little bookmarking doo-dads. They've learned to use email. They've learned what they like, and they've told their pals. No wonder traffic passing through ad-infested portal sites is down. What they like is not advertising. It's voice. Websites that have genuine voice are where people are beginning to congregate online, where they *do* hang out. Not in the huge aggregations demanded by traditional media-cum-marketing expectations, but in pockets, in ecological niches too small to attract the notice of the Eisners and the Murdochs. However, the size of these audiences is directly proportional to the perceived quality of the voice that attracts them and the cogency of what it has to say, whether the delivery vector is a word processor, an overdriven guitar amp, or a can of spray paint. An entirely new class of micromarkets—small, but growing fast—are forming around such micromedia sites today.

Micromedia

Because entry costs require high returns on investment, broadcast media rarely offer emergent voices a hearing. The Internet reverses this trend, providing many low-cost vectors for small-scale publishing—micromedia, as opposed to mass media. Low-budget bottom-feeder webzines don't worry much about size of readership. With little investment at risk, the primary motive is personal gratification, seldom profit, and the style of such publishing is therefore often quirky and experimental. If there's an audience that clicks with the material, *that's* the market—and it shows up via word of mouth. The process works bottom-up, by attraction, not top-down by intrusive demographic targeting.

A handful of webzines such as *Salon* and *Feed* are professionally produced, including the work of many journalists. They emulate the "controlled circulation" model of offline publications wherein subscription is free, with costs and profits covered by advertising. These sites have had a hard go of it, as this model requires a relatively large audience. But *Salon* and *Feed* are exceptions. Most zines and other forms of micromedia—email lists, web conferencing sites, chat boards, Usenet newsgroups—typically do not have business plans, advertisers or investors. Instead, they are independent efforts by individuals or small groups with nothing much to lose, and a possible audience to gain

One of the latest and most interesting additions to the suite of micromedia tools are weblogs—simply "*blogs*" to the faithful. There are a lot of faithful. Blogging exploded across the non-commercial regions of the Internet like a global pandemic—the real thing, not a drummed-up marketer's dream of manifesto destiny.

A weblog is a little like an online diary. Date-stamped entries are usually in the form of short observations or opinions of the moment, often including hyperlinks to news items and other web pages of interest to the author. Several startups now offer free weblog services to make such postings a piece of cake. At first glance, weblogs don't seem like anything new. Given a little effort, anyone with a text editor, an FTP client and a web page could put one together. But how much effort is too much? The requirement to write HTML would probably exclude most people right off the bat. Remember when URLs that came in email had to be cut and pasted into a web browser? Once it was possible to click directly on emailed links, the web took a huge leap forward. As Malcolm Gladwell demonstrates in *The Tipping Point*, little things can have disproportionately large consequences.[10] Weblogging appears to be one such wrinkle in the web today. And one thing you can count on: there will be more. Such tools will keep getting better, connecting more people entirely outside the big-media sphere of influence.

Dave Winer created weblogs.com to advance the phenomenon. "A weblog is kind of a continual tour," he says, "with a human guide you get to know. Each guide develops an audience, and there's camaraderie and politics between the them. They point to each other in all kinds of structures, graphs, loops, etc. They also point to the sites they read."[11] If you look at a few random weblogs, you might come away thinking that they're simply another form of random link lists. In a way, they are. But they're also much more. Something profound is going on here. The incestuous linking and camaraderie Winer talks about constitutes a powerful form of bottom-up news filtration and consensus building. The best voices emerging via weblogs and other micromedia are forming the kernels around which new networked communities of interest will coalesce—micromarkets *in potentia*. The Internet has always demanded that business read between the lines. Weblogs raise the bar. Now the challenge is to read between the sites.

And the micromedia phenomenon is growing—in the number of tools available to create and support them, in the number of sites coming onstream, in number of links among them, in number of loyal fans they are attracting. How many times have you gotten email—"Trust me, you really *need* to check this out!"—accompanied by some exceedingly strange URL like www.goatsatemywashingma-chine.com or www.sweetfancymoses.com. It might be the worst garbage you've ever seen. Or it might have you laughing so hard inside of ten seconds that you marvel once again at the inventiveness of the human species. And instantly you know your friend was right: you *did* need that.

Fortunately, *Goats Ate My Washing Machine* is not a real site. Not so fortunately, *Sweet Fancy Moses* is. Be forewarned, you could end up wasting a lot of time on this utterly bent "online journal of wit." And you're too busy for that, I know. But trust me, you really *need* to check this out! To illustrate the point, I asked Brian Crowley if I could quote a clip from his "Pretty Damn Good Dream Analysis." He agreed to this, writing back via his editor: "And feel free to tell Mr. Locke that the author toils each day in the marketing world, so he writes from experience." See? These are not just a bunch of kids fooling around. These are dedicated professionals.

Dream: "I am in my childhood home standing in front of the door to my bedroom, which is closed. I reach out to pull the door open, but someone inside the bedroom is holding it shut. I pull harder and harder, but the person is too strong, almost inhumanly so. After struggling with the door for many moments, I slump to the floor and catch my breath. 'Why won't you let me in?' I whisper into the door. A voice from inside the room answers, 'Because you are not ready.' I immediately recognize the other voice as my own."

Analysis: The dreamer is most likely troubled by pressures at work—an upcoming financial report for stockholders, perhaps. The dreamer's inability to open the door signifies his real-life failure to make third-quarter earnings reflect a significant growth to stockholder market shares. His ass is really on the line this time.[12]

What's more interesting about this piece than its high hilarity (though I think it's pretty funny) is the level of audience sophistication it depends on. The site says of itself: "Our obsession is to build a collective work where intellect, humor, and voice come together in orgiastic triple climax." And this expectation has not gone unmet. Traffic to *Sweet Fancy Moses* has done a hockey-stick ramp in the few months since a handful of writers got together and decided to launch it on the web. This is not stuff you'd be likely to encounter in the Sunday supplement of your local paper, or even in online publications with a broadcast-oriented business charter. Nonetheless, unsuspected and unpredicted by market segmentation analysis, there is a smart and avid audience emerging here. And new audiences hold the potential to become gateways to new micromarkets. This potential, however, will not be fulfilled through the usual traps and snares of traditional advertising.

In a moment of advanced procrastination—of which I experienced several thousand in the course of writing this book—I decided that I should explain this core principle of gonzo marketing in exhaustive detail on *Sweet Fancy Moses* itself, thus using the site as both example and delivery vehicle. Sparing you the full scope of my self-indulgence (masochists see endnote), here's part of what I wrote there:

In general, vice presidents of marketing working in large corporations think we are morons. Takes one to know one, I guess they figure. For decades, they have been sponsoring "content" that fits their bell-curve-driven dreams of mass market penetration. Bend over, here comes another sitcom. They will tell you they only sponsor this sort of thing for the mindless, shuffling Thorazine-Drooler category, which however, comprises 98.74% of all Americans. Because when they ask them "Who wants to be a millionaire?" every hand in the house goes up. Of course, they'd get the same reaction if they said, "Who wants to go to Arts and Crafts now?" or "Who needs to use the bathroom?" But the marketeers will tell you they've conducted extensive, expensive research. They'll tell you this is what the people *want*.

Yeah, but look who they asked! Forming a focus group is like jury selection at the OJ trial. "Not that one. He sneered. Swear to God, I saw his lip curl! And not the one laughing into her laptop, either." They never ask the smart people. They never ask us. And you know why? Because they know what we'd tell them. To stick it up their Nielsen ratings. Sure they do these multiple choice questionnaires. "Do you like *Friends* better than *Cheers?*" And maybe for the octogenarians: "Did you like *Cheers* better than *Mork and Mindy?*" But they never give you any *real* options, like: "If given half a chance, would you strangle Robin Williams with a length of rusted barbed wire dipped in botulism toxin?"[13]

While it's a perennial favorite, black corporate humor is obviously not the only focus of such micromedia attractors. It might be artistic, a real-time performance piece in which the Zapatistas take over Mexico—like www.ezln.org. Or political—like www.artcrimes.com. Slashdot is a community of Linux users that hacked together a web conferencing platform that has served to connect people who share that particular interest (maniacal obsession perhaps comes closer). The Slashdot platform is open-source software, which means it can be modified by other groups with different interests. The latest site to adopt the Slash code is *Plastic,*[14] masterminded by Joey Anuff, one of the original founders of *Suck.com*[15]—spawned out of *HotWired*— and Steven Johnson, co-founder and editor of *Feed.*[16] *Suck, Feed* and *Plastic* have recently shut down. But their problems have little to do with content quality, and much to do with the advertising model on which they depend. The audience size of any single micromedium is minuscule compared to broadcast media. But taken together, micromedia could easily eclipse television. And soon.

Whether hotshot media management types in New York and L.A. choose to believe it or not, these net-based publications are overt acts of journalism. In 1998, Jamie Heller, then executive editor of *TheStreet.com*, wrote a piece in *The New York Times* titled "Online Journalism Coming Into Its Own." It ends: "whatever the conventional media elite may think, online journalists might have decided that they're already arrived—and are happy to stay right where they are." Sounds good. Change comes to MediaLand. However, what has lent the Internet validity—for Heller, as he says in the article, and many others who originally came from the print side—is the immigration of known and respected members in good standing of the *legitimate* press.[17] This is a rather colonial perspective. A view from the Raj. Gin and tonics with the natives. A spot of hunting. "Indjya, old man, nothing like it! Great fun. Take the missus."

This is not to denigrate professional journalists—if their expertise is in researching issues and events and articulating their findings in—as the *Miami Herald's* Carl Hiaasen suggested—a kick-ass delivery modality.[18] As in when you go, "Wow, that piece whomped serious butt!" But if—how should I put this?—the *specialness* of having worked in conventional media is based on the mystique of the secret "objectivity" handshake. . . well, we've been over this already, haven't we? Don't get me started. Don't make me have to come over there! In fact, by jettisoning (or more likely, never having thought of) such primitive beliefs about "objective" and emotionally disengaged reporting, many *un*known, *un*credentialed *non*-pro web journalists are already doing—effortlessly, unselfconsciously, without a second thought—what public journalism has had so much trouble attempting to accomplish within the institutional framework of commercial broadcast, online or off. That is, these new web journalists are engaging people's real-live vital concerns and exploring issues percolating from the bottom up, not imposed top-down by polls and pundits. This is bona fide journalism, even if nobody official gives it official sanction. Badges? We don't need no steenkin badges![19] In *The World Wide Web and Contemporary Cultural Theory*, Steven Jones writes:

> Journalism on the web is not journalism as we have known it thus far. It creates a different order of content. . . It asks us less to attend to "the latest" and more to attend to what we find interesting; less to synthesize and understand a "who, what, when, where, how, and why" and more to attend to "what's next?"; less about a "them" and more about an "us". . . The range of possibilities has widened: we are no longer certain of what is reported in the news, and we are much more likely to allow alternative explanations. . . It

is not so much that we do not believe what we read, see, and hear in the news as it is that we are inclined to believe that there is more . . . As Marshall McLuhan put it, "'content' . . . is always another medium. The content of the press is literary statement, as the content of the book is speech, and the content of the movie is the novel." It is now more clear than ever that the content of the web is news, though not necessarily journalism.[20]

In an article called "The Dotcom Brain Drain," *The American Journalism Review* reported that a surprising number of reporters are abandoning print publications to write on the web. "Web sites are basically about conveying information in engaging ways," says veteran journalist Nick Denton, adding: "That's what journalists do."[21] And that's what Denton did. For eight years, he wrote for *The Economist* and *The Financial Times*. Then in 1998 he founded Moreover.com, which delivers news stories from thousands of sources to websites across the planet. "Traditional Internet technology leaves a significant blind spot around dynamic content," says Moreover.com. "Information that changes quickly is either omitted or delivered too late to be useful."[22]

The New York Times writes about the company in "Mining the 'Deep web' With Sharper Shovels," noting that only a tiny fraction of the estimated 500 billion "pieces of content" on the net are visible to conventional search engines.[23] The cliché has it that 99% of this stuff is junk. But the cliché reflects the primary bias of broadcast media. It's "junk" only because the people who want to find it don't aggregate into large enough segments to constitute sufficiently lucrative advertising targets. It's "worthless" only because media moguls like Michael Eisner and Rupert Murdoch can't figure out how to make a buck off it. Randall Rothenberg frames the problem neatly in *Advertising Age*:

. . . while the Internet destroys many existing economic models, it doesn't necessarily replace them with something equally viable. I've written about the radio's problem: with universal broadband penetration, the individual listener has access to thousands of stations, serving every niche interest imaginable. With any 17-year-old with a handful of MP3s and some time on his hands able to have his own global network, the value of brick-and-mortar stations, which has skyrocketed in recent years as conglomerates tried to assemble national networks, erodes. How do you rebuild—or sell advertising within—an industry composed of a kazillion stations, each with a handful of listeners? [24]

And he answers his own question: "Damned if I know." At least he's honest. But the real problem lies in automatic assumptions of how to parse "equally viable"—usually construed to mean something you can sell advertising in, around, about, over, under, sideways, down. But many "insignificant" niches can add up to a lot of people. *The Times* "Deep Web" story reports that in December 2000, some 340,000 people hit the Moreover site, adding "and that is without any consumer marketing from the company."[25] Advertising isn't the only way to make a buck. Moreover is both giving away its service to smaller independent web sites, which spread awareness of the company and its tools, while licensing its core engine to major corporations, where it's being used to assemble and annotate distributed topical knowledge bases on the fly.

So far, most of the news stories served by moreover.com come from traditional publishers: newspapers, the financial press, big-media web sites. But that's changing fast. The company has partnered with Blogger, an explosively expanding online startup that produces software for creating and maintaining personal weblogs.[26] The result is newsblogger.com, which not only lets small sites publish links to late-breaking news stories, but lets editors at those sites add their own commentary.[27] This constitutes something completely new in the world, a form of populist metajournalism. The commentary is often sophisticated media criticism—noticing how the publication plays up certain aspects of a story and plays down others. For an example of such media criticism, you really *need* to go check out *Online Journalism Review.*[28] It's not a weblog, it's a website, but here the point is not the mechanism, but how these tools are being used to comment and expand on mainstream news, to which people previously had no way to respond outside of token letters to the editor. In a similar (though non-populist) vein, *Slate*'s excellent Daily Papers feature is worth looking at. This email-cum-web column is teaching many thousands how to read and deconstruct the deep rhetoric of newspaper layout decisions, such as the significance of how an article is placed on or absent from Page One at publications like *The Wall Street Journal*, *The Washington Post* and *The New York Times*.[29] Such unprecedented and fast-growing popular sophistication with respect to media is a direct result of the net.

But back to blogs. Because moreover.com also indexes an increasing number of small indie weblogs, things are starting to get recursively tangled beyond all recognition out there. It's getting hard to tell who's "in the business" and who's doing it for love. "ALL THE NEWS THAT'S FIT TO BLOG" reads the motto on the newsblogger site. "What could be more intuitive than a list of chronological, commented links?" asks a piece in *digitalMASS* about Moreover's offbeat alliance. "It's only natural that a company like Blogger would be helping publish blogs with names like Deadman and Brainsluice alongside corporate news services."[30]

On Tom Peters' web site, Tom or someone near and dear to him explains weblogs and their significance. "A lot of people keep on-line 'blogs'—or 'weblogs'—as personal journals, or just as a running series of observations about anything under the sun. We've created a series of blogs in order to make a running commentary of neat, weird, or odd ideas that have to do with corporate culture, work, online commerce, or a variety of other topics."[31] Thus a phenomenon that grew bottom-up out of the deep, invisible web wins endorsement from the world's numero uno business consultant. Hands have been laid on. Yeah, it's dangerous, out of control. Yeah, it trashes all sorts of sacred-cow boundaries. But it's cool to like this stuff. Tom Peters turns serious webhead. I love it.

The stars of this new medium are just now emerging. Don't think Matt Drudge, think Walter Cronkite. Individually, their audiences will be much smaller than those of today's mass-market broadcast channels, but taken together, the total audience will be much larger. Within a few years, many thousands of quality news, entertainment and information sources will spring up on the Internet to serve highly specific communities of interest. These micromedia sites will constitute an increasingly important vector for electronic commerce, serving as possible points of entry into a huge collection of web micromarkets.

Micromarkets

Microsoft's *Slate* represents an interesting modification of the strictly advertising-based webzine model: corporate underwriting. The company owns the site and pays the considerable costs of producing it. But this begs the age-old journalistic question of influence— the separation of powers (or lack thereof) between editorial and business interests. How credible is *Slate* in reporting on the Microsoft antitrust case? Ownership isn't everything. In cases like this, it can be an impediment. What if, instead of launching *Slate* itself, Microsoft had bankrolled an indie zine with proven editorial appeal, then adopted an ironclad hands-off policy with respect to content? If corporations underwrote externally produced webzines and were careful to preserve site independence, the resulting sites could be far more credible attractors than are most current corporate web pages. This sort of enlightened patronage first appeared in the Renaissance when the Medici banking family supported artists like Botticelli, Michelangelo and Leonardo da Vinci. Strangely perhaps, it could work again today, financially rewarding quality site producers and enabling companies to better connect with nascent web micromarkets.

But these are hints of things soon to come—both in the next chapter and the near future. At present, micromarkets don't yet exist. Micromedia do exist, and are growing rapidly. Audiences are coming together around these new bottom-up sources of news and views. But these audiences will not become markets until business finds a viable way to interact with them. Markets exist only in the eye of the beholder—this is the view from the world of commerce. If business doesn't learn how to behold online markets—doesn't come to perceive them for what they really are—these markets will *never* come into being as such. Like any market, micromarkets are relational affairs. They do not exist independent of their observers in quite the same way as shoes and ships and sealing wax. This may seem an abstruse philosophical point, but it has critical ramifications for business, so pay close attention here. People in the microaudiences coalescing around micromedia do not think of themselves as micromarkets. *They think of themselves as people.*

This is perhaps the greatest shift in the balance of power between companies and what they have viewed until now as "consumers"—people whose only function was to buy products. The net has helped human beings to rediscover other, and often more interesting, uses for their humanity. Because of this shift in perspective—which has caused online markets to radically realign priorities and allegiances—business needs to be especially wary of using old broadcast terminology as if it still applied in familiar ways. "It looks like a medium, so it must be like television." Or "I see a lot of eyeballs out there, so it must be a branding opportunity." Just because some of the words sound the same doesn't mean they describe the same realities. In *Principles of Marketing*, Philip Kotler and Gary Armstrong talk about *micromarketing* in the following terms:

> Segment and niche marketers tailor their offers and marketing programs to meet the needs of various market segments. At the same time, however, they do not customize their offers to each individual customer. Thus, segment marketing and niche marketing fall between the extremes of mass marketing and micromarketing. Micromarketing is the practice of tailoring products and marketing programs to suit the tastes of specific individuals and locations. Micromarketing includes local marketing and individual marketing.[32]

What they mean by *local marketing* is street-level GPS coordinated with point-of-sale data. Real sophisticated. Real complex. Real spooky. I don't mean that. What they mean by *individual marketing* is mass customization, one-to-one stuff, "personalization." I don't mean that either. In fact, I don't talk about "micromarketing" at all. Or marketing *to* anybody, for that matter. That's still the whole targeting trip. Ready, aim, *sell!* Instead, I talk about *gonzo* marketing *for* and *with* micromarkets. As used in this book, "*micromarkets*" are not hash-browned or refried databases. Neither are they individuals, so-called "markets of one." Instead, they're genuinely *social* social groupings. Little ones perhaps, at first, but they're collections of people, communities joined by shared interests. And (this part is probably important too) they're groups you actually *belong* to, that you *interact* with—not by punching buttons and entering your zip code, but by exposing something real about who you are.

This kind of interaction—unlike Michael Eisner's variety—applies to *everyone* who wishes to be part of the community. Even businesses. Companies that want to relate to these communities as markets, must first become active participants. No more remote-control media buys. No more painting bull's-eyes on the backs of abstract demographic segments. So maybe this is a good time to let you in on a little wrinkle in the unified revised standard theory—gonzo marketing isn't really marketing at all. It's market advocacy.

On the net, advertising works against itself. Because it relies on scattergun tactics guaranteed to repel more attention than it attracts, it needs as large an audience as possible. If only 2 percent of the audience will even register an ad, much less act on it, the advertising model needs sites 50 times larger than sites in which everyone is paying attention. However, sites that much larger cost that much more. Therefore they must be even bigger to cover costs and bring in more eyeballs to satisfy more advertisers so more people will buy their products more often. It's a rat race. Critically, this never ending upward spiral directly degrades the quality of content. To attract a larger audience, content must be less challenging, more popular—less focused on specific interests, more broadly appealing. In other words, more generic. And because every other site with mass media pretensions is offering the same kind of generic information, it becomes a commodity, readily available in so many places that no one site can attract a critical mass in terms of audience share. This may have been OK for early TV, where the audience was captive and all the broadcast networks offered essentially the same fare. And by God, anyone who didn't like it could move to Russia! But on the web, it's not so OK. We don't have to move anything but our index fingers. Click. We weren't looking for commodity information anyway. We were looking for voice.

Meeting market expectations is a way for a business to be predictable, yes, granted. It's also a way to be *boring as hell*. Some will be tempted to argue here that at least it's safe. Don't. It's not safe. Boring is dangerous. Boring communicates that you have no guts, no heart, no soul. Conventional market research offers black-and-white certainty—or at least insinuates that it can provide powerful predictors of future market directions. Let's take a look at how this works. Say Nirvana hits big in Seattle, and OK so your big-assed record company missed it, but you pick up on the trend right away—and sign a thousand mediocre grunge bands. If Apple makes a sort of blue computer housing and it catches on because every other computer ever made was that puky off-ivory, then hey, you make yours sort of chartreuse. If everyone suddenly wants to be a millionaire, you launch a game show where the contestants get a wheelbarrow, a truss, and 10-minute pass to Fort Knox. Your time-slot competitor hits you with brilliantly creative programming about people stranded on a desert island with no sex? No problem. You strike back with strongly competitive programming about people stranded on a desert island with lots of sex and rabid half-starved monitor lizards. See? Difference is minimized. Expectations preserved.

Only by then, your market's gone. Your audience has long since split.

The Internet is entirely different. It's not an opportunity for viral marketing. We *are* a virus and we want to multiply. We *are* the audience. We *are* the market. We are in it and of it. This is not just our "positioning," it's our position. And we won't recant or renege or back down. Where would we go? What else *is* there? This is market advocacy. This is gonzo marketing. You don't have to be nuts, but it helps to have been there. Because when you get personal with so many people, you begin to get stretched, to blur at the edges. You don't define your product—you discover who you are. Prepare for deep existential terror at times. And, if you really connect, for the rush of your life.

Let's turn to Kotler and Andreason one last time. These guys are all right if you overlook their proclivity to prepend "target" to "audience."

Marketers who constantly keep attuned to their target audience are confronted again and again by the market's diversity. As a consequence, they assume markets almost always must be segmented with strategies fine-tuned to the needs and wants of each subpopulation. Closeness to consumers also leads to recognition that *traditional demographic approaches are seldom adequate* to capture the rich diversity in target audience's needs, wants, life-styles, perceptions, and preferences.[33]

Within a few years, thousands of quality news, entertainment and information sources will spring up on the Internet, each serving a highly specific community of interest. Around many of these micro-media, a web of intercommunicating micromarkets will emerge in a band of spectrum invisible to conventional marketing. The stars of this new medium are just now emerging. Don't think Dan Rather, think Chaucer, Cervantes. Think Dante. Don't think Jerry Springer, think Rabelais and Shakespeare. Don't think George W., think Winston C. Don't think Oprah, think the Oracle at Delphi. Human beings have always discovered magic and magnificence within themselves. It wasn't created by media marketeers—they just saw an opportunity to make a killing. The magic was there all along. It still is.

The Gonzo Model

"As the chief and only true gonzo, Thompson, in his famous 'Fear and Loathing' reportage for Rolling Stone *magazine, wasn't just a passive observer but played his own freaked-out part as unofficial Tom O'Bedlam to the events he covered."*

—THE OXFORD ENGLISH DICTIONARY QUOTING *NEWSWEEK*[1]

"Orr was crazy and could be grounded. All he had to do was ask; and as soon as he did, he would no longer be crazy and would have to fly more missions."

—JOSEPH HELLER, *CATCH-22*

THOUGH MANY READERS MAY SKIP TO THIS CHAPTER FIRST, ITS LOGIC will probably be perplexing without the circuitous route that leads to the gonzo model being proposed here. That route is not defined by the previous chapters in this book, but by the history of business in the 20th century. Let's briefly recap the essential elements. Mass production and its attendant economies of scale typified business for most of the past 100 years. Because this mode of production was so enormously successful, it has continued to shape and color the conduct of business even long past the ascendancy of the industrial model out of which it grew. Perhaps the major reason for this long and painful hangover is the persistence of mass media, which were spawned in response to the needs of business as critical vectors to mass markets. Like the management of large industrial corporations with many thousands of workers and millions of customers, broadcast advertising partakes of the same top-down style of command

and control. Both employees and customers were told what to do—whether to work hard or shop hard—but not asked in any substantive way for their input or opinions.

This basic mass marketing–mass media scenario was already changing in fundamental ways long before the advent of the Internet. Because of the vastly expanded range of products and services that became available through global competition once mass markets began to fragment into many segments and niches. The same competition brought enormous pressure to bear on companies, forcing them to turn to their entire workforce in search of process improvements and new product ideas. Though loudly proclaimed by many companies, the "empowerment" of workers to contribute such insights—as though this were a "privilege" granted thanks to corporate largesse—has done little to change the inherently authoritarian nature of management. Command and control remains the order of the day. And the same is true with respect to markets. Through there is much talk these days about the empowerment of the customer, companies still communicate their demands by broadcasting them to demographically determined abstractions about which they know very little, and with which they have little in the way of genuine relationships.

The coming of the Internet has greatly accelerated these trends. While the net did not cause these long-term shifts, it has catalyzed a much faster evolution of business than would have been possible without global networks. This change in the speed of business has also produced a change in the *kind* of business that will be viable from this point forward. With the reality of interconnected audiences and markets, something fundamental has changed in the world, and the world continues to change as a result. The catalyst has triggered an irreversible chain reaction.

However, both mainstream media and corporate marketing are blind to these changes inasmuch as they continue to rely on deep-seated yet tacit assumptions attaching to the pre-Internet broadcast model. The strategy of the ostrich notwithstanding, blindness never offers protection, only higher—since unacknowledged—risk. Four decades ago, one of best minds in marketing, Theodore Levitt, wrote about the catastrophic impact of a similar blindness on an earlier business era.

Even after the advent of automobiles, trucks and airplanes, the railroad tycoons remained imperturbably self-confident. If you had told
them 60 years before that in 30 years they would be flat on their
backs, broke, and pleading for government subsidies, they would
have thought you totally demented. Such a future was simply not
considered possible. It was not even a discussable subject, or an
askable question, or a matter which any sane person would consider worth speculating about.[2]

Using only slightly different language, anyone daring to challenge
the "obvious" and unshakable supremacy of the railroad barons
would have been considered gonzo. Whacko. A nutcase. Today,
anyone failing to genuflect to the similarly "obvious" and unassailable hegemony of AOL/Time Warner, Disney, News Corp and other
such media empires is also thought to be demented, deranged—or
perhaps just hopelessly ignorant and naïve. But these Masters of the
Mediaverse betray a confidence just as blind as that of the railroad
companies a century ago. And they don't have 60 years, or 30, to
figure it out. They don't even have three.

So what happens if the great "iron horses" of broadcast are about
to encounter the media equivalent of the automobile and the airplane? What if their millions of miles of inflexible track, laid at such
great cost, are about to be made superfluous by alternate routes appearing out of a dimension invisible to the imperturbably self-
confident chieftains of these great conglomerates? But "what if" has
nothing to do with it. These eventualities are not forthcoming;
they've already materialized. A quick change of transportation
metaphors is now called for, from railroads to shipping, because
however cleverly Michael Eisner, Rupert Murdoch, Steve Case and
the rest of these broadband tycoons rearrange the deck chairs on
their respective *Titanics*, an even more titanic iceberg with their
names carved into it has already calved off some remote Arctic ice
shelf and is inexorably drifting their way. That iceberg, of course, is
the Internet. If a just God grants my fervent prayer that I may be the
James Cameron of their fateful rendezvous, my heart will go on and
on. Film crews are standing by on seven continents. The revolution
will be streamed in MPEG.

And what will happen to business then? What will happen if companies are left with no way to advertise? But this is the wrong question entirely. Companies don't give a damn about advertising—any more than they did about railroads. What they cared about 100 years ago was getting goods to market by whatever means was most effective. What they care about today is connecting with potential customers by whatever means is most effective. In the pre-Internet days, when broadcast was the only way to accomplish that—the transcontinental railway of marketing—advertising was a foregone conclusion. But advertising is not only exorbitantly expensive, it's a ridiculously inefficient means of attempting to reach and form productive relationships with an increasingly fragmented array of networked markets. Many of these markets are just now emerging bottom-up from the web, and are completely invisible to the traditional analytic tools of market research.

These micromarkets are forming around micromedia, myriad small online publications that are beginning to attract millions beneath the notice (and contempt) of convention marketing radar, and which *could*—given a framework radically different from broadcast advertising—serve to mediate between companies and potential customers. This framework is what the gonzo model aims to provide.

Implementing the Program

The balance of this chapter describes how, by adopting this model, companies can open up to new markets in ways that are smarter, friendlier and far more effective than outmoded legacy marketing methods—the unnecessary baggage business has so far brought to the Internet. If you skipped over Chapter 1, pretend *this is a hypertext link*. Before you read on, go back and scan the section about what Ford Motor Company is up to—"Ripping Out the Wall"—and the speculative "Preview of the Gonzo Model." We're about to delve into the nuts and bolts. Without the contextual connections those previous bits provide—the conceptual bolts—the following may strike you as merely nuts.

Motivation and Resources

Paradoxically perhaps, there are several reasons why Global 1000 corporations may have the best advantage in the early stages of the transition from traditional marketing to more intimate micromarket relationships. This does not mean that smaller companies are excluded from adopting this model, or that they would reap less benefit. It's just to suggest that very large companies may well be first in to the pool (last one's a rotten investment).

First, these companies are most dependent on broadcast advertising, and therefore most at risk from its failure to port from conventional media to the Internet. While most are unaware of the reasons for this failure, many are exploring other avenues to reach networked markets. Given the near-religious fervor with which some of these companies have responded to approaches like permission marketing, this exploration often telegraphs to markets a counterproductive aura of desperation. These companies are ready for something different, but they're not quite sure what it is. The old broadcast model does not offer much help in assessing why one method is more likely to work, or fail, than another. Or worse, it leads to false predictions. This has caused much costly thrashing—companies going overboard for flavor-of-the-moment nostrums such as "push," "personalization" and "permission," which turn out to have the half-life of late-August fireflies.

Second, these companies are currently spending prodigious sums on adverting—in both offline media and on the more broadcast-oriented forms of web marketing. The funding for initial gonzo-model testbeds will come out of such supersized media budgets. And testbeds will be crucial. No company is going to shift a major portion of its marketing resources into this mode without testing the waters first. Micromarkets are not mass markets, or even the type of large market niches business has typically pursued. While this may seem obvious, it's important to understand the implications. Each micromarket will represent a much smaller percentage of revenue potential than the markets currently targeted through conventional segmentation. Therefore, companies will need to establish a much broader array of micromarket partnerships. Using a fairly random example, if each external micromarket partner represented 1/10 of 1% of overall revenues, the company would eventually need to establish 1,000 such relationships to replace earnings generated by its current marketing methods.

Third, these large global companies have very sizable and diverse workforces. This is critical, as what underpins the gonzo model are personal interests and passionate engagement around those interests. The first tactical step for companies is to determine what these interests are. Today, most corporations have little idea.

Intellectual Capital Audit

Intellectual capital has been the subject of much discussion in business journals, conferences, and high-level corporate think tanks. And lately, nascent ideas about social capital have been folded into the mix. However, most of this discussion has focused on knowledge about products and production processes, or social relationships within the organization. This self-reflexive and insular examination leaves the lion's share of existing intellectual and social capital lying on the table. It's there in plain sight, but the legacy of command and control prevents most companies from seeing it. They are blind to enormously valuable assets they're already holding.

In the first half of the twentieth century, nearly all industrial companies had a "check your brain at the door" policy. While not explicitly written into official employee handbooks, workers knew it was there, and behaved accordingly—keeping perfectly viable process improvement ideas to themselves. When Total Quality Management began to reverse this trend, and self-directed teams were given unprecedented authority to design their own work environments, management was often surprised to learn how much these workers knew. "How come you never told us any of this?" the bosses inquired. "How come you never asked?" the workers replied.

But here we're talking about a different sort of intellectual capital that has been undervalued to the point of invisibility. What are employees interested in *outside* the framework of "the job"? Human Resources never asks, except perhaps to fill in those trivial "other" fields in the resumé database—hobbies, club memberships, neigh-borhood action groups, whatever. The company yawns. The com-pany doesn't really care. But it should. What drives the self-selec-tion process whereby communities of interest come together on the Internet is not products—Seth Godin's notion of "consumer net-works" is little more than a convenient fiction. Instead, what unites these communities of interest is—duh!—their common *interests*.

Sometimes these shared interests have a political dimension, as with "interest groups" that make common cause to advance some desired change. More often, though, these are common, garden-variety interests, as in rock music or opera, historical biographies or mystery fiction, home schooling or scuba diving, or any of thou-sands of other interests workers pursue outside of their paid in-volvement with the company. While most of these are understand-ably avocational, many are related to the individual's professional work, whether it be accounting practice, computer programming or some aspect of business management. Whatever form they take, all are potential points of intersection with external communities of in-terest currently emerging on the net. As such, these interests are like diamonds in the dust in a networked economy.

Companies need to understand the worth of these interests, then identify their specific focus. This will require more than vague state-ments about valuable employees. It will require the establishment of serious programs to encourage and showcase such interests, and to develop and nurture communities of interest within the company.

Long ago, AOL created a content incubator, a "greenhouse" in which to let various creative talents show what they could produce. AOL promoted those it thought best into its commercial offering. Companies can follow a similar model. It's not rocket science. All that's required is a large and unconstrained web space behind the corporate firewall—and a top-management-blessed invitation for people to build sites around subjects they really care about. Given the "check-your-brain" hangover, most employees will contribute nothing. Incentives should be carefully considered, such as time off regular work to produce these sites. However, incentives that are too enticing across the board could remove an important quality fil-ter. Those who are naturally inclined to contribute will be driven by an extra degree of enthusiasm to communicate their passions—and this is the most valuable stuff a company can elicit. Such passion and enthusiasm forms a good fit with the Zeitgeist of the web.

Once the program gets underway, the developers of these internal sites will begin to realize that they share interests with other workers they've never met. In a company with 100,000+ employees, this is no big surprise. The company should encourage collaboration between such individuals and groups. The goal is a single site on each topic of interest, incorporating whatever talents and expertise members of the community can bring to the party. In themselves, such initiatives are likely to surprise the companies that seriously encourage them, if only through the *Hawthorne effect*—the phenomenon whereby the productivity of workers increases any time management pays attention to them, that being such a rare event. A less academic way of describing this is to recall the question, "How come you never asked?"

Identifying best of breed

However, the point is not productivity. The point is marketing. There is a trajectory to such work, and it's vector is through and beyond the corporate firewall. The point is to connect with external micromarkets. To accomplish this, the company needs to assess the sites it has nurtured through such a greenhouse program, and select the best results for further development. There are two critical measures of what "the best" means here. The first could be a serious challenge for many corporations. It entails understanding what "voice" is. A good metric to use in this regard—a worst practice, if you're keeping track—would be to select sites as distant as it's humanly possible to get from the vacuous rhetoric of the typical corporate home page. Elements to look for include personal style, differences of opinion, humor, deep knowledge of the territory—and an ability to articulate it—plus, if you're lucky, that indefinable quality of gonzo. Companies that promote the bland, the vanilla—in other words, the kind of crap they're used to delivering through their current "marketing communications"—might just as well not embark on this route. They'd be wasting their time.

The other measure of what constitutes best of breed entails fit with the company's markets. This is tricky ground. In the earlier Ford example, there is a distinct (if non-obvious) connection between organic gardening and the company's products—specifically, no one is going to haul manure in the family four-door. But such an explicit tie-in need not exist. If enough people outside the company are interested in cooking, say, such a focus could be attractive to certain web micromarkets even if the company offers no products that are directly related. If the markets it wants to attract are fairly general, it makes little difference. As long as its products or services *could* be useful to such an audience, such topical interests should not be excluded out of hand. However, if the company makes molybdenum gears for bulldozers, cooking might be a bit far afield. In making decisions about which areas to focus on, companies will use whatever insight they've garnered from previous demographic segmentation efforts. They'll also use gut feel. And they'll make mistakes. The latter is unavoidable, but since this is not a mass market strategy, and dozens or hundreds of sites will be offered to the web at large, no one bad call will be fatal. On the other hand, the near certainty of error makes it critical to establish out front a way to reset from such missteps such that none is catastrophic or ends up generating bad will either inside or outside the organization.

Identifying external partners

The challenge here is to locate independent external websites that form a natural fit with the internal employee interests identified in the previous step. Matching the interests of people in the company to those of people in the marketplace offers the potential for engendering conversations on matters of actual interest to emergent web micromarkets. No matter how hard companies wish for it, these micromarkets are unlikely to give their permission to talk about the wonders of your company's product. However, they may well grant permission for individuals who happen to work for you to join in discussions already underway—the nature of which discussions being what brought the micromarkets into existence in the first place.

Actually, these are not markets at all until the company is able to sell to them, and—critical paradox alert!—they will never *become* markets as long as the company's main purpose is to do so. It is crucial to understand that the primary objective of such internal/external intersections is to establish relationships of genuine trust among people sharing specific focal interests. Any attempt to undermine or short-circuit this process using intrusive marketing techniques will have devastating instant-karma consequences.

In looking for external web partners, the knowledge of employees already engaged in these programs will be critical. The most knowledgeable and articulate voices on the company side will also tend to be intimately familiar with relevant external web resources. They will know which sites are best, which worst, which marginal, and this information will be essential to making good micromedia partnership decisions. Usually, such expertise will be closely related to an individual's specific interests. However, some employees may have more general web sleuthing skills and a good nose for promising sites, whether or not they are well versed in the particular subject area. Companies should consider turning these generalists into dedicated web scouts, analogous to the A&R (artist and repertoire) scouts that major music recording labels employ to search out new talent. Identifying newly emerging web micromarkets will be an ongoing involvement, and such A&R scouting will soon form an important aspect of corporate marketing—as it should have from the beginning of corporate entry onto the web.

The best external candidates for partnership will not necessarily be the best established. The slicker the site and the greater the size of its existing audience, the more expensive the relationship is likely to be. This is where "radar for voice" can pay enormous dividends. A nascent site that is interesting, engaging, compelling, creative, independent, and again, if you're lucky, a little gonzo, is the ideal candidate. Such a site will have great potential to draw an audience. It is less likely to be encumbered by restrictions stemming from previous marketing or venture capital relationships. And critically, it will need resources of the sort that corporate underwriting can provide.

Underwriting

What exactly does *underwriting* mean? In essence, underwriting is a form of patronage, in the sense the term was used in the Renaissance. In fact, the practice it describes largely kicked off the Renaissance. In the 14th century, the Medici banking family served as a powerful patron to artists such as Botticelli, da Vinci and Michelangelo, whose work we might never have heard of without such corporate support. True, the word *"patronizing"* has come to have extremely negative connotations—as in, "don't patronize me!" We'll deal with these in the section below on the problem of influence.

Isn't *underwriting* just a fancy word for sponsorship? As the term is being used here, the answer is a resounding and definitive no. In the corporate marketing mindset, sponsorship is indissolubly linked to advertising, and underwriting does not involve advertising. In fact, it is a more effective alternative to advertising's inherently distanced and impersonal methods. The aim of underwriting external sites is to establish strong *personal* relationships between a company and emerging web micromarkets in which the company has a perceived future stake, and in whose subject matter company employees have a preexisting *personal* interest.

There is one important sense in which underwriting and advertising are linked. As the former will increasing replace the latter, the financial resources required to support these micromarket initiatives will come out of current media budgets. For this reason, the marketing department has to fully buy in. Achieving consensus on this point will constitute a substantial challenge for many corporations—an insurmountable hurdle in some cases. As this book has shown, marketing is set in its ways, and many of those ways are grounded in realities that ceased to apply decades before the Internet became a major avenue to markets. On the positive side, the decreasing effectiveness of current methods should act as a strong incentive, encouraging marketing to look beyond "best practices" that have long since become liabilities in a networked world.

So, what sorts of resources do these external sites need? The usual: time and money. Micromedia sites tend to be labors of love. Their developers are typically working to make ends meet while keeping their sites afloat on nights and weekends. The first contribution of corporate underwriting is to enable these creative principals to quit their day jobs in some cube farm, thus freeing them to devote full time to their primary passion. Companies can simply underwrite external partners by giving them money with which they can purchase needed resources. However, other forms of support tend to forge closer relationships—and as that's the whole idea, this should be considered. Companies can lend or donate computer equipment, disk space, bandwidth, and render various forms of technical, design and artistic assistance. They can also develop or license content relevant to the specific interests of these communities and make it freely available to them. Such content would be more welcome, and therefore more effective in creating recognition and goodwill, than the majority of current expensive-but-empty "branding" ploys.

Companies can also direct traffic to these partner sites from their web pages—a sort of reverse advertising. The objective is to grow these sites in which the company is investing. Just because they're micromarkets today doesn't mean they have to remain so. It is in the mutual interest of underwriters and external partners to announce the existence of partner sites and encourage customers and prospects to visit them. The set of micromarket partnerships a company engages in becomes an important component in its brand. Think of Benetton here. Its employees care—so the company tells us—about issues like AIDs and racial equality and capital punishment. The company further assumes that its market shares similar concerns. So it welds its brand to those issues. If it loses some customers in the process, it figures it will attract others more sympathetic to its positions. Benetton's radical experimentation along these lines is understandably terrifying to most companies.

However, the issues that interest people need not be "issues" at all; these interests extend far beyond the realm of heated political or cultural debate. A company may underwrite micromedia sites focusing on subjects as commonplace and uncontroversial as baseball, wine collecting, javascript programming, film noir, telecommuting, or notable bassoon performances. Though the last is a little unlikely (unless, of course, the company manufactures bassoons), a company will identify itself with emergent markets by the underwriting positions it takes, and the collection of these positions will say a lot about the character of the company as a whole. Companies should neither embrace nor sidestep controversy based on ulterior marketing considerations, but should take positions their employees truly support and consciously choose to align themselves with. This is a roundabout way of stating the obvious: that companies should tell the truth about who they are instead of representing themselves as airbrushed fictions.

Bottom line: *the fundamental message of marketing must change from "we want your money" to "we share your interests." In this respect, corporate underwriting is a way—perhaps the only viable way at present—for companies to put their own money where their mouth is.*

Structuring the relationship

If money is changing hands, you can bet that lawyers will be involved. They will. These won't be casual handshake deals but formal contractual relationships. Both parties will want to maximize the value of what they give and what they get for it. Both parties will want to minimize their risk. One tradeoff involving both value and risk will be the term of such contracts. As noted already, a company might find a smaller, newer micromedia partner attractive because the relationship will be relatively cheap. The site has little but sweat equity and voice to show; the rest is potential. The company is investing in this voice in the reasonable expectation that the audience it is able to attract will become more valuable over time. Plus, the company is agreeing to provide certain other valuable resources (as described in the last section) to assist in the success of the site. The company will want to extend its relationship for as long as possible at the same level of financial support, and not be penalized—through a ramping schedule of payments—for a success it has helped to secure. But too long a term might not be in the company's best interests either. There is no rule of thumb at this point on the optimal length of these relationships, and there may never be—many factors will have to be taken into account, and these will differ from company to company and site to site. The two parties will have to work out a compromise amenable to both. Exit protection for both sides therefore becomes especially important—one form of which might be yearly or biannual renewal options with plenty of notice given if one party intends to bail, or feels that renegotiation is warranted.

One protection the company will (and should) require is *exclusivity with respect to the domain*. While a site may have many underwriters—the more the merrier, for reasons we'll see below—it should be precluded from having more than one in any single competitive market arena (hereinafter, as those lawyers might say, the *domain*). In simpler terms, if a site enters into an underwriting relationship with Ford, it will not be able to ink a similar deal with General Motors. In the case of a coveted potential web partner, this will engender competitive bidding, which is good for the site. However, the site should take many other factors besides money into account. Prime among these is cultural fit. Do the parties "speak the same language"? Do they see eye to eye on expected results? Are both being honest and above board? If these questions are not explored, nasty surprises could result. If the answers are not in the affirmative, one party or both is going to be unhappy with the marriage.

But back to competitive bidding for a moment. If a company identifies a candidate site early enough, and offers it fair underwriting terms, price inflation due to bidding may be avoided. There are tradeoffs here on both sides. Should the site wait to get other companies interested, or are immediate funds more valuable than a potentially greater sum later? This is simply the old bird-in-the-hand question—though exclusivity considerations make it crucial to chose well here. As to the company, should it invest in the relationship now, at a lower price, or wait to find a possibly better candidate? The company is not explicitly bound by exclusivity—it would be too difficult to define, for one thing—but a) will not usually wish to underwrite competing sites, and b) resources are, after all, finite. So the company will obviously need to choose well too.

Despite these tradeoffs and admittedly gnarly considerations, companies will clearly attempt to sign quality partners before competitors can scoop them up. Without pretending to cover all the details here—as we say on the net, IANAL: I Am Not A Lawyer—contracts will have to spell out who gets what, for how long, and how the relationship will be continued beyond the contract term—or dissolved with the least damage to either party. More important than the letter of the law, however and as usual, is a sense of goodwill and a spirit of enthusiastic collaboration. These hookups should be joyous affairs. If they're not, they'll be disappointing. Or nightmares. There's not a lot of middle ground. Sure, problems will arise and need to be ironed out. Sure unforeseen factors will come to light and need to be dealt with. But this will only work if both sides basically respect each other.

Influence: Church and State

Mutual respect already has a deep tradition in conventional media. And this is one convention worth preserving. The separation of "Church and State" refers to the longstanding rule that editorial content must not be swayed by advertising dollars. The number of ad pages Microsoft buys in a magazine, for instance, should have no bearing on the review of Windows 2010. While this principle is often honored in the breach, it remains an excellent idea—for both the publication *and* the sponsor. If corporations are too often successful in influencing content decisions, readers begin to notice that the publication has sold out, and they soon go elsewhere for opinions they can trust. Ultimately, this is a pyrrhic victory for the advertiser, as it thereby loses a critical path of communication with the market. Understanding how this works is hardly a new thing in mainstream media. The general outlines of the principle were articulated by Adolph Ochs, publisher of *The New York Times*, as far back as 1916:

> It is an axiom in newspaper publishing—'more readers, more independence of the influence of advertisers; fewer readers and more dependence on the advertiser.' It may seem like a contradiction (yet it is true) to assert: the greater number of advertisers, the less influence they are individually able to exercise with the publisher.[3]

Within the framework under discussion, an important difference lies in the "more readers" argument, which itself reflects old broadcast and advertising axioms. Micromedia sites are not playing quite the same numbers game. A site far too small to attract broadcast advertisers can be highly sought after by multiple underwriters. But aside from considerations of audience size, Ochs's dictum still applies, albeit in somewhat restated form: the more *underwriters,* the more independence of voice is assured. Agreeing not to bring undue influence to bear on editorial content will be an important item in contracts. An underwriter attempting to do so will automatically be in breach and risk losing its long-term exclusive position. If competitors are avidly waiting in the wings for this to happen, it very likely won't. A company would have to be crazy to hand such advantage to a rival.

This is a delicate aspect of the relationship between companies and their micromedia partners. The diciest situations will be where the content of the external site has a direct bearing on the company's products—for example, if Toyota were to underwrite a site equivalent to *Car & Driver* magazine. This might be a dynamite idea. It's certainly not one to be avoided. But in cases like this, the company will need to sit on its hands and count to ten when the site reports that its latest product bites. Of course, it can argue and debate the opinion—it just can't threaten to penalize the site. If it does so, it paradoxically opens the door to Mitsubishi taking over its slot. This would obviously constitute a Very Bad Move. As a result of this dynamic, micromedia underwriting partners will be *better* protected from corporate manipulation than are their mass media counterparts in the broadcast world.

However, the influence problem probably won't be a very big deal overall. If Ford underwrites an organic gardening site, for instance, the company is highly unlikely to use its financial clout to sway readers' views on the best way to mulch carrots. So everyone can just relax. An excellent tactic in any case.

Why do it?

So far, this book has mostly looked at the negative motivations for gonzo marketing. Radical alternatives tend to appear when nothing else really works. The main agenda up to this chapter has been to show that marketing as currently practiced is badly mismatched to the culture and dynamics of the Internet. But the gonzo model goes beyond critique. Following the steps outlined above, companies can encourage authentic voice and genuine conversation within their walls, then break down the walls and connect those conversations to related exchanges already underway in the networked marketplace. Let's take a brief walkthrough of how this could work.

Say you're currently interested in K–12 education. You've got two kids and you're worried they're getting shortchanged in the public schools they go to. You want to know why and you want to explore your options. There's a lot of debate on this topic and sorting it out isn't easy. The conclusions that seem most obvious turn out to be questionable. The "definitive sources" you once might have trusted seem like mouthpieces for the status quo, or seem as if they've got hidden vested interests. But you've got little time to research all this. You care, but you also have to go buy a computer. Otherwise the kids won't be able to keep up with their schoolwork.

You go to the Dell site—let's say; this is entirely hypothetical—to start trying to figure out what system you need and how much it's going to set you back. To your amazement, right there on the homepage, you see a banner saying something like "Visit Our Home Schooling Community." As you watch, the banner changes. Next it says, "Visit Our Personal Investing Community," then "Visit Our Gonzo Tasmanian Chinchilla Ranching Community," but you're not interested in those (you're not even sure what that last one means). When the home schooling banner rolls back around, you click, and—hey, look at that!—there's a well produced web magazine addressing all your questions. The first thing you notice is a graphic saying "Underwritten by Dell." This is strange. And now you're curious. You click on this graphic assuming it will take you back to the Dell home page you've just come from. But another surprise: it doesn't. Instead, you end up on another sections of the Dell site where employees of the company are writing and talking about the very issues that have been bugging you. Intrigued but skeptical, you click around and scan a bunch of articles. The site is substantial and there's more to explore than you possibly could in one sitting. You bookmark the main entry point and pop over into email to send the URL to the half dozen friends you've lately been talking to about these school issues. "Look what I just found," you write. "I know, it's weird to find this on a computer company site, but what's even weirder is that there isn't any advertising."

Of course, there are links to Dell's regular site—this is a company page, so the frames are the same, with buttons for products and support and such. There are also links to many more of these "communities" Dell seems to be "underwriting." You explore the school pages some more and discover contributions by Dell people who think home schooling is the greatest, and Dell people who tried it and thought it sucked. They talk that way too—as if no one is controlling what they say. And they all have email addresses listed with invitations to comment on their views. You decide this must be bogus, some kind of advertising gimmick after all. But you email one person whose perspective you particularly agree with. To your astonishment, you get a reply 20 minutes later answering the question you asked, then adding "You know, it's a highly individual decision. Ask around, but go with your gut." Aside from a signature block that identifies this person as a Dell employee and a URL back to the Dell home schooling site, the message contains no pitch to buy anything. You forward it to the same six friends. "I can't believe these people have time to respond to stuff like this. Their company must be supporting this in a big way. I don't know why." But your skepticism is melting. You're impressed. You write back to the person who mailed you from Dell. "Wow, that was fast. Thanks. By the way, what do you do there?" The reply comes back even quicker this time. "I'm in customer service. Let me know if you ever have questions on that side of things. Doesn't matter if you have a Dell or something else. I know how they all work. ;-)"

As you browse around—you've come back several times now—you do find an article or two about Dell products. Aha, you think, this is where they get the payoff. But both sound like good advice on buying systems best suited to kids. "Forget the more expensive lines" one says. "Those are either for road-warrior business types or they're servers. Unless your kid is making a full-length movie (mine is, actually), you don't need that much power." Accompanying the piece is a chart laying out an optimal configuration for homework, gaming and Internet browsing. For less than you thought you'd have to pay. You click again. You buy it. While the price was a nice surprise, it wasn't the reason you bought the computer—and you didn't shop around as you were planning to. You bought it because you were impressed by what this company was doing. The next week, in the school parking lot, another parent mentions she's been thinking about a new computer for Billy. "Have you looked at the Dell site?" you ask. "I know you're interested in K–12 education. . . Here, let me write down this URL. It's really quite amazing."

Notice that there's nothing particularly gonzo about this little scenario—except that its approach to marketing breaks every accepted "rule" and notion of best practice. Also note that it focuses mainly on the company side of the micromarket partnership. In fact, the boundary between the two would be pretty permeable. There would be lots of links back and forth between the company site and its external underwriting partner, to content and resources existing on both sides. The partner would provide many pointers to Dell, and Dell would send as many people as it could to the partner site. They would be complementary, building in-depth understanding of the related issues, familiarity with regular contributors, and confidence in the company's intentions. They would also build customers. Loyal customers. But more than that, this combination would create more credible *evangelists* than any company could ever hope to generate, no matter how big its advertising budget.

There are other reasons why this model would be a major win for companies. Like attracting and holding onto the best and brightest talent—environments like this would be highly seductive to creative individuals. Like giving stockholders a better view of employee morale and the corporate culture's overall health than can be conveyed in a quarterly spreadsheet and a glad-handing annual report. Like giving journalists a thousand reasons for writing about the company. Like giving the net-at-large a million reasons to link to your web pages. Like the fact that what the gonzo model actually creates is a gigantic wide-area knowledge-acquisition filter attached to thousands of intelligent agents—a.k.a. knowledgeable human beings— and that this speaks directly to the capacity for innovation and the ability to remain competitive. There are many reasons for adopting the gonzo model, but the best will only be discovered in the course of exploration and experiment.

Why do it? Wrong question. The real question is, why not?

The Coming Internet Land Rush

I've always wanted to write The Coming Something-or-Other in a business book. It sounds so, you know, business-bookish. Don't worry, though, this is no convoluted consulting jive, compadres. You may think the net has been a big deal up to now, but you ain't seen nothing yet. Frankly, reviewing most of the corporate Internet gambits we've seen to date is not essentially dissimilar from watching a monkey trying to. . . (down, RageBoy, down!) fondle a football. In contrast, though mistakes will certainly be made, the model we've been circumambulating here will spur greater and faster development than everything that's happened on the net so far.

All it will take to torch it off is a few major corporations establishing the first micromarket partnerships. As soon as word leaks out that this is happening, their competitors will freak—with good reason. A company moving quickly to lock in relationships with the best voices in its areas of interest will reap substantial first-mover advantage. The next company to go looking will be looking at candidates of lesser quality. Competitors who wait a year or more to get started will find themselves picking over factory seconds. It's so simple. Deadly simple.

The result will be an Internet land rush of nearly unimaginable proportions. Imagine corporate buckboards lined up along the Internet border. Imagine B-movie thunder and lightning, sturm und drang. Imagine a light. . . over at the Frankenstein place. . . Imagine joyful anarchy and wild-eyed chaos as the empires of business-as-usual finally come crashing down of their own top-heavy weight. It's just a jump to the left. And it's about bloody time.[4]

So, if you run a website worth its salt, be prepared to see company A&R agents come calling, and soon. If it's not worth its salt, get busy. Gonzo marketing is market advocacy, remember? Despite the very real advantages to corporations, this one's for us. Be prepared to work with companies who get what you're up to and want to help circle the wagons around real—not bogus "consumer"—communities. As for the rest, the arrogant bastards had it coming all along. Enjoy the last laugh. Take no prisoners.

CHAPTER 8

Champions of the World

"Devil or angel, I can't make up my mind. . . "

THE PLATTERS [1]

"You don't know where you belong. . . "

CYNDI LAUPER, *SISTERS OF AVALON* [2]

SOMETIME BACK AROUND THE 3ʳᵈ CENTURY A.D., IF YOU CAN REMEMBER back that far, a certain meme got loose in an area roughly corresponding to what we now call the Middle East. Historically, quite a few whacked out ideas have originated in this region, most of them involving, in one way or another, the sacrifice of goats. Dave Barry can laugh at Santería all he wants, and we can all wonder what was up with those Aztecs, but this ancient proclivity to off the living in the pursuit of supernatural favor must reflect some deep, bloodthirsty need in the human soul. Or maybe—not to be insensitive to multicultural considerations, you understand—it was just an atavistic form of influence peddling. "Hello, God? Got a nice goat here for you. Uh-huh, hope you like it. Now about that Babylonian land development deal I was telling you about . . ." In all likelihood, we'll never know for sure.

Anyway, this meme came to be called *Manichaeism*—or if you happened to be in any way attached to a pope back in those days, the Manichean heresy. The core idea here was that nature and spirit are opposed and at war. Now, you can see right away how this would cause papal heartburn, as this was clearly encroaching on the monopoly turf of the whole Judeo-Christian setup. Gnostics and Buddhists horning in on the act clearly wouldn't do. To get the general flavor of this, think Microsoft and Netscape without Janet Reno. As if that weren't bad enough, Manichaeism also ticked off the Zoroastrians, from whose tradition it had borrowed certain critical elements, to the point that they finally did a drive-by on the rapper who was laying this stuff down—the dude's street name was Mani— and that was basically that. Or so everybody thought.

But these ideas continued to spread. They held a powerful attraction. God all-knowing and powerful, man stupid and weak. Spirit pure, flesh evil. Heaven good, earth bad. (You can see how the top-down thing got going.) This perspective simplified things a lot. And it had a straightforward agenda: the end of life and the destruction of the world. Talk about your perfect elevator pitch. What's to not understand? Much as I disapprove the fire-in-the-belly CEO-like qualities of Torquemada—who, granted, didn't get the Spanish Inquisition into high gear until much later—I think I might have been among the inquisitors on this particular Manichean issue. Fundamentalist dualism fundamentally sucks. Let's not quibble: any kind of dualism sucks. It's dumb. But it's understandable, I guess.

Historically, human beings have attempted to reduce the world to fit some overarching paradigm, some all-inclusive explanatory framework. Without such a worldview, the thinking goes, we would be left with only confusion and chaos. But the complexity of the world is such that every attempt to reduce it to fit such conceptual models impoverishes not only the world, but ourselves. Nonetheless, we can't seem to resist asking questions of the form: *which side are you on?* In the case of the Manichean debate: are you for the world or against it? But this attempt to simplify matters is naïve in the extreme, simplifying—and signifying—nothing. Instead, such black-and-white categorical distinctions mask what is truly interesting about the diverse ways in which people have come to perceive and value experience.

However, extreme naïveté never having posed much of a hurdle to human judgment, it should come as no surprise that the ancient Manichean war between matter and spirit has continued unabated to this day. Benjamin Barber writes of *Jihad vs. McWorld* and the binary, zero-sum implications seem unavoidable. This is a war between fundamentalist spirituality and fundamentalist materialism. Which side are you on? Are you for the world or against it? Come on, join up, take sides! But let's back up a minute. I want to make two points about materialism, the first personal and contemporary, the second cultural and historical, revisiting the dawn of business.

I have not been easy on business in this book. I have kicked asses and taken names. Applying the which-side-are-you-on filter, many may therefore conclude that I'm down on "materialism"— which translates into being rabidly anti-business. In fact, that stance is increasingly popular these days. You know the catechism. Business is evil, money is theft, corporations are rapacious juggernauts out of control, which left unchecked will destroy the quality of life on earth and the earth itself.

Paradoxically, the old Manichean agenda to put an end to the world, once based on spiritual opposition to the material plane, is now within the reach of the worldly powers. And this is no joke. Think global warming. Think industrial pollution, acid rain, breakneck deforestation. Business often seems to be at war with "the environment"—our more sophisticated way of referring to what the ancients simply called the world. It would be a serious mistake for business to take such anti-business sentiment lightly or to think that opposition to the bright and shiny vision of McWorld is safely localized in Islamic nations with unreasonably resistant notions about modernization and the wonders of a global economy. Next time you get a chance, drop by a demonstration against the World Trade Organization. Those are your children getting their heads busted open in the street.

So yeah, I share these concerns. But does this make me an "antimaterialist"? The quotation marks here and above, around "materialism," are necessary because these are essentially silly conceptual categories, setting up a bogus straw-man opposition between options that are not really optional. Abstruse philosophizing aside, the material world is not a concept. Whatever I may think about it, I remain in it and of it. If I question the attitudes and actions of business, does this mean I must "renounce the world" in favor of penitential sackcloth and ashes? If I think that business assumptions that applied in an earlier epoch have become dysfunctional in a networked society, does it mean I must go to the desert, wear funky sandals and eat locusts? It better not. Such either-or thinking constitutes a conceptual booby trap. Although the "logic" is usually transparent and invisible, when we think this way we are invoking extremely old binary opposites. Spirit good, world bad. World good, spirit bad. But such zero-sum, heads-I-win-tails-you-lose alternatives are suffocating and insufferable. I don't want to take sides. I don't want to be lumped into such confining categories. I want an olive tree *and* a Lexus. I want a Big Mac *and* a jihad.[3]

Let me try to explain this a different way. In the course of writing this book, in which I have admittedly given business a bad time, I have also given business quite a lot of . . . well, business. As you might expect, I pretty much have no life. I'm plugged into this monitor every damn day, online more than off. It's pathetic, I know. I'm a slave to the web. But I also eat and drink like mere mortals. I drive a car. I even wear clothes on occasion. The point is, I buy stuff. It's just that, being lazy, I buy it, whenever I can, on the net. Just while I was laboring over the last couple paragraphs, two delivery trucks arrived. The first brought ink cartridges for my printer; the second some really cool cooking software (I eat therefore I cook) and two boxes of *Harry Potter* audio CDs (they're not for my kid, they're for me). In the past several months I've ordered lots of stuff off the web: a Maxtor 80 gigabyte hard drive, a super-nifty Iomega Predator CD burner, an HP OfficeJet all-in-one printer/scanner/copier/fax combination, Iris OCR software and handheld text scanner, a Microsoft Encarta DVD encyclopedia upgrade, a Sony handheld digital voice recorder, a Sony digital camera, a CD Walkman, music CDs, DVD and VHS videos, a stereo with an integrated DVD player, (yet another) desktop computer, an online subscription to the *Grove Dictionary of Art*, an offline subscription to *Harvard Business Review*, and, of course, endless and innumerable books.

"Sure," you say, "you're an information junkie. That kind of stuff is all you net-heads ever buy." But *au contraire, mon frere*. I also purchased—again, from the web—all manner of clothing, toothpaste, vitamins, deodorant (very necessary in my line of work), several items of furniture and luggage, a pasta maker, a waffle iron, a crepe maker, a bread machine, a food processor, a microwave oven, a cast-iron barbecue grill, and—against all my better judgment, of which I haven't much to begin with—a Roland guitar synthesizer whose technology is sufficiently advanced as to be indistinguishable from magic.[4] OK, so maybe this doesn't qualify me as the world's greatest online shopper, but neither does it exactly brand me as a sworn enemy of e-commerce. While I strongly resist the idea that my identity is defined and bounded by my role as consumer, all in all, I think I've more than earned the sanguine salutation so typical of spammers: Valued Customer. Aside from a certain gender disparity, I'm right there with Madonna when she says, "I am a material girl."

But am I therefore a material-*ist?* I don't think so. And perhaps the information-junkie dimension constitutes some sort of skeleton key here, not just to my own behavior, but to that of the hundred-million-plus who have come online since I started writing about the Internet a decade ago. My personal buying habits aren't very interesting in themselves, unless you're my accountant (be glad you're not). They aren't interesting at all unless they represent some larger trend. But I think they do. I think they represent an enormous shift, not just in market attitudes and expectations, but in—for lack of a better phrase—collective consciousness. A deep and profound shift.

Among many attempts to explain the rising importance of computer-generated data was what Nicholas Negroponte saw as a critical differentiation between informational bits and "atomic" matter, upon which he expounded in *Being Digital.*[5] However, I've never been able to get very excited about this distinction. It seems to me yet another binary opposition. Bits good, atoms bad. Or—in the amphetamine-jazzed rhetoric of *Wired* magazine, where Negroponte flogged this simplistic concept to within centimeters of the grave—bits wired, atoms tired. While I know it's true that you can jam a webzine down a net connection a lot easier than, say, a pair of Nikes or a Ford Mustang, this doesn't do much to reduce my need for shoes and transportation. At the end of the day, after finally getting my head around the crucial difference between an HDTV signal and a chunk of Wisconsin cheddar, I'm not entirely sure what conclusion I am meant to draw from the bits-v-atoms argument—except maybe, the blur between content and advertising being what it is today, that I need to renew my subscription to *Wired.* Get some more hot tips on technofetishism.

But here's a tip of an altogether different stripe. Information is halfway between matter and spirit. I want to be very careful here. I don't mean that information is somehow sacred or spiritual in itself. I'm not trying to launch a new religion. Neither do I mean that information is superior to hula hoops but inferior to the angelic choirs. Instead, what I mean is that information mediates the spirit in which we perceive and value the material world. This mediation, which is neither inherently "spiritual" nor "materialistic," has a bearing on what we mean today by *"media,"* and how our cultural perception of that concept has changed over time.

Take the neologism *"multimedia,"* for example. This term partakes of a sort of meta-ambiguity, referring as it does to two distinct meanings of media without being very clear about either. In the first case, the multiplicity of multimedia refers to various *media of expression*, such as words, pictures, and sound. In the second case, the term refers to various *communication media*—such as newspapers, radio, television, and the Internet—through which such hybrid assemblages can be delivered. This latter sense has all but eclipsed the former, and in doing so has turned yet another of those sleight-of-tongue pop-philological tricks that serve to make meaning opaque, and eventually meaningless. As when someone protests— one of my personal all-time favorites—"Come on, that's just semantics. You know what I *mean*."

No, I don't know what you mean. Yet it's never been more important for all of us to understand what we mean by *"media"* and what it is that media mediate. Business understands this mediation as providing a vector for advertising—a channel through which to connect the dots from product to consumer. But let's go back to the older sense of *media*. A writer's medium is inscribed language; a painter's, color and form; a sculptor's, stone or metal; a musician's, sound and time. The medium is the means of conveyance, but what is conveyed is (usually) more than the material employed. Art communicates a *sense* of the world, not in literal terms, but by attempting to reproduce in another soul some deep, intangible and otherwise inexpressible quality of how the artist *experiences* the world—how the world *feels*. Art mediates spirit.

It is in this spirit that human beings, unbidden and uninstructed, have begun to use the Internet. Just as we used colored earths and

stone tools to create mimetic images of bison and horses in Neolithic caves. Just as we constructed monumental architectures hon-
oring gods now long forgotten. Just as we invented symbols and
emblems that pointed beyond themselves, hieroglyphics, pic-
tograms, alphabets, stories, epics, novels, histories. Just as we invented ecstatic dance and ritual music. Yeah, and so what? What
does it all *mean*, Mr. Natural? While nobody can say with any certainty, it is certain that whatever human beings have been attempting to express all these millennia continues to hold huge fascination
for human beings today. And this isn't some academic exercise in
art history. We practice what we preach. It's in our bones. It's in our
blood. It's in the beat of some larger heart. Perhaps the Stones said
it best. "I know, it's only rock and roll, but I like it."[6]

Billions of people will soon be connected to the Internet. They're
not all here yet, but they're coming. Writing in *The New York Times*,
Thomas L. Friedman reports that "Chinese will be the most popular
language on the web by 2007."[7] They're coming, and what they're
coming for is what the net mediates: the beat of that larger heart.
The net is not intrinsically a medium for advertising. They're not
coming for product brochures or lower prices. They're not coming
for some ersatz Disney World "experience." Instead, the net is an
artistic medium. It mediates spirit. Whatever spirit we bring to it, we
are coming for that. We are coming to discover who we are.

But let's not set up another Manichean spirit/matter dichotomy
here. Rock and roll good, e-commerce bad. The problem with materialism is not that it loves the world too much, but that it does not
love the world *enough*. If the dictates of business are causing the
exhaustion of planetary resources, something is clearly wrong with
its system of valuing matter. Not all value reduces to dollars and
cents. Most people I know detest being addressed as "Valued Customer" because they understand precisely what they're being valued
for: the chance that they'll fork over the purchase price. Any other
dimension of our existence is outside business's concern, beneath
its interest, immaterial. And, that's exactly right. This dimension *is*
immaterial. What does a company care that your dog can speak
Urdu? That your daughter is dying of leukemia? That you almost
broke under the pressure once, but somehow you survived. That
tonight the air feels the way it did the first time you fell in love?

These are matters that matter to people who appreciate and value your spirit. They are not material to a materialism that views human beings only through monetary criteria of value.

In adopting such a one-dimensional perspective, business has devalued the world it once represented. This stance is not an intrinsic aspect of business. It's not a given, not irreversible. Historically, the only-money-is-material attitude is fairly recent. I'm always amazed to hear people singing the Queen lyric—"we are the champions of the world"—after their team wins a football game.[8] I suspect the inspiration for this song had about as much to do with sports as the Star Spangled Banner had to do with web advertising. It's not about taking home the trophy. It's about *championing the world*. Four definitions are listed for *"champion"* in *The American Heritage Dictionary*. The first two involve contending and winning prizes. But the second two entail speaking on behalf of, or defending the honor of, some other entity. "3. An ardent defender or supporter of a cause or another person: a champion of the homeless. 4. One who fights; a warrior." Business was once a champion of the world in this larger sense.

Do you remember the sublunary sphere we talked about back toward the beginning of all this? Skipped that bit, did you? It figures. Well, for you slackers then, the sublunary sphere was the material world and *all* its material girls—the world, literally, under the orbit of the moon. In the eyes of the early Christian Church, the "things of this world" were mundane—that is, *"worldly"* in a highly pejorative sense. The other world (as in *"otherworldly")* was the only world worth having any truck with: the destination of the just: heaven. What happened down here below on earth was of no interest or importance except as it related to getting *out* of this world, escaping this vale of toil and tears for a purely spiritual realm, "a better place." This was echoed in the Manichean dualism with which we opened this final chapter: world bad, spirit good. Simply put, matter didn't matter.

To say the least, this is a dim view of life on earth. What changed it was largely business. Business championed the world as no other segment of society had dared. It concerned itself with people and their needs, their hopes and dreams. It trafficked in desire and traded in "filthy lucre." It made the world its home base and permanent headquarters. It also made the world a better place. Less toilful for many. Less tearful for most. It did not eradicate pain and injustice. It did not create heaven on earth. But that was never its aim. Always in favor of the pragmatic business plan, its aim was earth on earth. And no apologies.

Historically and culturally, this was a huge accomplishment, and in many respects, a great leap for civilization. Significantly, business did not accomplish this by opposing matter to spirit and winning in a head-to-head contest, but rather by accommodating itself to the world of spirit and showing that the two were not incompatible. Commercial and ecumenical values were shown to be non-exclusive. But over time, business came to recast *all* values that were once commonly held by the inhabitants of this worldly sphere in terms that were conducive only to its own interest in maximizing profit. In an ironic reversal, business has become the new Church, with an equally inflexible, if secular, binary dogma. Now money is everything, and personal wealth the Promised Land. The produce-market-consume cycle is all that matters, and anything falling outside it simply noise. Simply a challenge that can be steam-rollered with a better jingle, a shinier brand, a bigger advertising budget. If something comes along that business doesn't quite understand, something that doesn't fit its value proposition, hey, no problem: invoke the ancient catechism. But first, give it to the boys in marketing to give it a bit of a hook and a better spin. Disney World good, Internet bad.

And so the thrashing continues, from pole to pole, until we're exhausted and ready to scream. Black vs. white. White vs. black. It's been going on for centuries. But quick, choose camps. Which side are you on?

It doesn't have to be this way.

We are people of earth. Feet firmly on the ground, we dream, but we also buy shoes. We explore each other's heads and hearts, but we also rent the occasional video, buy the occasional car or house or—whoops, there goes the neighborhood, honey—Eminem CD. Explicit lyrics and all. We value the spirit of the world that holds our lives in the balance so tentatively, but we also buy computers and carpets and zucchinis and vacuum cleaners and a million other things we need or want or decide—though we know it's not true—

that we just can't live without. And it's OK. All of it. It's OK that business makes stuff and tries to get us interested in buying it. It's OK that we're often interested in more than what business has to offer. We *might* be interested if only business came across a little less lame, a little less blind to what we're all about. We are not the devils of McWorld. We are not the angels of Jihad. We are both and neither. We are people of earth.

While dogma tends to limit and shut down the realm of the possible, contradiction and uncertainty enrich it. We have a name for people who deal with confusion without trying to reduce and simplify it, who enter into an open conversation with the world. We call them artists. Without artists, the world would be one big billboard. Without artists, the human dream would be over. Fortunately, it's not. Around populist artists—though most wouldn't call themselves that—new communities are emerging bottom-up on the net. An artist who connects with such a community is a shaman, a healer. And the disease that's gone truly viral, the malady that most needs a cure today is Either-Or Syndrome. Paradoxically, given where this emergence is taking place, being an artist is about being *non*-digital, *non*-binary. Not this versus that. Not that versus this. We are both and neither. We are more than is dreamed in your marketing plan, Horatio.

But isn't all this talk about artists (*artists* for God's sake!) really just more harebrained, impractical net-head bullshit? One last time, here's Philip Kotler, perhaps the world's most highly credentialed marketing authority, writing in *Harvard Business Review* five years ago—just as the Internet was getting off the ground and the notion of community as local and geographically bounded was being redefined as borderless and globally connected.

By supporting the arts, businesses demonstrate good citizenship, add polish to their corporate image, enhance their community's quality of life, and promote goodwill among customers, clients, and employees. Moreover, a thriving cultural community helps businesses recruit and retain highly educated and talented people. The collective power of these benefits allows businesses to attribute many of the cash expenses of collaborative ventures to marketing rather than philanthropic budgets.[9]

The most critical factor in creating collaborative alliances between business and the arts, says Kotler, is trust. Internet artists and corporate underwriters must come to understand each other's view of the world. There is nothing written in stone that says the two must forever remain incompatible. But trust, says Kotler, "cannot be built in the abstract by thinking, planning, and talking about it. The best way to build trust is to get to work."[10]

Commerce and culture don't need to be at war. They need to be reintegrated. The bellicose imagery of business—waging campaigns, penetrating markets, beating the competition with killer-apps—won't be changed by adopting a new net-correct vocabulary or more worshipful protestations about Valued Customers. Fears about a global economy replacing indigenous customs with cheap made-in-America media trash, and enslaving the populations of poor countries as indentured sweatshop workers, won't be ameliorated by breaking windows at anti-WTO rallies. Maybe there's no hope for such an integration. Maybe business and society are bound for head-on collision or head-on collusion and there's no other way out. In which case, we are all well and truly fucked. Either way, the end of life and the destruction of the world are guaranteed. The Manicheans get the last laugh. And we can all go to heaven happy.

On the other hand, the challenge may not be so daunting after all. That's what I'm betting. That's what this book has been about. The dot-com meltdown of 2000 didn't prove that commerce is unworkable online. It only proved that get-a-bigger-hammer tactics based on antiquated notions about mass markets and broadcast media are unworkable online. Even for high-latency MTFTTB (Mean Time From Tail To Brain) dinosaurs, the message is slowly sinking in. Business is tired of playing the clueless bad guy. People are tired of working for and buying from clueless bad-guy businesses. The gonzo model is a way that companies and Internet communities can begin to work together in genuine partnership. The net has heightened our consciousness of ourselves as a species. This is a profound shift, the implications of which we can barely glimpse, still only guess at. There is more to the world that's coming than electronic commerce. For one thing, there's a potential Renaissance waiting in the wings, an explosion of art and culture greater than that touched off 500 years—not incidentally, by a form of corporate underwriting. Florentine bankers wanted to be remembered for their patronage of the arts. We remember them today because it worked. But the rifts between workers and companies, between companies and their markets, are profound and the negative effects of these rents in the social fabric touch nearly everyone on the planet today. The healing has to begin somewhere. Commerce is an excellent starting point.

The ideas in this book will be only ideas at first, bloodless and abstract. But as people in corporations and Internet communities begin to get to know each other *as* people—as acquaintances, friends and even sparring partners—begin to expect the unexpected. You know the cartoon that shows a scientist working out the formula for the Big Bang, and right in the middle it says "then a miracle occurs"? Expect that. Gonzo marketing is market advocacy. It's not zero-sum, not us-against-them. It's about lighting up the human network, creating a more humane global society—and achieving undreamed-of market efficiencies in the process. While the reasons the gonzo model is necessary and inevitable may be complex, the method is simple. Hook up, connect, co-create, procreate. Redeploy. Foment joy. Brothers in arms, sisters of Avalon, champions of the world get to work.[11]

notes

Introduction

1. *Encarta Book of Quotations,* developed for Microsoft Corporation by Blooms-bury Publishing, 1999.

2. Look for the January 2001 Forrester Report "The Snooze Factor: Sleepy Time in the Management Aisle." You won't be able to find it, however, because it does-n't exist. If you believed it did, seek immediate help from a professional gullibility counselor. Harley Manning, on the other hand, is a real research director at For-rester who reads Entropy Gradient Reversals and does, in fact, believe that most business books are better than Valium for getting to sleep at night. Much to the credit of both Manning and his company, this gratuitous chain yanking is published with knowledge aforethought and prior consent. Whatever those mean.

3. Johan Huizinga, *Homo Ludens: A Study of the Play Element in Culture,* Bea-con Press, 1955. First published in Dutch, 1938. Quotes from the original foreword.

4. *Encarta Book of Quotations,* op. cit.

5. Claude Levi-Strauss, *The Savage Mind*, University of Chicago Press, 1966. Originally published in French as *La Pensee Sauvage*, 1962.

6. David Gates, "Will We Ever Get Over Irony?," *Newsweek*, January 1, 2000, p. 90.

7. Nitin Nohria and James D Berkley, "Whatever Happened to the Take-Charge Manager?" *Harvard Business Review*, January, 1994, p. 128.

8. No, we're not really putting down the fine indigenous cultures of Borneo and New Guinea. See irony, supra. Even better, see a headshrinker.

9. Huizinga, op. cit.

10. http://www.ibm.com/lous-grooves.html Unfortunately, this page now re-ports "Our apologies. . . 404 multifail."

11. Daniel J. Boorstin, *Hidden History*, Vintage Books, 1989.

12. Shunryu Suzuki, *Zen Mind, Beginner's Mind*, Weatherhill, 1972.

13. Hunter S. Thompson, "The Kentucky Derby is Decadent and Depraved," in-cluded in Tom Wolfe, *The New Journalism*, Harper & Row, 1973. p. 179.

14. Hunter S. Thompson, *Fear and Loathing in Las Vegas: A Savage Journey to the Heart of the American Dream*, Vintage Books, 1971.

15. Motley Fool, http://www.fool.com

16. Gary Snyder, *The Practice of the Wild*, North Point Press, 1990.

17. *The I Ching or Book of Changes*, translated by C. F. Baynes and R. Wilhelm, Princeton University Press, 1967.

18. Hunter S. Thompson, op. cit.

Chapter 1

1. Taken from an obscure and badly translated Japanese arcade game, this meme burned up the net for a time. If you have to ask what it means, it's already too late. http://www.scene.org/redhound/AYB.swf. See also Jon Carroll, "All your base are belong to us," *The San Francisco Chronicle*, February 20, 2001. "The Net revealed how slow the media were, maybe how slow they had always been. By the time something hit the mass media, it was over." http://tribalwar.com/forums/showthread.php?threadid=24539

2. William Gibson, *Neuromancer*. New York: Ace Science Fiction Books, 1984.

3. Part of this section appeared on *Feed*.http://www.feedmag.com

4. Courtney Love, speaking to the Digital Hollywood online entertainment conference in New York on May 16 2000, as reproduced on *Salon* –http://www.salon.com/tech/feature/2000/06/14/love/index.html

5. This section originally ran on Byte's web site on February 21, 2000.

6. Entropy Gradient Reversals lives at http://www.rageboy.com

7. *The Economist*, "Lost in cyberspace," December 16, 1999.

8. For a sampling of the companies from which EGR draws subscribers, see http://www.rageboy.com/domains.html

9. As transcribed from the RealAudio file on Ford's website.

10. *The New York Times*, May 13, 2000; "Ford's Admission Perplexes the Neighbors in Henry's Hometown."The full Ford "1999 Corporate Citizenship Report" is at: http://www.ford.com/default.asp?pageid=399&storyid=387. The Ford "Sport Utility Vehicle Case Study" is online at: http://www.ford.com/default.asp?pageid=399&storyid=742

11. Jac Nasser, "Letter to Ford Stakeholders" at http://www.ford.com/default.asp?pageid=399&storyid=733

Chapter 2

1. Charles D. Schewe and Alexander Hiam, *The Portable MBA in Marketing*, John Wiley & Sons, 1998. Quotes taken from the glossary section, p. 473.

2. Thorsten Veblen, *The Theory of the Leisure Class*, 1899.

3. Pink Floyd, "Money," on *Dark Side of the Moon*, 1973. Lyrics by Roger Waters.

4. Philip Kotler, *Kotler on Marketing*, Free Press, 1999, pp. 17–34.

5. The Grateful Dead, "Touch of Grey," on *In the Dark*, 1987. Lyrics by Robert Hunter.

6. Dylan Thomas, "A Refusal to Mourn the Death, by Fire, of a Child in London," from *The Poems of Dylan Thomas*, New Directions, 1971.

7. Clifford Geertz, "Thick Description: Toward an Interpretative Theory of Culture," in *The Interpretation of Cultures*, Basic Books, 1973, p. 6.

8. Ibid. p. 5.

9. Peter L. Berger and Thomas Luckmann, *The Social Construction of Reality: A Treatise on the Sociology of Knowledge*, Anchor Books, 1966, pp. 59.

10. William Gibson, *Neuromancer*. New York: Ace Science Fiction Books, 1984.

11. Friedrich Nietzsche, *The Will to Power*, Random House, 1987. See also http://plato.stanford.edu/entries/nietzsche/

12. Marc Cohn, "Walking in Memphis," on *Marc Cohn*, 1991. Also performed by Cher on several albums and probably at least once in Las Vegas, home of the pyramids. The Talking Heads, "Cities," on *Fear of Music*, 1979. While it's not clear how many Greeks were in Memphis at any one time, David Byrne seems to have believed they were there in force. On the other hand, he's on the money about The King. Perhaps he believed, as I do, that Elvis said it best: "we can't go on together with suspicious minds."

13. Philip Kotler, *Marketing Management: The Millennium Edition*, Prentice Hall, 2000, p. 15.

14. http://www.ey.com/global/gcr.nsf/US/First_Mover_to_First_Prover _-_Thought_Center_-_Ernst_&_Young_LLP (emphasis in original)

15. http://www.ey.com/global/gcr.nsf/US/Marketplaces~Business_Model_ _eBusiness_-_Ernst_&_Young_LLP

16. *The American Heritage Dictionary of the English Language, Fourth Edition*, Houghton Mifflin, 2000.

17. Benjamin R. Barber, *Jihad vs. McWorld: How Globalism and Tribalism Are Reshaping the World*, Ballantine Books, 1995, p. 4

18. Ibid, p. 220.

19. Kris Kristofferson, "Me & Bobby McGee." Also performed by Roger Miller (1969), Janis Joplin, and Jerry Lee Lewis (1972). "Freedom's just another word for nothing left to lose."

20. For instance: Duane E. Knapp, *The Brand Mindset: Five Essential Strategies for Building Brand Advantage Throughout Your Company*, McGraw-Hill Professional Publishing, 1999. See also the related site where the quote appears http://www.brandstrategy.com/m_ebrand.htm. Also: "Our brand is everything to us," says Valerie Oberle, Vice President of Business Development at the Disney Institute – http://www.qualitydigest.com/jan97/disney.html Also: "The brand is everything," says Bloomingdale's CEO Michael Gould – http://www.columbia.edu/ cu/business/botline/marketing.html

21. William Shakespeare, Sonnet 116.

22. Charles Hardin and Norman Petty, "Not Fade Away." Originally performed by Buddy Holly in 1957. Recorded by the Rolling Stones on their first album in 1964 and again in 1972 on *Exile On Main St.*

23. Gampopa, *The Jewel Ornament of Liberation*, translated by Herbert Guenther, Shambala, 1959.

24. *Webster's Third New International Dictionary: Unabridged*, electronic edition, Merriam Webster, 2000.

25. *The Oxford English Dictionary*, second edition, Oxford University Press, 1989.

26. *The Business of Alchemy: Science, Culture and the Holy Roman Empire*, Pamela H. Smith, Princeton University Press, 1994. pp. 7–8.

27. Ibid. p. 9.

28. Hamish Pringle and Marjorie Thompson, *Brand Spirit: How Cause Related Marketing Builds Brands*, John Wiley & Sons, 1999, p. 57.

29. Dire Straits, "Sultans of Swing," on *Dire Straits*, 1978. Thank you, goodnight, now it's time to go home.

30. Recast from *The Old Testament*, Genesis 1:2, King James version.

31. Tracy Kidder, *The Soul of a New Machine*, Little Brown and Company, 1981. See also, Laurie Windham, *The Soul of the New Consumer: The Attitudes, Behavior, and Preferences of E-Customers*, Allworth Press, 2000.

32. Barry Heermann, *Building Team Spirit: Activities for Inspiring and Energizing Teams*, McGraw-Hill, 1997. From the introduction, online at http://www.coax.net/spirit_at_work/intro.htm. See also, John W. Newstrom and Edward Scannell, *The Big Book of Team Building Games: Trust-Building Activities, Team Spirit Exercises, and Other Fun Things to Do*, McGraw-Hill, 1998.

33. *The Oxford English Dictionary*, second edition, Oxford University Press, 1989.

34. Lou Reed, "Take a Walk On the Wild Side," on *Transformer*, 1972.

35. Jefferson Airplane, "White Rabbit," on *Surrealistic Pillow*, 1967.

36. Homer, *The Iliad,* translated by Samuel Butler.

37. Homer, *The Odyssey,* translated by Samuel Butler.

38. See "Content is King," a talk delivered by Bill Gates, Chairman of Microsoft Corporation, January 3, 1996. http://www.microsoft.com/billgates/columns/1996essay/essay960103.asp

39. David Noble, *A World Without Women: The Christian Clerical Culture of Western Science*, Knopf, 1992.

Chapter 3

1. Aldous Huxley, *The Olive Tree And Other Essays*, 1936.

2. Adolf Hitler, *Mein Kampf*, 1933.

3. http://adage.com/news_and_features/special_reports/mktg100–1999/index.html

4. http://adage.com/century/jingles.html

5. Rob Walker, "Biz.Com: Four e-business journalists offer a guide to the new capitalism in the Internet age," a review of *The Cluetrain Manifesto* in *The New York Times Book Review*, March 26, 2000.

6. Leslie Kaufman, "Tuning In the New Way: The Internet Scene May Just Have a Lot in Common with the 1960's," *The New York Times*, April 10, 2000.

7. Philip Kotler, "Reflections on Marketing," the preface to The Kellogg Marketing Faculty, Northwestern University, *Kellogg on Marketing*, Dawn Iacobucci (editor), John Wiley & Sons, 2001.

8. Philip Kotler, "Marketing in the Age of Information Democracy," in The Kellogg Marketing Faculty, Northwestern University, *Kellogg on Marketing*, Dawn Iacobucci (editor), John Wiley & Sons, 2001, p. 387.

9. Christopher Locke, "Take My Word for It," *Journal of the Wild-Assed Guess*, September, 1995.

10. http://www.kraftfoods.com/html/brands/brands.html

11. U2, "Even Better Than the Real Thing," *Achtung Baby*, Island Records Ltd., 1991.

12. Richard Earle, *The Art of Cause Marketing: How to Use Advertising to Change Personal Behavior and Public Policy*, NTC Business Books, 2000. Italics in original.

13. After writing this, I discovered that the *Harvard Business Review* Paperback Series does include two volumes with "marketing" in their titles, though both are much older. *Sharpening the Marketing Edge* was published over 10 years ago, and *Consumer Marketing Strategies* is out of print.

14. Randall Rothenberg, "What Makes Sense, and Doesn't, or How to Resist Internet's Song," *Advertising Age*, August 5, 2000. http://adage.com/news_and_features/rr_viewpoint/archives/rr20000508.html

15. Theodore Levitt, "Marketing Myopia," *Harvard Business Review*, July-August 1960.

16. Theodore Levitt, "Marketing Myopia," *Harvard Business Review*, reprinted September-October 1975. The quote is from Levitt's "Retrospective Commentary" on his original 1960 article.

17. Jill Rosenfeld, "Experience the Real Thing," *Fast Company*, January/February 2000.

18. David Byrne (director), *True Stories*, 1986. A highly satirical look at a small Texas town during its "celebration of specialness." Jamie Uys (director), *The Gods Must Be Crazy*, 1980. A Coke bottle falls from the sky in the Kalahari desert causing severe cultural disruption to a tribe of Bushmen.

19. Jill Rosenfeld, "Experience the Real Thing," *Fast Company*, January/February 2000.

20. Sergio Zyman, *The End of Marketing As We Know It*, HarperCollins, 2000.

21. Quoted with the permission of the poster.

22. Thomas Scoville, "Legends in Their Own Minds," *Salon*, December 16, 1999. http://www.salon.com/tech/books/1999/12/16/renegades/index.html

23. Jerry Della Femina and Sergio Zyman, "It's a Mad, Mad, Mad Ad World," *Context*, December 2000/January 2001. http://www.contextmag.com/setFrameRedirect.asp?src=/archives/200012/thelastword.asp

24. Courtney Love, speech at the Digital Hollywood online Entertainment Conference, New York, May 16, 2000. Published on *Salon* as "Courtney Love Does the Math" http://www.salon.com/tech/feature/2000/06/14/love/index.html

25. Susan Sesolak, "Discovering Sources for Segmentation Data." from the companion website to Philip Kotler, *Marketing Management: The Millennium Edition*, Prentice Hall, 2000. The quote is from an "Internet exercise" dealing with chapter 9: Identifying Market Segments and Selecting Target Markets. http://cw. prenhall.com/bookbind/pubbooks/kotler5/chapter9/deluxe.html

26. Ibid. Susan Sesolak, "Discovering Sources For Segmentation Data."

27. Harry Webber, *Divide and Conquer: Targeting Your Customers Through Market Segmentation*, John Wiley & Sons, 1998. Michael J. Weiss, *The Clustered World: How We Live, What We Buy, and What It All Means About Who We Are*, Little, Brown and Company, 2000.

28. Regis McKenna, *The Regis Touch: New Marketing Strategies For Uncertain Times*, Addison-Wesley, 1986.

29. Regis McKenna, *Relationship Marketing: Successful Strategies for the Age of the Customer*, Addison-Wesley, 1991.

30. B. Joseph Pine II, *Mass Customization: The New Frontier in Business Competition*, Harvard Business School Press, 1993. See also: James H. Gilmore and B. Joseph Pine II, *Markets of One: Creating Customer-Unique Value Through Mass Customization*, A Harvard Business Review Book, 2000.

31. See for instance, Don Peppers and Martha Rogers, *Enterprise One to One: Tools for Competing in the Interactive Age*, Doubleday/Currency, 1997.

32. In 1999, I created personalization.com for Net Perceptions. At the beginning of 2001, I handed off my position as editor in chief to Eric Norlin. In June 2001, Net Perceptions decided to close down the site. http://www.personalization.com

33. See a somewhat more detailed discussion in Christopher Locke, "Beyond Purchase Circles," *personalization.com*, November, 1999. http://www.personalization.com/soapbox/columns/clocke-column-3.asp

34. Malcolm Gladwell, "The Science of the Sleeper: How the Information Age Could Blow Away the Blockbuster," *The New Yorker*, October 4, 1999. http://www.gladwell.com/1999_10_04_a_sleeper.htm

35. Theodore Levitt, "Marketing Myopia," *Harvard Business Review*, July-August, 1960, pp. 45–65.

36. Theodore Levitt, "Marketing Myopia," *Harvard Business Review*, reprinted September-October 1975. The quote is from Levitt's "Retrospective Commentary" on his original 1960 article.

37. Some of the material in this section is from an interview I did for the journal of the American Association of Advertising Agencies: "The Fortune Tellers," *Agency* (Vol. 10, No. 1), Winter 2000.

38. Steven M. Cristol and Peter Sealey, *Simplicity Marketing: Relieving Customer Stress in the Digital Age*, Free Press, 2000. Much of the material in this section is from my article "Smart Customers, Dumb Companies," *Harvard Business Review*, November-December, 2000.

39. Ibid. Cristol and Sealey, p. 201.

40. Ibid. Cristol and Sealey, p. 190.

41. Ibid. Cristol and Sealey, p. 7.

42. Tom Petty, "I Won't Back Down," on *Full Moon Fever*, MCA Records, 1989.

43. http://www.thestandard.com/people/display/0,1157,1043,00.html

44. Personal communication.

45. Seth Godin, *E-Mail Addresses of the Rich & Famous*, Addison-Wesley, 1994. p. viii.

46. Seth Godin, *Permission Marketing: Turning Strangers Into Friends and Friends Into Customers*, Simon & Schuster, 1999.

47. Peter Sealey, "How E-Commerce Will Trump Brand Management," *Harvard Business Review*, July-August 1999.

48. Seth Godin, "Unleash Your Ideavirus," *Fast Company*, August 2000, p. 115. http://www.fastcompany.com/online/37/ideavirus.html

49. Seth Godin, "Unleash Your Ideavirus," *Fast Company*, August 2000, p. 115. http://www.fastcompany.com/online/37/ideavirus.html

50. Christopher Locke, "Internet Apocalypso," *The Cluetrain Manifesto*, Perseus, 2000.

51. Seth Godin, "Unleash Your Ideavirus," *Fast Company*, August 2000, p. 115. http://www.fastcompany.com/online/37/ideavirus.html

52. Seth Godin, "Unleash Your Ideavirus," *Fast Company*, August 2000, p. 115. http://www.fastcompany.com/online/37/ideavirus.html

53. Seth Godin, *Unleashing the Ideavirus*, electronic edition, Do You Zoom, Inc., 2000. http://www.ideavirus.com

54. Emanuel Rosen, *the anatomy of buzz: how to create word of mouth marketing*, Doubleday/Currency, 2000, p. 195.

55. With the exception of this statement, all Seth Godin's remarks in this section are direct quotes from his book, *Permission Marketing: Turning Strangers into Friends and Friends into Customers*, Simon & Schuster, 1999.

56. Parts of this section previously appeared in different form as "The Halcyon Days of Broadcast Ad Model Fade," *Digitrends*, October 2000. Also online at http://www.digitrends.net/marketing/11542_12584.html

57. Thomas S. Kuhn. *The Structure of Scientific Revolutions*, third edition, University of Chicago Press, 1996. Originally published in 1962.

58. From an interview on C-SPAN's Booknotes, March 7, 1999. http://www.booknotes.org/transcripts/50506.htm

Chapter 4

1. A different version of this chapter ran in Esther Dyson's *Release 1.0* in February, 2000.

2. http://www.personalization.com. After creating the site and getting the core community together, I passed the project on to Eric Norlin, who is now editor in chief.

3. http://www.opensource.org

4. Elizabeth Weise, "Future Will Be Up Close And Personal," *USA Today*, November 23, 1999.

5. I forget the publication this interview appeared in. Email me if you know.

6. Theodore Levitt, "Marketing Myopia," *Harvard Business Review*, July-August 1960.

7. Theodore Levitt, "Marketing Myopia," *Harvard Business Review*, July-August 1960.

8. Emily Warn, *The Novice Insomniac*, Copper Canyon Press, 1996.

9. IBM press release, "Web Integrators, Hosters and Incubators Now to Provide IBM Offering for Internet Start-Ups," Partnerworld, Atlanta, GA, February 26, 2001.

10. http://www.cluetrain.com

11. Olu Oni, "Ashby's Law Revisited," http://members.home.net/onis/articles/feature1.htm

12. Brian Millar, "Modern Life is Rubbish," *personalization.com*, www.personalization.com/soapbox/contributions/millar.asp

Chapter 5

1. Robert D. Putnam, *Bowling Alone: The Collapse and Revival of American Community*, Simon & Schuster, 2000, p. 171.

2. Philip Kotler and Gerald Zaltman, "Social Marketing: An Approach to Planned Social Change," *Journal of Marketing*, July 1971, pp. 3–12.

3. Philip Kotler and Eduardo L. Roberto, *Social Marketing: Strategies for Changing Public Behavior*, Free Press, 1989, p. 24.

4. Doug McKenzie-Mohr and William Smith, *Fostering Sustainable Behavior: An Introduction to Community-Based Social Marketing*, New Society Publishers, 1999.

5. Neill McKee, *Social Mobilization & Social Marketing in Developing Communities: Lessons for Communicators*, Southbound, 1993.

6. *Chin Saik Yoon,* "Participatory Communication for Development," in Guy Bessette and C.V. Rajasunderam (editors), *Participatory Development Communication: A West African Agenda,* Stylus Publications, 1996.

7. *Encarta World English Dictionary*, 1999. Developed for Microsoft by Bloomsbury Publishing Plc.

8. Rudyard Kipling, "The White Man's Burden," *McClure's Magazine*, February, 1899. http://www.boondocksnet.com/kipling/kipling.html in Jim Zwick, (editor) *Anti-Imperialism in the United States, 1898–1935* http://www.boondocksnet.com/ail98–35.html (January 8, 2001).

9. Ariel Dorfman and Armand Mattelart, *How to Read Donald Duck: Imperialist Ideology in the Disney Comic*, International General, 1984. While it pre-dates the net by a bit, this seems relevant to the general theme.

10. Elaine Lawless, *Holy Women, Wholly Women: Sharing Ministries Through Life Stories and Reciprocal Ethnography*, University of Pennsylvania Press, 1993. Special thanks to my sister, Elizabeth Locke, who pointed out the potential relevance of reciprocal ethnography to gonzo marketing.

11. *Chin Saik Yoon,* op. cit.

12. *The Blues Brothers*, Universal Pictures, 1980.

13. Shirley Sagawa and Eli Segal, *Common Interest, Common Good: Creating Value Through Business and Social Sector Partnerships*, Harvard Business School Press, 1999, p. 117.

14. Sue Adkins, *Cause Related Marketing: Who Cares Wins*, Butterworth-Heinemann, 2000, p. 11.

15. Stuart Elliott, "Advertising: Absolut to Salute GLAAD," *The New York Times*, February 22, 2001.

16. Share Our Strength is online at http://www.strength.org

17. Bill Shore, *The Cathedral Within: Transforming Your Life by Giving Something Back*, Random House, 1999.

18. Richard Earle, *The Art of Cause Marketing: How to Use Advertising to Change Personal Behavior and Public Policy*, NTC Business Books, 2000, p. 3.

19. Philip Kotler and Alan R. Andreason, *Strategic Marketing for Nonprofit Organizations,* fifth edition, Prentice Hall, 1996, p. 304.

20. Philip Kotler and Alan R. Andreason, *Strategic Marketing for Nonprofit Organizations,* fifth edition, Prentice Hall, 1996, p. 389.

21. Philip Kotler and Alan R. Andreason, *Strategic Marketing for Nonprofit Organizations,* fifth edition, Prentice Hall, 1996, p. 388.

22. Hamish Pringle and Marjorie Thompson, *Brand Spirit: How Cause Related Marketing Builds Brands*, John Wiley & Sons, 1999, p. xix. Edward de Bono has written many books, perhaps the best known of which is *Lateral Thinking*.

23. "A Short Course in Social Marketing," Novartis Foundation for Sustainable Development, 2001. http://www.foundation.novartis.com/social_marketing.htm

24. "Social Marketing for Epilepsy," *Novartis Foundation for Sustainable Development, 2001*. http://www.foundation.novartis.com/social_marketing_epilepsy.htm

25. Dan Bischoff, "Consuming Passions," *Ms.* magazine, December 2000/January 2001, pp. 61–65.

26. Philip Kotler and Alan R. Andreason, *Strategic Marketing for Nonprofit Organizations,* fifth edition, Prentice Hall, 1996, p. 306.

27. Philip Kotler, *Kotler on Marketing*, Free Press, 1999, p. 14.

28. Evantheia Schibsted, "Shock It to You," *Business 2.0*, May 1, 2000.

29. "Advertising and death," *The Economist*, February 17, 2000.

30. Luciano Benetton, March 1998, http://www.benetton.com/wws/aboutyou/peopleplaces/file2063.html

31. Debra Ollivier, "The Colorful Dissenter of Benetton," *Salon*, April 17, 2000. http://www.salon.com/people/feature/2000/04/17/toscani_int/index.html. Some quotes are from the associated interview, "Toscani in His Own Words," which begins at http://www.salon.com/people/feature/2000/04/17/toscani_int/index1.html

32. Ibid.

33. John Rossant, "The Faded Colors of Benetton," *Business Week*, April 10, 1995.

34. Benetton corporate press release, "Benetton Advertising: Toscani Passes The Baton," Ponzano, Italy, April 29, 2000. http://www.benetton.com/press/sito/press_releases/press2000/communication/oting.html

35. *Talk* magazine, "the Players" (editorial team), http://www.talkmagazine.com/players/index.html

36. Reviewing *Talk* magazine, Alex Kuczynski writes: "Of 22 articles in the first four issues written by people in the film industry or about people or characters in the film industry, 11 featured people recently or currently affiliated with Miramax or Disney Projects." As reported in "The Critics: Mainstream Media," *Columbia Journalism Review*, March/April 2000. On the other hand, Michael Wolff reports on an interview with Tina Brown about *Talk*. "We want it to have the feeling of the voices of the Web." Wolff notes that she adds "Of course we want it to be accurate." Michael Wolff, "All Talk," *New York Magazine*, January 25, 1999.

37. Oliviero Toscani, *1000 Extra/Ordinary Objects*, Taschen America, 2000. http://www.benetton.com/wws/aboutmake/colors/index.html

38. Rosabeth Moss Kanter in the preface to Shirley Sagawa and Eli Segal, *Common Interest, Common Good: Creating Value Through Business and Social Sector Partnerships*, Harvard Business School Press, 1999.

39. See for instance: NikeWatch at http://www.caa.org.au/campaigns/nike/index.html; Corporate Watch at http://www.corpwatch.org/trac/nike/announce/nikes.html; and the Boycott Nike site at http://www.saigon.com/nike/. These are just near-random examples of the kind of public corporate oversight the web has enabled.

40. Garrett Hardin, "The Tragedy of the Commons," *Science*, 162, 1968, pp. 1243–1248.

41. Robert D. Putnam, *Bowling Alone: The Collapse and Revival of American Community*, Simon & Schuster, 2000, p. 19.

42. By Farrell, "Bring Back the Quilting Bee," a review of *Bowling Alone* in *Business Week*, June 26, 2000.

43. Robert D. Putnam, *Bowling Alone: The Collapse and Revival of American Community*, Simon & Schuster, 2000, p. 171.

44. Eric L. Lesser, *Knowledge and Social Capital: Foundations and Applications*, Butterworth-Heinemann, 2000.

45. Eric L. Lesser, *Knowledge and Communities*, Butterworth-Heinemann, 2000.

46. John Seely Brown and Paul Duguid, "Organizational Learning and Communities of Practice: Toward a Unified View of Working, Learning, and Innovation," originally published in *Organization Science*, February, 1991. The George W. Bush quote is purportedly from a talk he gave in Arlington Heights, Ill., on Oct. 24, 2000. "It's important for us to explain to our nation that life is important. It's not only life of babies, but it's life of children living in, you know, the dark dungeons of the Internet."

47. John Seely Brown and Paul Duguid, *The Social Life of Information*, Harvard Business School Press, 2000.

48. Jay Rosen, posted to Amazon.com November 22, 1999. http://www.amazon.com/exec/obidos/tg/stores/detail/-/books/0300078234/reviews/

49. Tom Goldstein, "Good Question" (review of *What Are Journalists For?*), *The New York Times*, November 14, 1999.

50. James Fallows, *Breaking the News: How the Media Undermine American Democracy*, Vintage Books, 1997, p. 260.

51. Rosen, *What Are Journalists For?*, Yale University Press, 1999, p. 34.

52. From an interview on C-SPAN's Booknotes, July 25, 1999. http://www.booknotes.org/transcripts/50525.htm

53. Howard Kurtz, *Media Circus: The Trouble with America's Newspapers*, Times Books/Random House, 1993, p. 341.

54. Jon Katz discussing his book – *Virtuous Reality: How America Surrendered Discussion of Moral Values to Opportunists, Nitwits & Blockheads Like William Bennett* on *Booknotes*, Air Date: March 23, 1997. http://www.booknotes.org/transcripts/50404.htm

55. James S. Ettema and Theodore L. Glasser, *Custodians of Conscience: Investigative Journalism and Private Virtue*, Columbia University Press, 1998, p. 61.

56. For an interesting note on McGuffins, see http://nextdch.mty.itesm.mx/~plopezg/Kaplan/Mcguffin.html

57. Tom Wolfe, *The New Journalism*, Harper & Row, 1973.

58. Kevin Kerrane and Ben Yagoda (editors), *The Art of Fact: A Historical Anthology of Literary Journalism*, Touchstone Books, 1998. Also: Norman Sims (editor), *The Literary Journalists*, Ballantine Books, 1984. Also: Norman Sims (editor), *Literary Journalism: A New Collection of the Best American Nonfiction*, Ballantine Books, 1995.

59. Jack Fuller, *News Values: Ideas for an Information Age*, University of Chicago Press, 1997, p. 136.

60. Hunter S. Thompson, "The fix is in," *ESPN, Page 2*, http://espn.go.com/page2/s/thompson/001127.html

61. David T.Z. Mindich, *Just the Facts: How "Objectivity" Came to Define American Journalism*, New York University Press, 1998.

62. Mary Linsky, "The Public Interest in Journalism," *The American Prospect*, January 17, 2000. See also, Walter Lippmann, *Public Opinion*, Free Press Paperbacks (Simon & Schuster), 1997. Originally published by Macmillan in 1922.

63. Jurgen Habermas, *Legitimation Crisis*, Beacon Press, 1975. German edition originally published in 1973. Jürgen Habermas, *The Structural Transformation of the Public Sphere: An Inquiry into a Category of Bourgeois Society*, MIT Press, 1991. German original published 1962.

64. Scott Sonner, "Publisher Sees Newspapers Flourishing in Internet Era," Associated Press, dateline: Reno, Nevada, April 1, 2000, available at http://www.sfgate.com/cgi-bin/article.cgi?file=/news/archive/2000/04/01/state0401EST0107.DTL.

65. Bartholomew H. Sparrow, *Uncertain Guardians: The News Media as a Political Institution*, Johns Hopkins University Press, 1999; Martin A. Lee and Norman Solomon, *Unreliable Sources: A Guide to Detecting Bias in News Media*, Lyle Stuart,

1990; Robert W. McChesney, *Rich Media, Poor Democracy: Communication Politics in Dubious Times*, University of Illinois Press, 1999; *Republic of Denial: Press, Politics and Public Life*, Yale University Press, 1999; Doug Underwood, *When MBAs Rule the Newsroom*, Columbia University Press, 1993; Martin Plissner, *The Control Room: How Television Calls the Shots in Presidential Elections*, Free Press, 1999; Howard Kurtz, *Media Circus: The Trouble with America's Newspapers*, Times Books, 1993; James Fallows, *Breaking the News: How the Media Undermine American Democracy*, Vintage, 1997.

66. Gary Snyder, *The Practice of the Wild*, North Point Press, 1990.

67. Dawn B. Sova, *Banned Books*, Facts on File, 1998. The series includes four volumes: *Literature Suppressed on Political Grounds, Literature Suppressed on Sexual Grounds, Literature Suppressed on Religious Grounds,* and *Literature Suppressed on Social Grounds*—the Florida (Chaucer) case appears in the last, pp. 64–65. All the authors listed in this paragraph are included in the series.

68. *Better Than Sex: Confessions of a Political Junkie—The Gonzo Papers, Volume 4*, Hunter S. Thompson, Ballantine Books, 1994. p. 243. Italics in original.

69. Dave Barry, *Big Trouble*, Berkeley Books, 2001, pp. 14–15.

70. Edward S. Herman and Noam Chomsky, *Manufacturing Dissent: The Political Economy of the Mass Media*, Pantheon Books, 1988, p. xi.

71. Ben H. Bagdikian, *The Media Monopoly*, Fifth edition, Beacon Press, 2000.

72. Herbert J. Gans, *Deciding What's News: A Study of CBS Evening News, NBC Nightly News, Newsweek, and Time*, Vintage Books, 1989, p. 313.

73. Herbert Gans, *Popular Culture and High Culture: An Analysis and Evaluation of Taste*, Basic Books, 1999, p. 175. Originally published in 1974.

Chapter 6

1. Gary Armstrong and Philip Kotler, *Marketing: An Introduction*, fifth edition, Prentice Hall, 1999, p. 183.

2. Ben H. Bagdikian, *The Media Monopoly*, Fifth edition, Beacon Press, 2000. pp. x–xxi.

3. Saul Hansell, "Disney to Abandon Portal Site," *New York Times,* January 30, 2001.

4. Nico Detourn, "Was Disney's Go.com a Goofy Idea?," *Motley Fool,* January 30, 2001. http://www.fool.com/news/2001/dis010130.htm

5. Walt Disney Internet Group investor relations page, http://disney.go.com/investors/wdig/invest.html

6. Michael Wolff, "Eisner Un-Moused?" New York Magazine, July12, 1999, http://www.newyorkmag.com/page.cfm?page_id=143.

7. Source is a timeline accompanying Christopher Parkes, "Disney ends Go.com portal," *The Financial Times*, January 29, 2001.

8. Brad King, "Placing Product Before Art," *Wired News*, February 1, 2001.

9. Abbot Joseph Liebling, "Do You Belong in Journalism?," *The New Yorker,* May 14, 1960.

10. Malcolm Gladwell, *The Tipping Point: How Little Things Can Make a Big Difference,* Little Brown, 2000.

11. Personal communication

12. http://www.sweetfancymoses.com/crowley_dream

13. Christopher Locke, "Writer's Bloc," *Sweet Fancy Moses,* http://www.sweetfancymoses.com/locke_bloc.htm

14. http://www.plastic.com

15. http://www.suck.com

16. http://www.fccdmag.com

17. Jamie Heller, "Online Journalism Coming Into Its Own.," *The New York Times,* August 3, 1998.

18. Carl Hiaasen, *Kick Ass,* University Press of Florida, 1999.

19. "Badges? We ain't got no badges. We don't need no badges. I don't have to show you any stinking badges!" Dialogue from *The Treasure of the Sierra Madre,* 1948.

20. Steven Jones, "The Bias of the Web," in Andrew Herman and Thomas Swiss (editors), *The World Wide Web and Contemporary Cultural Theory,* p. 177. The embedded quote is from Marshall McLuhan, *Understanding Media, The Extensions of Man,* Penguin, 1964, p. 266.

21. Paul Farhi, "The Dotcom Brain Drain: Print Journalists Are Heeding the Siren Song of the Internet," *American Journalism Review,* March, 2000.

22. http://w.moreover.com/site/about/team/index.html#nickdenton

23. Lisa Guernsey, "Mining the 'Deep Web' with Sharper Shovels," *The New York Times,* January 25, 2001.

24. Randall Rothenberg, "What Makes Sense, and Doesn't, or How to Resist Internet's Song," *Advertising Age,* August 5, 2000. http://adage.com/news_and_features/rr_viewpoint/archives/rr20000508.html

25. Lisa Guernsey, "Mining the 'Deep Web' With Sharper Shovels," *The New York Times,* January 25, 2001.

26. http://www.blogger.com

27. http://www.newsblogger.com

28. http://www.onlinejournalism.com

29. Scott Shuger and others, "Today's Papers" (ongoing column), *Slate,* http://slate.msn.com/code/TodaysPapers/TodaysPapers.asp

30. Julia Lipman, "Weblogs Crawl Out from Underground," *digitalMASS,* December 13, 2000. http://digitalmass.boston.com/columns/internet/1213.html

31. http://www.tompeters.com/content/weblogs/index.html

32. Philip Kotler and Gary Armstrong, *Principles of Marketing,* 9th edition, Prentice Hall, 2001, pp. 247–248.

33. Philip Kotler and Alan R. Andreason, *Strategic Marketing for Nonprofit Organizations,* fifth edition, Prentice Hall, 1996, p. 397. Italics added.

Chapter 7

1. *Newsweek*, May 12, 1980, as quoted in *The Oxford English Dictionary*, second edition, Oxford University Press.

2. Theodore Levitt, "Marketing Myopia," *Harvard Business Review*, July-August 1960.

3. Adolph S. Ochs, in an address to the Philadelphia convention of the Associated Advertising Clubs of the World, June 26, 1916. Cited in Elmer Davis, *History of the New York Times, 1851–1921*, which is in turn cited in Walter Lippmann, *Public Opinion*, Free Press Paperbacks (Simon & Schuster), 1997. Originally published by Macmillan in 1922.

4. Thanks and a tip o' the hat to *Rocky Horror*. If you're not familiar with this film, go rent it, Frederick. Give yourself over to absolute pleasure. Find out what bottom-up is all about. Oh, Frankie!

Chapter 8

1. Blanche Carter, "Devil or Angel." Performed by The Clovers in 1956; also by Bobby Vee in 1960.

2. Cyndi Lauper and Jan Pulsford "You Don't Know," *Sisters of Avalon*, Epic (Sony), 1997.

3. Benjamin R. Barber, *Jihad vs. McWorld: How Globalism and Tribalism Are Reshaping The World*, Ballantine Books, 1995. Thomas L. Friedman, *The Lexus and Olive Tree*, Farrar Straus & Giroux, 2000.

4. "Any sufficiently advanced technology is indistinguishable from magic." The line appears in Arthur C. Clarke, *Profiles of the Future: An Inquiry into the Limits of the Possible*, 1962.

5. Nicholas Negroponte, *Being Digital*, Knopf, 1995.

6. Mick Jagger and Keith Richards, "It's Only Rock & Roll," performed by The Rolling Stones on *It's only Rock & Roll*, 1974.

7. Thomas L. Friedman, "Hype and Anti-Hype," *The New York Times*, February 23, 2001.

8. Freddy Mercury, "We Are the Champions," performed by Queen on *News of the World*, 1977.

9. Joanne Scheff and Philip Kotler, "How the Arts Can Prosper Through Strategic Collaborations," *Harvard Business Review*, January 1996, p. 52.

10. Joanne Scheff and Philip Kotler, op. cit.

11. Mark Knopfler, "Bothers in Arms," performed by Dire Straits on *Bothers in Arms*, 1985.

index

Christopher Locke
clocke@panix.com

Named in a 2001 Financial Times Group survey as one of the "top 50 business thinkers in the world," Locke is author of *Gonzo Marketing: Winning Through Worst Practices*, co-author of *The Cluetrain Manifesto*, president of Entropy Web Consulting, and editor/publisher of the widely acclaimed and justly infamous webzine *Entropy Gradient Reversals*. Now based in Boulder, Colorado, has worked for Fujitsu, Ricoh, the Japanese government's "Fifth Generation" artificial intelligence project, Carnegie Mellon University's Robotics Institute, CMP Publications, Mecklermedia, MCI, and IBM. He has written extensively for publications such as *Forbes, Release 1.0, Information Week, Publish, The Industry Standard*, and *Harvard Business Review*, and his professional work has been covered by *Fast Company, Wired, Advertising Age, Business Week, The Economist, Fortune, The New York Times, The Wall Street Journal* and many others.

He has never recanted anything.